Contents

If we do not care what we eat, we do not care for ourselves, and if we do not care for ourselves, how can we care for others?

Andrew Payne, *Pie in the Sky* (Witzend Productions Limited/SelecTV plc)

About this book

Food in Care is about the part that food plays in caring. Food is an essential part of life, affecting our health, well-being and happiness. It is automatically important, therefore, in caring for people, whether their care is temporary or long term. Sometimes its importance can be overlooked or taken for granted in the midst of all the other elements of caring for others. But we cannot just say 'food is important' and then change the subject. If carers understand what food is and where it fits into our daily lives they are more likely to provide better, higher quality, compassionate care.

Clients are individuals, and their diet – the food they eat – is often very special to them. Religion, habit, upbringing, the amount of money available, all shape what and when people eat. Some enjoy shopping for food, cooking and eating. Others do not. These individual preferences need to be considered in caring, when diet and life style may have to be modified for health and therapeutic reasons.

Who is this book for?

The book will be helpful if you are working in the care sector, if you are training for this kind of work, or if you are involved in caring in a more informal way – looking after a relative or friend, or as a volunteer worker. It will also be helpful:

- if you are preparing for assessment for a National Vocational Qualification (NVQ) or Scottish Vocational Qualification (SVQ) in care or child care and education, up to and including level 3. It gives you the knowledge needed for you to show competence in areas such as: enabling clients to eat and drink; enabling clients to choose, prepare and store food; preparing food and drink for a client; contributing to the health, safety and security of individuals and their environment; enabling clients to manage their domestic and personal resources; supporting clients during specific treatment, therapeutic and development programmes (NVQs/SVQs in care); providing food and drink for children; caring for and promoting the development of babies in the first year of their lives (NVQs/SVQs in child care and education);
- if you are studying for a General National Vocational Qualification (GNVQ) in health and social care at Intermediate or Advanced level. You will find that it gives you the background knowledge needed for those areas of the qualification which deal with the part that food plays in people's lives, as well as diet and healthy eating and how client groups experience and influence health-care provision;

- if you are a full- or part-time worker in the health services, social services, in an education setting or with a voluntary organisation. The book provides information which has a practical application in your work. You might use it on an in-service training course;
- if you are following a training course leading to a professional qualification in dietetics, nutrition, social work or catering. The book gives a useful summary of food issues in relation to caring.

The aims of the book

The book aims to give basic information about food, diet and nutrition and to show how this is applied in caring for different clients in a range of care settings.

The people you are caring for may:

- be in their own homes or sheltered housing, in residential or nursing homes, in schools, hospitals or hostels;
- be babies, children, teenagers, adults or older people;
- be from a range of cultural backgrounds and may not have English as their first language;
- be recovering from illness, accident or surgery or may be terminally ill;
- be suffering from the effects of drugs;
- have long- or short-term physical or mental impairment.

The book aims to show the roles of the professional dietitian, nutritionist and caterer in the care team. You, as a carer, need to be able to carry out their professional advice and instructions. You will be better able to do this if you understand the background to it, and so can be more confident and effective in your caring.

The structure of the book

Food covers a very wide field, and it is not possible to cover all areas in great detail. The main issues are discussed. The early chapters give an overview of food – food and people, food and diet, food and caring, different needs of different people. Special needs and special diets are then considered, followed by more detailed discussion of nutrients and nutrition, the kinds of figures and calculations that are involved in food issues, food and kitchen safety and, finally, bringing everything together, planning meals and menus.

Throughout the book, activities ask carers to become involved in discovering what facilities are available in their area, in understanding the needs of different groups, what provision is required for different groups and how to adapt where necessary.

It is important to note, however, that this book is not intended to replace the experience and knowledge of professional dietitians. There is no substitute for that. Their expert advice, however, can be put to better effect if carers understand the background to it and have some guidance on interpreting it practically in everyday situations.

Sources of information and further reading

Information in the text has been culled from a wide variety of published sources, some relating to statistical measurements. The book contains data, material and charts from the reports of the Committee on the Medical Aspects of Food Policy (called COMA) which was set up by government. Four of its main reports are referred to in the text:

No 41: The Dietary Reference Values for Food Energy and Other Nutrients for the United Kingdom, 1991;
No 43: Nutrition and the Elderly, 1992;
No 45: Weaning and the Weaning Diet, 1994;
No 46: Nutritional Aspects of Cardiovascular Disease, 1994.

Many of the observations in the text come from the professionals working in a variety of care settings who have generously given their time during the preparation of this book. Other information was first highlighted in the media. This material can add to our understanding of certain issues, and, after assessment and evaluation by experienced practitioners, may be put into practice.

Details of all sources are given at the ends of chapters, together with books and other material for reference or further reading. A complete listing of all the material referred to in the text appears at the end of the book.

How to use the book

The book is structured so that you can use it to suit your own individual situation and needs. It can be used as a reference source, in your workplace or when you are training. You may want to dip into various chapters, seeking out information on particular topics. The Index will help you to find what you want.

Some of the activities and exercises involve finding out about people and organisations. It is a good idea to check with your supervisor or tutor before tackling these, to make sure you approach the right person, and that you have permission – if necessary – to do so.

Whatever activity you do or information you obtain, you will find it useful to keep it, perhaps in a notebook or loose-leaf file. A card index may be suitable for some kinds of information. Ask your supervisor or tutor for guidance if necessary.

The wider context

As well as being part of the study of diet and nutrition and their relationship with health and caring, food is also part of social, political, economic and environmental issues.

- Food is a central part of human activity. Human beings are sociable – we eat together. We learn to share with and care for others through providing food. Food is important in the huge variety of cultures around the world.
- For most people, food is a source of pleasure and enjoyment. The success or otherwise of social occasions is often measured by the reactions to food.
- Food is a factor in evolution which has been driven partly by the availability of food and nutrients. Plants and animals have had to adapt to cope with changes in nutrient supply and will almost certainly continue to do so.
- Food is part of political and economic life as well as the environment. The food eaten in the UK comes from all over the world. Policies in relation to food are based on agricultural and economic considerations. In spite of the UK Government's Health of the Nation Programme, which

was set up to reduce the incidence of certain diseases by the year 2000 and which emphasises the role of diet in relation to some of these diseases, food policy in the UK does not yet relate to health.

● Food is very big business. In the UK alone the food industry gives work to one in seven of the population. Growing, processing, distributing, cooking and serving food are all part of the industry, which operates in a wide international context. The regulation of the UK food industry is determined to a large extent, now, by the European Union, and all aspects of the industry are becoming more international in their outlook and practice.

Food is not only a fact of life, it is a fact of living and enjoying life. So – enjoy learning about food and the ways in which it can be used to help and care for others.

1 Food and people

The subject of food covers many aspects and issues. Relating these aspects and issues to the people we care about and for, is the purpose of this book.

People are the most important element in all our tasks as carers. How we show our care for them includes our understanding of food and how they feel about it and react to it. Food, though, requires some understanding in itself.

Food is:

- the source of complex chemicals – nutrients – that living bodies need to stay alive and be healthy;
- the source of comfort and a means to human caring;
- a part of our social life and enjoyment;
- an industry that employs millions of people worldwide.

In Western countries food is plentiful, colourful, varied and appetising. It is also enjoyable. Human beings are a sociable species: we eat together; we learn to share, to give and to care for each other at meal times and through other food provision. Food is a central part of human community and interaction. For most people, food is a source of pleasure and enjoyment. The success or otherwise of social occasions is often measured by reactions to the food.

1.1 Thoughts on food

Although a very basic part of our lives, our understanding and consideration of food may be automatic, especially when we have so many other interesting things to do with our time. We tend to eat what we like and enjoy, often unconsciously turning to those foods which gave us comfort when we were growing up.

Life in developed countries involves people in many stimulating activities. Interest in providing food, even for the family, may wane and involvement in cooking can often seem too time-consuming.

Information about food is abundant, but it often conflicts and isn't always helpful. Information can be found in textbooks, from the media, on food labels, in advertisements, in cookery books and reference books. It is not always consistent and much of it cannot be understood by those who listen to or read it.

Many people prefer not to bother too much about food and some would be happy if they could do without it altogether. The food industry could become the main influence in our understanding and choice of food.

For some, even eating food has become a chore! With so many fresh, colourful, varied foods arriving from all over the world, it is sad to think that some people don't find them enjoyable.

ACTIVITY 1.2

An exercise to find information about food

1   Begin to build up a file of notes on as many sources of information about the foods you eat as you can. These may include magazine and television advertisements, food and cookery programmes on television and radio, newspaper and magazine articles, textbooks and other course-work books, the labels on packets and tins, information supplied by supermarkets and other chain stores.

2   Find out as much as you can about (i) milk, (ii) baked beans and (iii) margarine.

●   Is the information you find consistent? If not, how does it conflict?

You could make a chart of your findings:

Food	Food label	Advertisement	Textbook	Other sources

Where food itself has become regarded as a chore – whether it be in growing it, preparing it, buying it, cooking it – the people who are involved in these activities may be regarded as low in status. Many cooks in care settings may see themselves in this way, too, and may lack the self-confidence to contribute fully to discussions about the part food plays in the care of clients. They should be encouraged to play their important part in the total care plan; their expertise must not be passed by.

Food is fashionable

Food is subject to both superstition and fashion. Superstitions can be handed on from generation to generation. Some have the label 'Old Wives' Tales'. Others can be generated accidentally when foods gain the label 'good' or 'bad'. Some are generated deliberately by food advertisers, the producers of slimming products or regimes or government policies in relation to health.

Some foods just seem to go in and out of favour. For example, brown bread versus white bread has been going on for at least 500 years and perhaps even back to Roman times. Right now butter and margarine are battling it out!

Food is sociable

The sharing of food is basic to our growth as a species that can live in harmony in civilised groups. From very early childhood we learn to share

---

Food is sociable

The basic instinct to choose only appropriate foods, as many animals still do, may have diminished, but one basic human instinct lives on:

Human beings are a sociable species and food is part of the way human society functions. We are one of the very few animals that shares food together.

It is very rare for human beings to be together without some form of food or refreshments being offered and shared.

It is almost automatic to put the kettle on when someone calls especially if they are upset or have a problem. It is our instinct to care for each other and comfort each other with the gift of food.

A family eating together

with each other as we eat with parents and other adults around the meal table.

From the earliest days of human life on earth and at all stages through life, human beings welcome their guests with gifts of food. The more important the guest the more special or elaborate the food. Rejection of the food can cause offence in any group and culture. When living in multi-cultural communities, it is necessary for everyone to be aware of the traditions of others. Sensitivity and great care are required.

Religion, food and celebration

- Try to think of a wedding or a party without food!

Food is an essential part of the way human beings celebrate special occasions. For people of all cultural groups, religion has shaped their social lives and traditions, with many of the celebrations being shaped by religious observances. For some, these observances are still a religious necessity. For others, the traditional celebrations continue without the religious significance. Food is an integral part of religious festivals and special foods form part of the celebrations, often remaining long after their religious significance has been forgotten.

Religion cannot be separated from the way of life and conduct within society. This applies to religions that are traditionally practised in European and New World countries as well as those from other continents. The blessing and sharing of food is part of daily life and worship. In most cultures, children are taught to give thanks for their food – for some their thanks are simply offered to the person who cooked it.

Certain foods have become traditional elements of specific festivals – turkey at Thanksgiving; eggs at Easter (an example of a traditional food from a pre-Christian religion). Foods which are part of the tradition of practising Christians still influence menus for those who are not – fish on Fridays, pancakes on Shrove Tuesday, for example.

Food and celebration

Why do people eat food?

Most people eat food because they enjoy it. There are, of course, many reasons for eating food and choosing different foods at different times. Some of the reasons for eating food are:

- it is part of our social life;
- it is part of family life and activity;
- because we get hungry;
- comfort in times of depression and stress;
- we have got into the habit.

Why do different people eat different foods? What sorts of factors influence choices? Some of the reasons for differences would include:

- upbringing, habits, likes and dislikes;
- religious observances;
- availability of money;
- abilities of the cook;
- availability of time;
- shopping facilities;
- access to (or lack of) freshly grown produce.

What is food?

What constitutes food will vary according to the animal species. Some animals can digest things that human beings cannot. Animals such as cows and horses have the ability to digest cellulose (fibre in the human diet) and

---

ACTIVITY 1.3

Write down your favourite meal. Give your reasons for liking it.

When you eat it do you think about it in terms of your health and nutritional needs?

ACTIVITY 1.4

Make a list of the reasons why you eat food.

How many people of different cultures and religions do you know? Make a list of the foods they eat that are different from your own traditional foods.

ACTIVITY 1.5

What is 'normal?'

1   Select a group of three or four workmates or friends. Each of you write down your usual meal pattern (i.e. what is normal in terms of meal times, whether they are snacks or full meals and the types of foods you would include). List your likes and dislikes. Note the things that make you choose some foods and not others, such as:

- other members of the family don't like it;
- you're a long way from the shops;
- it's too expensive.

2   Now compare notes and talk about similarities and differences within your group.
Make a list of the most common similarities. Would you regard this as an example of what is 'normal'?
Keep these lists of the similarities and differences in your group's meals to compare with what others eat in later Activities.

ACTIVITY 1.6

What is food?

Try writing a definition or at least a sentence or two that just about covers it.

break it down into glucose. What constitutes food will also vary according to national and cultural traditions and these will change over time as understanding and availability change.

But what *is* food? 'Food' is a very hard thing to define. Try it!

Words like 'eaten', 'health', 'nutrients' or 'nutrition', 'energy', 'growth', 'life' come to mind.

Consider each of those in turn.

- Food is eaten, but milk is a food, too;
- Food promotes health, but some things are 'bad for you', they say;
- Food supplies nutrients; that's better (but nutrients are defined as essential ingredients found in food!);
- Food provides energy; sometimes it makes people sleepy;
- Food is necessary for growth; so is it necessary for adults?
- Food is essential for life; so are water and air and they are not classified as food.

'Food' clearly includes all of the above. The *Oxford Concise Dictionary* definition is: 'substances to be taken into the body to maintain life and growth' but even this could do with a bit more explanation.

What is food?

A definition of 'food' could turn out to be: 'Food is any substance which when eaten or drunk provides the body with essential ingredients (nutrients) necessary for proper growth and repair and optimum health. Optimum health includes mental health, happiness, well-being.'

> *The food people choose to eat will vary and may not fit with what some would see as nutritionally ideal, but people get their nutrition from the food they **do** eat which may not be the food that others think they **should** eat.*

Choosing food

Most animals inherit an instinct to choose only certain foods which they know will not be harmful. Some of their wild instincts can alter as they become associated with humans, and this may not always be beneficial.

Human instinct is no longer reliable when it comes to choosing food for health and survival. The choice of food is determined by upbringing, habits, emotional state, likes and dislikes, etc. and there are now many additional factors such as:

- television programmes;
- press;
- peer group;
- advertising;
- articles;
- school curriculum;
- supermarket displays.

These influences can alter from time to time. They may even be politically governed. During World War II, for example, people in the UK were encouraged to grow foods, cook in certain ways, eat foods they were not used to. If there was a glut of a certain food it became 'good for you'!

Is food good or bad?

When talking to older people, they will often say that they were taught that their food was 'good for them', especially if they didn't like it. Such things as cream, butter, eggs, cheese, meat (even dripping); cakes and pastries – as well as spinach, prunes and cod liver oil – would all have been thought essential for staying fit or getting over illness.

Many of those are now thought to be 'bad for you'. As we have seen, food is subject to fashions, superstition and prejudice. Food manufacturers want to sell us their products and will denounce others. Advertisers do not have to tell the whole truth. It seems sometimes to be very confusing and hard to decide; even the 'experts' don't always agree.

Just think though …. if our older clients or relatives have survived 80 or 90 years and are fairly fit, their early diet can't have been totally bad for them, can it? Of course, there are other factors that have helped them to live into healthy old age. It may be that some foods are not useful in the changed lifestyles of the Western world. It may be, however, that some of the 'old fashioned' traditional diets may need to be looked at again to see if they really were all that 'bad'. Researchers need to assess the other factors that appear to be contributing to ill health to see if they should be modified rather than blame everything on the diet.

1.2 Caring for others

> *Everyone is an individual with their own likes, dislikes, preferences and circumstances.*

Caring for others takes place all the time. Older people and other adults who are ill or need support are cared for in hospitals, in residential situations and in their own homes. Children are cared for in residential settings, schools, nurseries, hospitals and with their families at home.

People may have physical disabilities; visual, hearing or oral impairment; learning difficulties; behavioural problems; communication problems.

Rewards, bribes and punishments

'If you're good you can have some sweeties' is an offer that many a child will try hard not to refuse. In former times children would often be sent to bed without their supper as a punishment. It was a punishment as children would be hungry, cold and have no access to pocket money with which to buy their own supply. A modern child living in an affluent household would probably just raid the fridge and make off with tomorrow's dinner!

Food is still part of a system of bribes, rewards and punishments for many and it isn't only children who can be punished through food.

- Certain foods may be thought to be too good for a group of clients in a particular care setting even when that food is cheap and plentiful. External prejudice and a desire to be punitive can bring pressure to bear to remove it from the menu.
- Older people in care can become very distressed when their food is taken away because they are slow, perhaps. They may be told they can't have something they've been looking forward to.
- Sometimes, even, a special diet will be used as a threat in a misguided attempt to get a patient to achieve some desired change in their condition.
- During times of illness, distress and pain, people often comfort themselves with a special delicacy. Many people allow themselves a reward after a hard day's work or a very trying time. For some it will be chocolate, for others a whisky or a beer. They feel they've earned it – what others think about that food being 'good' or ' bad' will be irrelevant.

Food as punishment

Food as a bribe

Describing foods as 'bad for you' can give rise to feelings of guilt and resentment without altering what people choose to eat. This, in itself, could be a kind of punishment for people who have grown up liking some of these foods. There are better reasons for doing something than the fact that someone else thinks it will be good for you.

In general, using food for bribes, rewards or punishments is not good practice in any care situation. It leaves people of all ages with strong feelings about some foods which could lead to very unbalanced eating patterns or disturbed behaviour and resentment towards those who care for them.

Tea and sympathy

Food clearly provides people with a great deal more than nutrients and a means of survival. Health and well-being are dependent on food as well as love, shelter, warmth, security, self-esteem and fulfillment, all of which form the basis of a hierarchy of human needs. The comfort provided by food is often far more important than the nutrients it contains.

Looking forward to something gives a large boost to morale which can lift a state of depression and lead the way for a quicker recovery. Sensitivity, however, is required in being aware when a client is playing on a carer's good will. It is easy to fall into the trap of spoiling someone out of sympathy.

Providing both healthy eating and comfort without fuss involves knowing about food as well as about people. For healthy people living busy, active lives, choice of food is fairly automatic. It is part of our regular, often unconscious, planning. Sometimes, though, we have to give food a great deal more attention.

There are times in life when what we eat and when we eat it can make the difference between death or life, long-term illness or recovery, loneliness or belonging, depression or well-being. Often at these very vulnerable times, we cannot choose or prepare foods for ourselves. Someone who cares has to do it for us. It is not enough to rely solely on normal meals, usual foods, quick and easy solutions. At these times, someone has to really care about food – as well as about us.

> *'A little of what you fancy does you good'* – an old adage that is worth remembering at times.

CASE STUDY 1.1

Following the death of her husband, Mrs A did not want to cook meals for herself. She lived on breakfast cereals, bread and butter, cheese and biscuits and tinned soup. When she caught a chill it rapidly became bronchitis and despite antibiotics she became very weak and could not eat much at all.

She needed someone to care.

Mrs A had, by now, several problems to contend with:

- she was still grieving for her loss;
- she was lonely and depressed;
- she was suffering from a lack of some nutrients;
- she was recovering from a severe illness and from the effects of antibiotics;
- she did not even have the energy to readily make the digestive juices to digest her meals.

Caring involves giving time and trouble to food and a lot of thought and persistence.

The type of situation outlined here is quite common on admission to hospitals, nursing homes and in domestic situations, too. The answer lies in offering very small, very frequent meals.

- Small, dainty items served frequently throughout the day with a small drink in between.
- Glucose is the quickest source of energy. It can be bought in a powder and dissolved in a fruit juice or other drinks. A small glucose drink given before a meal is the best way to ensure that a debilitated person has an energy source to readily make digestive juices for that meal.
- Avoid large, main meals. However high in nutrients, however attractive:
  - they have to be chewed which takes energy;
  - they can overface someone who is very frail;
  - they may make the situation worse.
- Commercial high-protein supplements may seem like an easy option, but:
  - they do not provide enough Calories or protein on their own;
  - they may interfere with a person's food intake by depressing their appetite;
  - they may also imply that a carer does not really care that much after all.

Follow the guidelines for a high protein, high Calorie diet given on page 93 in Chapter 5 for about two weeks. This may seem a long time to be bothering, but in the long run it can reduce the length of time a client needs to be dependent and cared for. In the long term it can be the most cost-effective answer. Also, your client will be glad to be independent again.

Imagination and ingenuity

It is often a useful exercise to think yourself into someone else's place. Try to remember how you felt as a child. Try to imagine how you would manage if you were disabled and alone.

In almost every situation, ingenuity can solve what may appear to be a difficult problem. There is always a way around a difficulty and together, carers and clients can usually find it.

ACTIVITY 1.7

With one hand held behind your back, try to eat a soft boiled egg in an egg cup.

With your eyes shut, try to eat a plate of baked beans.

With a partner, take it in turns to feed each other.

Sit on your fingers for 5 minutes. Then try to use a knife and fork or open a bottle.

1.3 The biographical approach

Professional carers will use the biographical approach to get to know their clients, in order to plan a care package that fits their special needs. Part of this process will enable the carer to find out about the foods that the client likes and enjoys. Finding out about their diet history is one way of finding out other things, too.

In the case of very young children, details must be obtained from older relatives and their contribution can be valuable in all other situations too. However, carers must be sensitive to tensions that may exist within close relationships. It is sometimes necessary to have more than one session to achieve a reasonable assessment, checking up on points where there has been disagreement between client and relative.

It is important to remember always that everything a client relates is in the strictest confidence and may only be passed on to others with the knowledge of the client or, sometimes, their relatives.

ACTIVITY 1.8

Aim: to investigate a person's diet history.

1   Sit down with one of your older clients or relatives – someone in their 70's, say – and ask them about their childhood and early life. Many elderly people who are forgetful of recent events will happily remember 'the old days'.

2   As you ask them to remember their family, ask them what they ate at tea, at school, at weekends, etc. As you listen to the answers you will think of other things that you might find interesting. You will also begin to build up a picture of life in the early days of our older citizens and you may be able to relate some of the dietary factors with their present state of health.

Remember to treat everything you are told with strict confidence and professionalism.

Types of questions that you could ask include:

How many children were in your family?
What number child were you?
What did your father do for a living?
Where were you born and brought up?
Did you have a fairly good income or were you sometimes short of money?
What did you do during holidays?
What type of meals do you remember having?
Did you enjoy your food?

Did you have any meals at school?
When did you leave school?
Did you go out to work or did you stay at home to help your mother with the other children (assuming your respondent is a woman)/help in father's work (if your respondent is a man)?
Tell me about your own family. How did you meet your wife/husband (if there was one)?
How many children did you have (if there were any)?
Do you remember the pregnancies? Was this during the second war?
How did the rationing affect what you all ate then? And so on.

You might also ask: What is your favourite food? What is your favourite meal?

3   Write down their meal patterns, their reasons for their likes and dislikes and their food habits. Compare this with your responses in the exercise on page 4 where you did the same enquiry into your own group's food intake.

4   Make a note of the differences and similarities. Does this give you ideas about what to include in a menu for older clients or about advising older clients on planning meals?

2 Food and diet

A diet is just a daily intake of food.

We all have a diet of one sort or another.

The word 'diet' has come to mean a specific regime of food intake and in many cases it is assumed that it relates to slimming. The phrase 'I'm on a diet' is often used by women to refer to their attempts to lose a few pounds in weight. 'Dieting' is very fashionable and is a very lucrative business for many companies and distributors of slimming regimes.

Some of the many factors that affect choice in a person's individual diet were discussed in Chapter 1.

ACTIVITY 2.1

1 Look back at the lists on pages 4 and 6.
Add to the lists as many other factors as you can think of that affect what people choose to eat.

2 Write down what you ate and drank yesterday. Alongside each item write down why you chose that item. For example:

– it was there;
– it looked nice;
– it is one of my favourites;
– I could afford it, etc.

2.1 Balancing diets – what does it mean?

When people choose meals and menus, balancing the nutrients, however important, is not usually at the top of their list. Many aspects in our choice of food contribute to balance and there are many things to balance.

- *Well-being:* Food contributes a great deal to the feeling of well-being. Food can be a very good anti-depressant.
- *Taste, texture, colour:* Balancing meals makes use of the wide variety of these three characteristics.
- *Different foods and ingredients:* There are now so many that it is possible to experiment and increase variety, but the menu should include tried and tested dishes as well.

- *Money:* Food is often the most costly item in a household budget. However, not all foods are expensive, neither are expensive foods always the best; balancing costs can be achieved by careful planning. In a home or day centre or where food is prepared in bulk, staff salaries can add to the cost. Good menu-planning takes this into account.
- *Nutrients:* We cannot forget the nutrients altogether. Nearly all the nutrients work in conjunction with each other and need to be balanced together when planning meals. These nutrients are considered later in this chapter and in more depth in Chapter 6.

Balancing meals and menus

In all cases and in all cultures a balanced meal is based on a *staple food*. Staple foods include:

- all the cereal grains – wheat, oats, barley, rye, rice, corn;
- some root crops – potatoes, yams, cassava (tapioca);
- some pulses and seeds – lentils, millet;
- some tree crops – sago, okra, plaintain.

The staple food varies from country to country and from region to region within countries. In England the staple food for many centuries has been wheat, whereas in Scotland it has traditionally been barley and oats. For the last 500 years a second staple food in Britain has been the potato. This became the staple food in Ireland as it grew better than wheat in areas of high rainfall.

Other cereals and crops are now coming into the UK shops and adding to the traditional diet, for example bulgar wheat, buckwheat, millet. These can also give greater variety to the diets of vegetarians or people who suffer from allergies. Many of these crops will be made into traditional dishes and breads according to a region's tradition: dahl, pasta, oatcakes, porridge, for example. Others will be cooked and served as the basis of the meal.

Staple foods usually form the bulk of the meal. All staples are high in the carbohydrate, *starch*, and must be cooked, as raw starch is not digestible by humans. As well as starch, a staple food usually contains some *protein* and some *vitamins* and *minerals*. Staple crops are usually low in fat. Traditional diets have found ways to compensate where the staple food does not contain many nutrients other than starch.

> **KEY CONCEPT**
> A **Staple food** is the food, usually a cereal or vegetable crop, most heavily relied on to fulfil the energy needs for the majority of people within a country or region where it grows easily.

ACTIVITY 2.2

Change and you

How has your diet changed over the years? What was your favourite meal when you left school? What is it now?
Make a list of the meals and common foods in your diet 10 years ago and now.

If there is a change, can you say what made the change?
e.g. moved away from parental home; now have more money for convenience foods; have my own family now to provide for; television programmes and magazine articles and advertisements have made me change, etc.

ACTIVITY 2.3

Begin to keep a diary of your daily food intake for a week. Include all foods, snacks, beverages and drinks.
Keep this diary for Activities in later chapters.

When planning meals and menus, select the staple food that is most appropriate for the group or occasion. For example:

- many meals from Asia will be based around rice;
- Mexican dishes often include corn (maize);
- European bread and flour may be rye-based.

With the increase in global transport of food, many traditional recipes have been adapted to use staples other than the traditional crop of the region.

A *balanced meal* is based on the staple food with the addition of other foods to balance nutrients, colour, flavour, texture and cost. For example:

- nuts, pulses, meat, fish, cheese, eggs, milk or yoghurt to give extra protein and contribute to mineral intake;
- fresh vegetables, salad and/or fruit give fibre, vitamins A and C, colour, texture and taste;
- butter or margarine, ghee or oil provide fat and absorb the fat-soluble vitamins;
- cakes, pastry, puddings (preferably home-made) and extra fats or oil provide extra energy when needed, for example during growth or illness.

NB: To ensure an adequate intake of vitamin D in Britain (and other countries with low sunshine records), oily fish such as salmon, herring, sardine, etc. may need to be taken once a week.

> *EXAMPLE* Balanced meal
>
> Boiled rice: staple;
> Curried chicken and vegetables: added protein (chicken);
> Fibre, vitamins and minerals (fresh vegetables);
> Poppadums: second staple with added fat;
> Fresh fruit (mango): fibre, vitamins and minerals.

A balanced diet for a day should contain:

- three balanced meals as outlined above and
- 2 or 3 between-meal snacks.

It may not always be possible to achieve this but small, frequent meals enable the body to cope better than an intake of large, occasional meals. Quantities in each case, will be determined by the person's individual requirements.

ACTIVITY 2.4

Write down a meal menu similar to the example given. Either one that you have just eaten or one that is being provided for your clients.
Identify which parts of it provide the staple, the balancing nutrients, the colour, texture and taste. Is it 'balanced'?

Regional variations

Many traditional diets include much the same dish in a form that suits the region and climate. For example, people in the UK are familiar with the traditional Cornish pastie – a pastry shell with a savoury filling inside. The same idea occurs in many different guises including:

- meat and potato pie – Yorkshire;
- ravioli – Italy;
- samosas – India;
- curry puffs – Malaysia;
- spring rolls – China.

ACTIVITY 2.5

Look through recipe books – especially those which include dishes from non-British cultures. See how many variations you can find on the theme of a pastry or pasta shell with a savoury filling. Try the same exercise with another dish that you regard as part of your own tradition.

The effects of cooking and processing on foods

Many meals and menus include processed, convenience foods. In some types of catering most of the meal is composed of food which has undergone some form of processing whereas in others, caterers try to provide meals based on fresh, unprocessed foods. This is another area where balance is important. Convenience foods save a good deal of costly time and, where they do not affect the overall nutritional balance of a menu, need not give cause for worry.

In some cases the processing actually improves the taste, texture, colour or availability of nutrients. However, the more highly processed a food is, the less likely it will be to contain its original colour, taste, texture or nutrients. It may have laboratory-made nutrients added and may also have added colour, flavourings and preservatives. Some important nutrients are affected by cooking and processing, particularly vitamin C and the B group vitamins (see also page 19).

Achieving a balance for ourselves and others is not always easy. We may make ourselves a set of ideals only to find that we then have to make compromises. Our ideals might include:

- Eat small meals regularly.
- Try not to eat on the move.
- Where possible, choose foods which have undergone very little processing.
- In the main, buy locally-grown fresh produce, as opposed to imported goods.
- In the main, buy foods in their normal season.
- Make your own dishes. This has many advantages – lower cost, fresh ingredients, less processing and packaging.

Breakfast is considered by many to be the most important meal of the day. Its effect on metabolism acts as a stimulus for the body to return to its day-time operational mode after sleep. Some people can cope quite well

The National Food Guide

The Balance of Good Health

Fruit and vegetables
Choose a wide variety

Bread, other cereals and potatoes
Eat all types and choose high fibre kinds whenever you can

Meat, fish and alternatives
Choose lower fat alternatives whenever you can

Fatty and sugary foods
Try not to eat these too often, and when you do, have small amounts

Milk and dairy foods
Choose lower fat alternatives whenever you can

Reproduced by permission of the Heath Education Authority.
The balance of good health

without eating breakfast. Others find they are less well able to cope with work or school and that their reaction times are slower.

When taking diet histories (see page 10) you may hear people say that they miss breakfast to save time or because they think it's a meal they can do without or they prefer to sleep until the last minute. This may be just a current fashion or a sign that human bodies are adapting to external change. Only time will tell.

2.2 Grouping foods to achieve balance

Food can be classified broadly into five main food groups. This type of grouping can over-simplify the situation and may lead to some confusion. In terms of nutrients, for example, there is considerable cross-over between the groups and when looking at nutritional balance it is often necessary to consider the overall diet rather than just the food groups.

The *Balance of Good Health* 1994 reflects the guidelines for a balanced diet given on page 13. Emphasis is placed on the staple foods, supplemented by fruits and vegetables, milk and dairy foods, meat, fish, pulses, nuts and eggs, with fats and sugary foods carrying a warning. This scheme can be adapted to any traditional diet and forms the basis of the nation's guide to healthy eating.

The five food groups are:

- bread, other cereals and potato;
- fruit and vegetables;
- milk and dairy foods;
- meat, fish, and alternatives;
- fatty and sugary foods.

ACTIVITY 2.6

Make a chart with the help of the guidelines in *The Balance of Good Health* booklet (*The Balance of Good Health* 1994, published by The Health Education Authority/MAFF).

Food group	Main nutrients	What to eat	Which to avoid
Bread, etc.			
Fruit and vegetables			
Milk and dairy foods			
Meat and fish			
Fatty and sugary foods			

2.3 Nutrition in a nutshell

The main nutrients and their functions

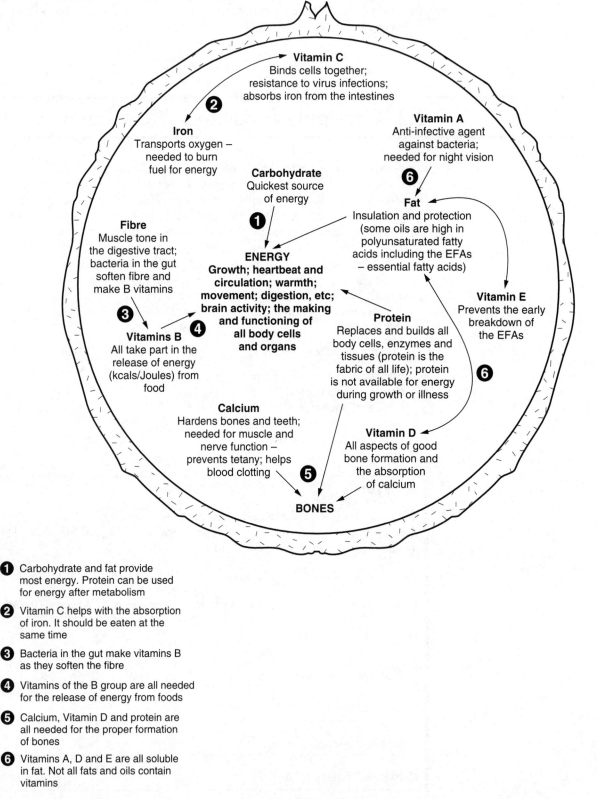

Vitamin C
Binds cells together;
resistance to virus infections;
absorbs iron from the intestines

❷

Iron
Transports oxygen –
needed to burn
fuel for energy

Carbohydrate
Quickest source
of energy

❶

Vitamin A
Anti-infective agent
against bacteria;
needed for night vision

❻

Fat
Insulation and protection
(some oils are high in
polyunsaturated fatty
acids including the EFAs
– essential fatty acids)

Fibre
Muscle tone in
the digestive tract;
bacteria in the gut
soften fibre and
make B vitamins

❸

Vitamins B
All take part in the
release of energy
(kcals/Joules) from
food

❹

**ENERGY
Growth; heartbeat and
circulation; warmth;
movement; digestion, etc;
brain activity; the making
and functioning of
all body cells
and organs**

Protein
Replaces and builds all
body cells, enzymes and
tissues (protein is the
fabric of all life); protein
is not available for energy
during growth or illness

Vitamin E
Prevents the early
breakdown of
the EFAs

❻

Calcium
Hardens bones and teeth;
needed for muscle and
nerve function –
prevents tetany; helps
blood clotting

❺

Vitamin D
All aspects of good
bone formation and
the absorption
of calcium

BONES

❶ Carbohydrate and fat provide
most energy. Protein can be used
for energy after metabolism

❷ Vitamin C helps with the absorption
of iron. It should be eaten at the
same time

❸ Bacteria in the gut make vitamins B
as they soften the fibre

❹ Vitamins of the B group are all needed
for the release of energy from foods

❺ Calcium, Vitamin D and protein are
all needed for the proper formation
of bones

❻ Vitamins A, D and E are all soluble
in fat. Not all fats and oils contain
vitamins

The main nutrients and their sources

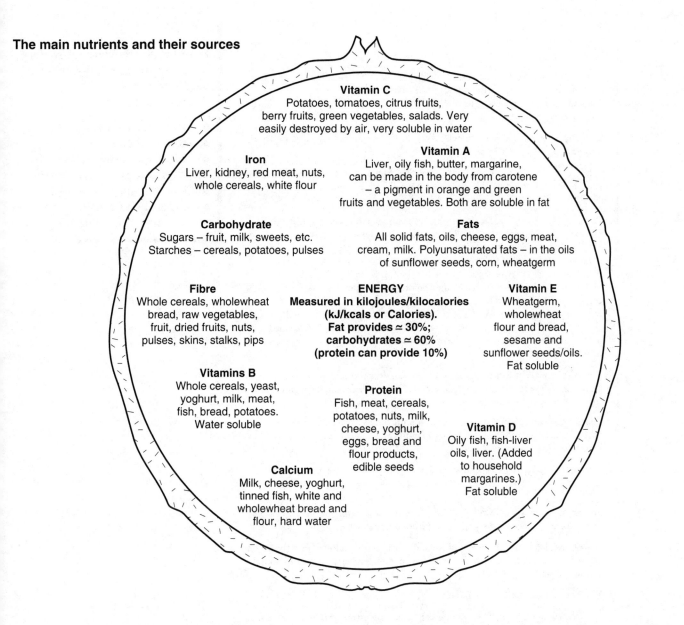

Vitamin C
Potatoes, tomatoes, citrus fruits,
berry fruits, green vegetables, salads. Very
easily destroyed by air, very soluble in water

Iron
Liver, kidney, red meat, nuts,
whole cereals, white flour

Vitamin A
Liver, oily fish, butter, margarine,
can be made in the body from carotene
– a pigment in orange and green
fruits and vegetables. Both are soluble in fat

Carbohydrate
Sugars – fruit, milk, sweets, etc.
Starches – cereals, potatoes, pulses

Fats
All solid fats, oils, cheese, eggs, meat,
cream, milk. Polyunsaturated fats – in the oils
of sunflower seeds, corn, wheatgerm

Fibre
Whole cereals, wholewheat
bread, raw vegetables,
fruit, dried fruits, nuts,
pulses, skins, stalks, pips

ENERGY
Measured in kilojoules/kilocalories
(kJ/kcals or Calories).
Fat provides ≃ 30%;
carbohydrates ≃ 60%
(protein can provide 10%)

Vitamin E
Wheatgerm,
wholewheat
flour and bread,
sesame and
sunflower seeds/oils.
Fat soluble

Vitamins B
Whole cereals, yeast,
yoghurt, milk, meat,
fish, bread, potatoes.
Water soluble

Protein
Fish, meat, cereals,
potatoes, nuts, milk,
cheese, yoghurt,
eggs, bread and
flour products,
edible seeds

Vitamin D
Oily fish, fish-liver
oils, liver. (Added
to household
margarines.)
Fat soluble

Calcium
Milk, cheese, yoghurt,
tinned fish, white and
wholewheat bread and
flour, hard water

Water is the main transport system of the body. Materials are carried in solution or suspension around the body and into or out of cells.

Energy in food and in the body is measured in kilocalories or kilojoules. A kilocalorie is equal to 1000 calories and is often abbreviated to **Calorie** (with a capital c). A joule is a very small amount of energy so the usual units are kilojoules (**kJ**) or megajoules (**mJ**).

One kilocalorie (kcal) is equal to approximately 4.19 kilojoules (kJ).

Table 2.1 *The foods we eat and the nutrients they provide*

Food	Nutrients provided and additional information
Bread and wheat flour products	Protein, carbohydrate, calcium, iron, B vitamins, fibre (wholewheat products contain more fibre than refined flour products) Calcium, iron, vitamin B_1 and nicotinic acid are added to refined flour in the UK, by law
Other cereal grains	Carbohydrate, protein (content will vary), B vitamins, minerals (fibre in wholegrain products)
Breakfast cereals	Made from unrefined cereal grains: see above. Made from refined cereal grains: carbohydrate. B vitamins, calcium and iron may be added to some products; check the label
Milk, cheese and yoghurt, fromage frais	Protein, fat, (carbohydrate in milk), calcium, B vitamins (some vitamin A especially in Channel Island milk). Low and lower fat varieties are available. Skimmed milk contains almost no fat and no vitamin A; semi-skimmed milk contains half the fat of full cream milk and much less vitamin A Evaporated milks may be made from full-fat or half-fat milks. The nutrient content of the milks will be concentrated by the evaporation of water. Some of the vitamin B content will be destroyed by the heat process Sweetened condensed milk may be made from full-fat or skimmed milk. A high concentration sugar syrup is added which helps to preserve the product. The nutrient content will depend on the milk used but it will provide a very high level of sugar
Cream	The fat and protein content of dairy cream will depend on its type. The ratio of fat to water increases (and protein decreases) from single cream, through sterilised (tinned) cream, whipping cream, double cream to clotted cream 'Filled' milks and creams are made from skimmed milk with added vegetable oils to reproduce the fat content of full-fat or semi-skimmed milk or dairy cream. They may have added vitamins A and D
Ice cream	Fat, refined sugar, some protein and calcium (dairy ice cream contains butterfat)
Eggs	Protein, fat, iron, B vitamins
Fish	Protein, B vitamins. In oily fish and fish-liver oils – fat, vitamins A and D. In tinned fish – calcium is increased especially if the bones are eaten
Meat	Protein, fat, iron, calcium, B vitamins; Poultry can be much lower in fat and iron content; liver and kidney are lower in fat content, higher in iron and contain vitamins A and D
Potatoes	Vitamin C, protein, fibre, B vitamins
Pulse vegetables	Protein, carbohydrate, B vitamins, calcium, iron, fibre (fat in soya beans, peanuts and cashew nuts); vitamin C is high when pulses sprout
Root vegetables	Carbohydrate, fibre (mineral content will vary according to the place where the vegetables are grown) Carrots provide carotene for the body to convert to vitamin A
Green vegetables and salads	Vitamin C, fibre, carotene to convert to vitamin A
Tomatoes	Vitamin C, vitamin A (as carotene)
Citrus fruits and berry fruits	Vitamin C, carbohydrate as fruit sugars, fibre, some B vitamins and some carotene to turn into vitamin A
Other fruits	Carbohydrate as fruit sugars, fibre, some vitamin C
Butter and household margarine	Fat, vitamins A and D. Low fat spreads contain about half the fat of butter and margarine Vitamins A and D are added to all domestic margarines and low fat substitutes in the UK

ACTIVITY 2.7

From the diagram on page 16 trace some important links between nutrients.
What is the link between:

- iron and vitamin C?
- iron and energy?
- energy and the vitamins B?
- fibre and the vitamins B?
- calcium and vitamin D?
- fat and vitamins A and D?
- vitamin A and vitamin C?

Food	Nutrients provided and additional information
Vegetable oils	Fat; there may be some vitamin E in some oils, e.g. wheatgerm oil
Lard, suet, dripping, ghee, etc.	Fat
Sugar, syrups, treacle	Carbohydrate in the form of refined sugar (black treacle contains some iron)
Jams, jellies, marmalades, honey	Carbohydrate in the form of refined sugar; some vitamin C in jams etc. that, are freshly made from fresh fruits; pure honey will contain some B vitamins
Squash, colas, and other fizzy drinks	Carbohydrate in the form of refined sugar
Chocolate	Protein, fat, carbohydrate (refined sugar), iron
Toffees, etc.	Mostly carbohydrate as refined sugar

The effects of cooking and processing on some nutrients

The effects of cooking and processing on taste, colour and texture of foods have already been discussed on page 14. Certain nutrients are altered or destroyed by the effects of heat, air and some chemicals used in processing or cooking. The effects on some of these nutrients include:

- *Protein* – largely unaffected by cooking. If overcooked, it can become very hard and may be undigestible for some people.
- *Starch* – has to be cooked in order for it to be digested. If cooked in acidic solution it can break down into glucose. Starch is partially broken down during cooking in dry heat, i.e. toasting, baking, roasting.
- *Fat* – is not altered by normal cooking methods. If overheated, cooking oils can lose some beneficial properties.
- *Iron* – is not altered by cooking or processing.
- *Calcium* – is not altered by cooking or processing.
- *Vitamins A and D* – can be dissolved out into the cooking or canning oil.
- *Vitamins of the B Group* – some are destroyed by heat and alkalis used in processing. They may dissolve out into the cooking or processing liquid and be discarded.
- *Vitamin C* – is destroyed by air (oxidation). This destruction is increased by heat, the presence of some metals, e.g. copper, and alkalis, e.g. bicarbonate of soda. It is water-soluble and will be discarded if soaked or if cooking liquid is thrown away. Vitamin C is fairly stable in cold, 'dry', acid conditions. For example, vegetables prepared and kept 'dry' in a refrigerator overnight will not lose much of their vitamin C.

Further details on this topic can be found in Chapter 6.

2.4   Healthy eating

Concepts of healthy eating vary and many people are faced with conflict and confusion. Different groups of people have different ideas about what is healthy. Advice can come from food companies, magazines, television and radio programmes as well as the health care professionals, and much of this advice may well be conflicting. Some of the apparent confusion comes from the way in which information is presented, which may not always be understood even by the presenters.

People often find it easier to take no notice of any advice from any source and may simply carry on with their traditional ways, for better or worse. When advising clients about their food in relation to health it is necessary for carers to be sure that they understand the information and are able to translate it into practical terms according to their client's situation.

Guidelines on healthy eating

The Health Education Authority (formerly the Health Education Council) began the process of issuing general guidelines in relation to food and health by publishing '*Proposals for Nutrition Guidelines for Health Education in Britain*' in 1983. These guidelines have been endorsed following the publication of the COMA Report, 46 (*Nutritional Aspects of Cardiovascular Disease*) and form the basis of all guidance being given by health professionals in relation to diet and food.

Current guidelines propose that the British diet should aim to:

- increase fibre;
- increase starch;
- decrease salt;
- decrease total fat, and alter the type of fat eaten;
- decrease sugar.

The aim, in the average diet, is to lower the percentage of kilojoules/Calories (energy) which comes from fats and increase the percentage which comes from carbohydrates, whilst at the same time altering the nature of the fats and carbohydrates consumed. Dietary fibre decreased after the Second World War as foods became more refined and a greater range of convenience foods became available.

The table on the right compares the traditional percentages of energy in the diet provided by proteins, fats and carbohydrates compared with current guidelines.

- *Altering the type of fat* – it is recommended that people should eat more vegetable and fish oils and less fat from meat and dairy products.
- *Altering the type of carbohydrate* – it is recommended that the carbohydrate should be in the form of starches and natural sugars contained in fruits and vegetables rather than as refined sugar and foods containing added sugar.

Is change possible?

The authors of the COMA report, *Nutritional Aspects of Cardiovascular Disease*, recognise that the alterations that they recommend are not easy and may not be achieved by many people. In order to achieve these recommendations it is necessary for the British people to change their traditional diet fairly drastically. For example, people may need to double their intake of starch, alter the type of fat they normally use and, since most British

Nutrient	Percentage of total energy	
	Traditional	Current guidelines
Protein	10–15	10
Fat	40	30
Carbohydrates	45–50	60

traditions use fat in conjunction with starch, they may have to alter their meals and menus. This will probably be unacceptable to many older people.

- Many people in their 50s and 60s were taught that bread and potatoes are fattening and had to be avoided in favour of meat, eggs, cheese, etc.
- Many people in their 80s and 90s who are fairly healthy will think that their traditional diet has not done them all that much harm.

It is possible to change people's thinking but ideas cannot be changed in a hurry. Many people do try to change their diet. Below is a comparison of two daily meal patterns chosen to provide the recommended nutrients for a moderately active man, requiring approximately 2550 kcals daily: 1 – a traditionally British day's menu and 2 – a day's menu using current guidelines. It seems that someone has taken note of the recommendations and tried to alter his diet.

When these two menus were calculated:

- the percentage contribution to total energy in the diet from fat *remains similar* although there is less meat and dairy fat in the second menu. Changing from butter to margarine has made a small contribution to this alteration;
- the percentage contribution to total energy in the diet from carbohydrate *remains similar* although there is a slight reduction in the amount of sugar taken in the second menu.

However, the total energy (Calories) has come down in Menu 2 to well below the recommended intake for that group of men.

On enquiry, it was discovered that Menu 2 was usually supplemented with wine at the evening meal. Adding half a bottle of medium dry wine brings the total Calorie intake up to the required figure. These Calories come from alcohol.

It is not always possible to produce accurate estimates as much depends on the portion sizes which are said to have been eaten. Some of the nutrients which are deemed undesirable will, also, be included in processed and manufactured convenience foods, making estimations even more difficult.

Changing our own diet can present problems. Trying to change someone else's can present even bigger ones as there are so many other factors involved.

ACTIVITY 2.8

Look back at Activity 2.2 that you began earlier in the chapter. Have any of the factors on 'healthy eating' listed on page 20 influenced your choice of food recently?

Menu 1	
Breakfast	Bacon and egg
	Bread and butter; marmalade
	Tea with whole milk
Mid-morning	Tea or coffee with milk
	Sweet biscuit
Midday	Beef casserole
	Mashed potatoes
	Cabbage and carrots
	Stewed fruit with custard
Mid-afternoon	Tea with milk
	Sweet biscuit
Evening meal	Cheese on toast with grilled tomato
	Bread and butter
	Cake
	Tea with milk
Bedtime	Ham sandwich
	Tea with milk
Daily	Whole milk for drinks and cereals

Menu 2	
Breakfast	Orange Juice
	Wheatflakes
	Bread and margarine; marmalade
	Tea or coffee with semi-skimmed milk
Mid-morning	Tea or coffee with milk
	Semi-sweet biscuit
Midday	Tuna or salmon sandwich with salad
	Fresh fruit
	Plain yoghurt
Mid-afternoon	Tea with milk
	Semi-sweet biscuit
Evening meal	Chicken and vegetables with pasta
	Coleslaw
	Cheese, biscuits and fresh fruit
	Coffee with milk
Bedtime	Milk drink
Daily	Semi-skimmed milk for drinks and cereals

When trying to alter meal preferences, do so gradually and with as little alteration to the preferred meals and menu pattern as possible.

It is especially important that older people are not made to feel that their traditional diet has been wrong and bad for them.

Children can react badly if they are always denied the foods that their friends have or that they **think** they should have.

Hints and notes on incorporating the recommendations into meals and menus

Altering fat intake

Fat provides energy, protection and warmth and is a very necessary nutrient in northern climates, especially in winter (refer to the section on fat in Chapter 6). It is a concentrated source of energy which is very valuable in the diets of ill and frail people who have little appetite. Recommendations made in the COMA Report 46 for reducing fat are for healthy adults. They do not apply to the frail and sick or to young children under 5 years of age.

Some fats (dairy fats and fish oils) contain vitamins A and D and levels of these vitamins will need to be monitored if these fats are reduced.

Some hints on altering the fat content of the diet for healthy adults:

- reduce hard fats and replace some with fish and vegetable oils;
- avoid dripping, lard, suet and hardened vegetable fat as much as possible;
- use olive oil or other vegetable oil where appropriate;
- avoid frying foods where possible. Many foods can be grilled, baked or roasted, e.g. bacon, sausage, fish, chops;
- use some table margarine instead of butter but note that people have preferences for one or the other. Some low-fat spreads may be acceptable in sandwiches or on bread, etc;
- skimmed or semi-skimmed milk may be used in sauces, custard, milk puddings, batters and porridge;
- keep cream intake (both dairy cream and cream substitutes) low; some would say avoid it altogether, if possible.

Low fat diets in the treatment of disease are discussed on page 87. Where a patient needs a high protein, high Calorie intake, use is made of fat as a concentrated source of energy (see page 93).

Hardened vegetable fats and margarines are of no greater value to the body than hard animal fats.

Vegetable oils lose some of their useful properties when heated repeatedly or to very high temperatures.

Vegetable oils do not contain the fat-soluble vitamins A and D.

Increasing fibre

Fibre is known as non-starch polysaccharide (NSP). Some people refer to it as cellulose or roughage. It is the indigestible (by humans) material found in plants, i.e. skins, pips, bran, stalks, etc. The function of fibre in the human diet is given in Chapter 6.

In recent years the foods that we choose to eat are more likely to be highly processed, to have undergone more controlled growing cycles and are often packaged as instant, convenience foods. Many of our foods will also contain additives and contaminants from the growing, processing, preserving and packaging areas of the food chain. This means that many of the foods we eat will be low in fibre, and may also contain substances which could be harmful if absorbed rather than excreted. These substances need to be removed from the gut efficiently, along with the waste products of digestion and the remains of some potent digestive juices.

Most people need to ensure that some fibre is included in each meal for the effective passage of that meal. Where the diet needs to be *nutrient-dense*, however, fibre should be kept low. Fibre is very bulky, and where someone is frail, ill or lacks the energy to chew and digest food, it should be kept to a minimum. In such cases, it is important that their food is high in essential nutrients. Fibre can reduce the concentration of nutrients in a meal quite considerably and it can also interfere with the absorption of some nutrients. A fibre gel can be given as a medicine if necessary. It should be given after meals as it may reduce appetite and prevent the patient from eating.

Sources of non-starch polysaccharide are given on pages 103 and 104. These foods can be used in a variety of ways. Sometimes it is possible to use them in ways which are not obvious but care should be taken to maintain the clients' confidence and not hide things from them.

Some hints on adding fibre to ensure an adequate intake in the meals of healthy adults:

- increase amounts gradually over several weeks;
- use some wholewheat flour in cakes, pastry, bread, scones and batters where appropriate. Oatmeal or rolled oats can also be used in teabreads, parkin, gingerbread, flapjacks;
- use porridge oats to thicken mince, Scotch broth, etc;
- use oatmeal in rissoles, meatloaf, meatballs and as a coating on herrings, mackerel, etc. when grilling or frying;
- use dried peas, beans or lentils in stews and soups, if acceptable;
- chopped salad can make a tasty sandwich filling;
- offer digestive biscuits or wholewheat crackers at break times;
- use fresh, stewed or dried fruit daily;
- offer a choice of porridge or wholegrain cereals at breakfast;
- include vegetables (including potatoes) and salads daily.

Increasing starch

Starch is the carbohydrate found in cereal grains, pulses, potatoes and some root vegetables so most of the foods listed in the section on fibre will provide starch in the diet as well as non-starch polysaccharides (NSP) and other indigestible substances. Starch is the main ingredient of most staple foods (see page 12) and is usually the cheapest, as well as being a quick source of energy.

A healthy diet does not have to be expensive. A number of vegetable-based dishes are well balanced and quite cheap to make. A great variety of cereals and other crops is now available. Menus can introduce these in a variety of ways, encouraging people to eat a great deal more starch while cutting down on fats. Most cereal grains, pulses and potato also contain protein, so it is possible to increase starch in the diet and, at the same time, include a variety of complementary proteins.

Decreasing salt

Salt (sodium chloride) is an essential ingredient in all body fluids. It is always in the same ratio with water in the body, i.e. water and salt balance go together.

In temperate climates, about 2 g of salt are required per day. Many people normally eat more than this amount. Salt is excreted via the kidneys, sweat, faeces and in tears. Babies and young children have limited control over the amount of sweat they produce and its mineral content. They may lose too much salt and become dehydrated in very hot weather.

Clients may also lose salt and water in any condition where there is vomiting and diarrhoea, when salt, other minerals and water can become so depleted that death can occur from dehydration.

The COMA Report, 41, *Dietary Reference Values for Food Energy and Nutrients for the United Kingdom* suggests an intake of fibre of 12–24 g per day for healthy adults. (These recommendations do not apply to children under 5 years old.)

A traditional British diet can provide up to 18 g of fibre so it may not be necessary to increase fibre intake too enthusiastically.

KEY CONCEPT
Nutrient dense – the meal must contain a high level of a number of nutrients in a fairly small amount of food. Fibre and water should be kept to a minimum as they are bulky and dilute the overall nutrient content.

It is unnecessary and can be dangerous to add bran to everything.

The harmful effects of salt

Damage to the kidneys, heart, liver or blood vessels often results in decreased bloodflow. Pressure builds up and the body begins to retain excess water. The effects of this high blood pressure (hypertension) can be dangerous and even life-threatening.

As the salt:water ratio in the body remains constant, it follows that reducing salt intake should reduce the amount of water in the body and so reduce blood pressure. Information about low salt diets is given in Chapter 5.

Some hints on decreasing salt in the normal diet for healthy adults:

- salt substitutes containing potassium are available but may not be suitable in some conditions. They are not recommended for use in cooking as they can leave a metallic taste;
- use cooking methods which do not need salt, for example roast, grill or fry meats; grill or fry fish; roast, sauté, bake or chip potatoes;
- use unsalted or slightly salted butter in baking and omit any salt from the recipe;
- reduce salt in cooking vegetables, soups and sauces;
- use other flavourings where appropriate, for example herbs, spices, onions, celery, vinegar, lemon juice;
- reduce intake of salted meats and fish and other items high in salt, for example bacon, ham, corned beef, sausages, smoked fish, tinned fish, crisps, cheese, salted roast nuts;
- eat less convenience foods (including sweet foods) in favour of home-made equivalents, which are likely to contain less salt;
- *check all labels* for added salt.

People who need very strict control of their salt levels must obtain a low sodium diet from a registered dietitian. Sodium in other forms will also be restricted.

Decreasing sugar

This refers to refined granulated sugars and syrups made from sugar cane or sugar beet, maple syrup and manufactured honey:

- where possible, reduce the amount of sugar in recipes containing sugar, for example in milk puddings, custard, crumbles and sponge mixes;
- offer a sugar substitute, if necessary, for tea or other drinks;
- where possible, use home-made products rather than bought, made-up or packet mixes for cakes, puddings, sauces, biscuits, jams, etc;
- for desserts include fruit, home-made yoghurt and cheese;
- where possible, use unsweetened fruit juices instead of concentrated fruit squash;
- look out for hidden sugar in processed foods, e.g. baked beans, tomato ketchup, other bottled sauces, tomato and other soups, breakfast cereals;
- *check all labels* for added sugar.

ACTIVITY 2.9

Plan a week's menu for yourself following the healthy eating guidelines.

- Do you find that some of them are conflicting?
- Could you keep to all the guidelines or would some of them be inconvenient?

References and further reading

COMA Report No. 41 1991: *Dietary Reference Values for Food Energy and Nutrients for the United Kingdom*. HMSO

COMA Report No. 46 1994: *Nutritional Aspects of Cardiovascular Disease*. HMSO

Coultate and Davies 1994: *Food – The Definitive Guide*. Royal Society of Chemistry

The Balance of Good Health. The Health Education Authority, Hamilton House, Mabledon Place, London WC1H 9TX

1993: *Enjoy Healthy Eating*. The Health Education Authority

3 Food and caring

Through the NHS and Community Care Act 1990, the UK government set out its objective to help people lead, as far as possible, full and independent lives; to give them a much better opportunity to secure the services they need and to stimulate public agencies to tailor services to the individual's needs.

Caring in the community

Caring for people in the community is now an increasingly important element of the provision of care to people at all stages of life. People who are ill, sometimes terminally, disadvantaged or in some way disabled will increasingly receive the care they need in their own homes.

Care plans

Local authority social services departments have the responsibility to assess the needs of individuals and offer a care package to meet those needs. The care can come from a variety of agencies including:

- health care professionals – both statutory and private;
- voluntary organisations;
- relatives;
- neighbours;
- friends.

The package should be arranged by the care coordinator and the client and will take into account the need for the client to be as independent as he/she wants to be and is able to be.

There are many factors to consider when caring for others and the care plan which is established for each client will need to include the food issues that relate to that client. As with all aspects included in the care plan, the client's diet must be well monitored and other advice given, if necessary, as a client's condition or circumstances change.

Within the care plan, food may be:

- prepared entirely by the client with or without the help of a partner;
- provided by relatives, friends or neighbours;
- provided by an outside provider and delivered to the door or at a day centre or club.

The food may also be subsidised by the local authority's social services department.

In the main this chapter will help those who care for others in their own homes but much of the information can be adapted for use in other caring contexts.

3.1   Giving advice to clients

Whatever the caring situation, you as a carer will be asked for advice or opinion on food at some point. Many people assume that because it's food, you should know all about it and because you are a carer, you will know all the answers. As we have seen, there are many conflicting ideas about food, diet and nutrition, and not all the 'experts' agree.

If you don't know the answer, say so. You can always add 'but I'll find out for you, if you would like me to'. However, you will find that both you, and your clients, know quite a lot.

A good carer can always learn from others' experience. It is necessary to know how far you can go alone in dealing with a client's request for advice or information and when to refer to a professional trained in food issues, such as a dietitian or clinical nutritionist.

Carers may be asked to advise individuals or their families on a wide variety of food issues. For example:

- healthy eating;
- special diets;
- feeding a young family;
- budgeting.

Some carers may be asked to suggest meals and menus:

- for someone who wants to be independent but has limited abilities and memory;
- for someone who is terminally ill and who wants to be nursed at home;
- to encourage an elderly person to revive their interest in cooking or a younger person to enjoy learning to cook;
- to help someone leaving long-term care and going into a hostel or bed-sitter.

Advice may be needed for the care of all ages from young babies to the elderly. The person may be physically disabled, have severe learning difficulties or have a chronic disease. Many will be struggling to cope on a very small, fixed income. At all times there is a need to ensure that clients stay as healthy as possible and enjoy their food. There are no rules that can be applied in all circumstances and at all times.

- Each client's needs and circumstances must be assessed individually. No two people will need the same advice.
- The advice given must be worked out for each client by considering all the individual circumstances.
- *Nutritional requirements* must be remembered and nutritional status may sometimes need to be assessed and monitored.
- *Well-being and happiness* are often the more noticeable factors and must be emphasised.
- Consistency is important.

In some households more than one care professional may be called in to help. Some clients will attend day centres or resource centres. Some clients will spend time in respite care or in hospital. Children will attend health clinics and, later, school.

ACTIVITY 3.1

Look at the diagram on page 27. Copy each heading and write underneath, the factors which would need to be considered by someone who came to look after you if you were ill.

Note the many variations of circumstances that you might encounter as a carer.

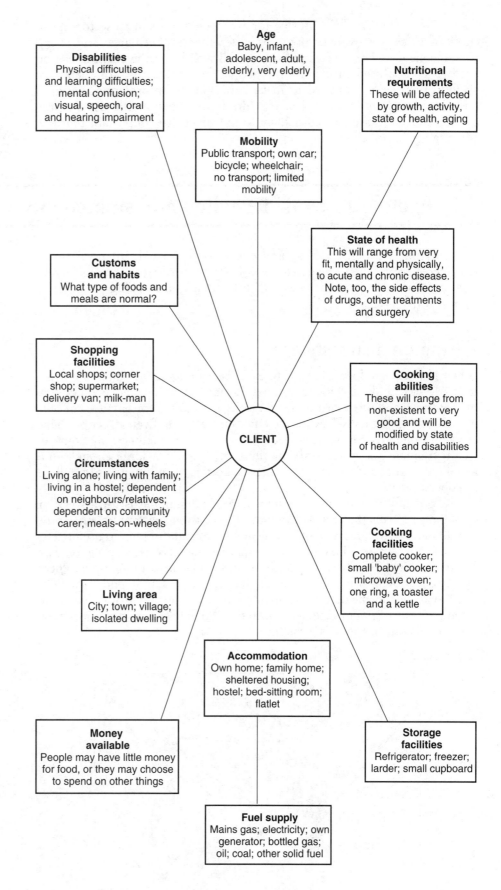

Factors to consider when advising a client on a healthy diet

Food information can be confusing for everyone. Carers in all sectors must check that they are aware of any information that has been given to a client by someone else. For the sake of health and well-being the client does not need to be confused further by the people who are caring for them. As an individual carer you need to make sure that the information you give tallies with others in the team. If it doesn't, talk with the other team members rather than contradict them to the client. It is important that the advice given is consistent.

3.2 Factors to consider when advising clients

The buying, storing, cooking and eating of food will all need to be considered from time to time. Advice will vary according to various factors relating to the status of the client, with financial status being particularly significant.

Eating on a shoestring

When finances are low it is hard to eat a healthy diet and almost impossible to do so if cooking skills are limited. In many cases the diet becomes very monotonous and often clients spend money earmarked for payment of bills in order to give themselves or their families a treat. Even if people have enough money to cover their needs in theory, their income may come in small, frequent (or infrequent) amounts, with never a large enough sum available at one time to make use of special offers or to buy items in bulk at a reduced price.

Advice on planning ahead is invaluable. Planning meals for a week or even longer means that clients can make use of oven space more efficiently, can do more than one batch of baking at a time, and can plan to use up leftovers without waste. Maximising oven space when it is on is also a good way to save on fuel bills. Ovens, especially electric ones, take a long time to heat up and cool down. Some dishes, such as jacket potatoes, milk puddings, flapjacks, will cook as the oven heats up or cools down. It is good advice to cook a complete meal *either* in the oven *or* on the hob, where possible; putting the oven on for just one item is wasteful.

Shortage of money isn't the only factor that determines whether people live on unbalanced and even nutritionally inadequate diets. People who have a good income may be very confused about diet and some find handling money so difficult as to be regularly in debt.

Tips for menu planning on a low budget

Good food, which provides all the nutrients in an attractive, acceptable and enjoyable way, does not always have to be expensive.

- A small amount of a concentrated protein food, together with a staple food (cereal grains), is all that is needed. Cheese, eggs, nuts, meat and fish can all be 'stretched' with pulses, vegetables and cereal grains and made very economical (see page 12 for balancing meals and menus).
- Combining two or three vegetable protein sources in one meal creates a total protein value as good as, if not better than that supplied by meat. For example, pasta can be served with a mixture of vegetables including pulses.
- Cheaper cuts of lean beef, pork and lamb will contain the same nutrients as more expensive ones, once cooked. Offal is always good value for money.
- Chicken and turkey are usually fairly low in price per pound or kilo, and the bones make a very good basis for soup. A homemade soup using fresh vegetables and pulses and served with a cheesey dumpling or topped with plain yoghurt makes a cheap and satisfying meal on a cold day.
- Oily fish (kippers, herring, mackerel) are usually cheaper than white fish and have a wider nutritional value. Tinned sardines, pilchards and tuna are very good value for money and make useful fillings for sandwiches or baked potatoes.

Shopping

The availability and accessibility of shopping facilities vary enormously.

- There is no guarantee that everyone will have a supermarket nearby, with the great variety that a large store can offer, even if they have the ability to visit one.
- Clients may not have the transport necessary to get to a supermarket, or they may not be able to carry bulky or heavy shopping.
- Although most large chainstore companies are aware of the problems faced by many of their customers, some shops and stores do not have disabled access nor facilities to help people who have visual, hearing or speech impairment.
- Some clients with a visual or hearing impairment may not be aware of the special money-saving offers around.
- Clients in wheelchairs or using walking sticks may not be able to reach items on high shelves and many older people are shorter in stature as a result of poor nutrition when they were growing up or due to more recent bone loss.
- People with severe learning difficulties may not be able to read or understand the instructions on the tin or packet. Some instructions leave everyone confused in any case.

'It says to stand in hot water for half-an-hour'

Supermarket shopping

The major supermarket chains in Britain have heeded the advice given by organisations which campaign on behalf of vulnerable groups: Age Concern England, the Royal National Institute for the Blind (RNIB), the Disabled Living Foundation for example, are all able to advise on facilities required for different people. Although some supermarkets provide a number of services, they are not very good at advertising them and making their customers aware of the help that is available.

Many modern stores now offer disabled wheelchair access, special trolleys for wheelchair users, special trolleys to carry up to two toddlers, extra wide aisles and checkouts, trained staff assistance for customers with visual and hearing impairment and help with bag packing at the checkout. Some stores compete with each to offer other services. The following are examples of services offered by some outlets of the large supermarket chains in Britain in the 1990s:

- *ASDA* – staff trained in sign language; special shopping evenings for older people; many own-brand as well as brand-name dietary products; 'sweetie free' checkouts to keep the bill as well as tooth decay down!
- *Marks and Spencer* – actively supports a great deal of work in the community; offers extra services in many stores including level access and at least one automatic sliding door, wide walkways and at least one extra wide food checkout point; permits entry of guide dogs for the blind and hearing dogs for the deaf.
- *Sainsburys* – offer extra information for customers including recipes, guidelines on healthy meals and menus and a variety of fact-sheets (some of these have been recorded onto cassettes for the visually impaired); many own-brand products for special diets and up-to-date booklets on these products as well as recipe books for some special diets; information on television carries subtitles for the hard of hearing; minicom telephone in several stores which assists deaf customers; new schemes set up with the help of the RNIB and the RNID include staff trained to provide practical help to customers with disabilities and staff trained in sign language; a variety of other initiatives in the pipeline to assist visually and hearing impaired shoppers.

However, even the most able-bodied person may find it hard to make sense of the shelf layout or the apparent need to regularly alter it.

Clubs and groups often arrange trips to the nearest supermarket for those who would otherwise not be able to get there. It may not always be possible, on such occasions, to test the store's willingness to help as the clients generally like to be independent, or rely on the carers or each other or simply go without. Some clients go along for the outing and just like to sit in the modern cafeterias chatting.

ACTIVITY 3.2

1 Visit your nearest supermarket. Find out what facilities it offers for people who:

- are elderly;
- not very tall;
- need wheelchair access;
- have a visual or hearing impairment.

If possible take a client with you and jointly assess the facilities offered. First ask to talk to a manager. Then ask to try the facilities out for yourself.

2 Try to visit other supermarkets and large stores. Begin to build up a picture of those that, in your opinion, offer good facilities for people with difficulties and those stores that still have a long way to go.

Supermarket facilities

Both the Royal National College for the Blind and Age Concern offer courses for shop managers and others to enable them to share the experiences of disabled customers. With this increase in awareness of the problems faced by quite a large sector of the population, shopping facilities should progressively improve.

Local shops

Clients often prefer to shop locally where this is possible despite the likelihood of higher cost. Older clients may have grown up in the area and will know the shops, their owners and the other customers. Even when housebound they may prefer their carer to buy their groceries in the shops they have known all their lives. From the carer's point of view, handy local shops can save a great deal of time and enable items to be bought quickly in an emergency.

The corner shop (open all hours) is becoming a rarity in many parts of the country. Most are now managed for a larger company. This gives the advantage of lower prices on the company's own-name items but the brand-name products are still much more highly priced than in the supermarkets.

Shopping services

For many housebound people, the best shopping delivery service and contact with the outside world is still the milkman. Most milk floats carry a range of basic food items and many others can be ordered.

Other shopping services are designed to deliver goods to the elderly, the disabled and the housebound. These services make use of computer technology to enable people to order what they want from a wide ranging catalogue and for these items to be delivered to their home or a centre. Some services are operated jointly by the social services department and a local supermarket. Others are wholly commercial.

Clients can order from a wide range of food and household items and other services may include delivery of prescriptions, dry cleaning and bakery goods. Orders are delivered by trained staff who can also keep a watchful eye on vulnerable clients. In addition to food and household items, some commercial services offer a range of frozen meals to allow clients a choice of menu. These services are available to clients whose needs and circumstances have been assessed by their local social services department.

Two examples of shopping services are given here. There will probably be similar services operating in your area.

- Gateshead Metropolitan Borough Council (social services department) together with Tesco Stores Ltd, operate the *Gateshead Shopping Service*. This service has been growing since its small beginnings in 1980 and has been copied in other areas. It uses centrally located telephone ordering points – local library, community centre, sheltered housing complex. One ordering point is within the local social services department itself so that contact can be made with clients deemed to be at risk.
- *Teleshop Services Ltd* is a commercial organisation, although its origins were similar to the Gateshead venture. The company is expanding to offer the shopping service to all social services departments in Britain.

Computer technology has increased the opportunities for distance shopping and delivery services. People are already able to shop from their club or community centre. They will become more accustomed to ordering their shopping using their own television sets linked through the telephone line.

ACTIVITY 3.3

Find out if there are any shopping services in your local area. If possible, make contact with them to investigate what they are able to offer. Your local social services department will advise you on suppliers and the policy for referring clients for these special services.

Teleshopping

A major disadvantage of this type of remote-control shopping and delivery is the increased risk of isolation and the problems that this could bring to vulnerable, lonely and depressed people.

Storing and cooking food

In this modern age, food storage facilities like refrigerators and freezers are taken for granted by many but not everyone is that privileged:

- not everyone has a refrigerator;
- not everyone has a freezer or cold larder;
- some are without mains electricity or gas;
- many people, especially single clients in flatlets and sheltered housing, have limited cupboard space for food;
- many fridges and freezers are inefficient, often due to ignorance on the client's part of the need to defrost and clean them regularly.

Advising people on buying food in bulk, even if they can afford it, must depend on the availability and type of storage space. Correct storage of food is vital for health and economic reasons (it is wasteful to throw spoiled food away). Chapter 8 covers food safety in depth and gives details of the requirements for correct storage.

The art of good cooking is no longer being passed on from generation to generation. Many people in all walks of life have become increasingly dependent on pre-prepared and pre-cooked meals. Far less emphasis has been placed on cookery and home-management in the school curriculum in recent years and many younger people in Britain have little or no idea where to start.

Encouraging people to learn basic cookery skills and enjoy cooking, where possible, could be one of the most cost-effective measures in the national campaign for the health of the nation. It will certainly make the task of the community carer easier when advising on diet in relation to health. Cooking meals for others is a very strong indication of our care for them.

Attitudes to cooking vary widely from total lack of interest or ability, through regarding it as a chore which someone else should undertake, to ecstatic reverence for all things culinary. Somewhere in the middle is the common-sense, practical, enjoyment of preparing and serving food for others, often the family.

Cookery is the subject of many entertaining television programmes, magazine articles and colourful recipe books with the emphasis being on entertainment. The effect may thus be to discourage people; they feel daunted and inadequate in the face of such exotic ingredients, so many varied implements and techniques and such slick methods. It may seem much easier to go out and buy a takeaway or a convenience frozen meal. It is worth remembering and passing on the fact that all dishes start out from a few, very simple, basic, tried and tested recipes and methods. Basic cookery can sound very dull and unexciting but all cooks, at whatever level, learn the basics and adapt them to produce a whole range of different dishes. Programmes, magazines and recipe books have to appear to be different in order to keep the public interest. Probably, the only real added ingredients are imagination, initiative and a sense of adventure.

Younger clients may be intimidated by the thought of producing meals for themselves or their families, especially if they haven't learned much cookery at school. Carers can help by encouraging them to learn a few basic recipes and build meals around them. Sometimes it is useful to include a convenience product as an encouraging starter, for example a pastry mix or a canned sauce. The client can go on to learn that recipe later. Being able to make a meat pie for themselves, using packet pastry and tinned meat, gives many a novice the encouragement to be more adventurous.

When money is scarce, a young family may be eating a very poor diet unless some home cooking is included. It is not really possible to obtain all the nourishment that a family needs using convenience foods, without spending more money than is available on current UK state benefits.

Many single people are discharged from long-stay hospitals into hostels, small flats or self contained bed-sitters within the community. On a very small income, they find it very difficult to feed themselves and need advice from their carers about shopping, cooking and eating well. Carers will need to take into account their cooking equipment or, in some cases, lack of it. Young people leave care at 16. They need advice on many aspects of living in the world and they are in particular need of sensitive help with food. The NCH Action for Children's Leaving Care project provides some advice but this needs to be backed up by health care professionals.

Most women and some men in the older age group will have been good cooks for much of their lives. If and as their health deteriorates or disabilities interfere, they will often become very resourceful and invent ways of carrying on. Carers can watch and listen and pick up tips to help others. Help and advice from dietitians and local adult education centres can also be very useful. Courses designed to help people cope with the sudden or

---

ACTIVITY 3.4

List examples of meals or snacks that require:

(i) very little preparation;
(ii) a larger amount of preparation;
(iii) some basic cooking skills.

For example:

(i) baked beans on toast; fresh apple.
(ii) minced meat or chicken with a canned sauce; boil-in-the-bag rice; frozen peas; tinned pineapple and custard.
(iii) grilled fish and lemon; mashed potato; sprouts; fresh apple crumble.

gradual onset of disabilities will usually offer guidance on cooking and the specialised equipment that is available for different needs. Details of such help is available through the nearest occupational therapy department.

There will inevitably be some clients who cannot be expected to learn to cook and in such cases an alternative will need to be sought. Many vulnerable people rely on others to shop and cook for them and it may be necessary to assess the skills of these relatives or neighbourly carers and advise them as well as the client.

Fuel for cooking and storage

As has been already stated, some people do not have mains electricity or gas. Even those that do may find themselves cut off, especially in a harsh winter.

- Some remote communities rely on their own oil-fuelled electricity generators.
- Others use bottled gas and solid fuel for cooking, refrigeration and heating.
- Deliveries of oil and solid fuel may be interrupted.
- Modified cooking and refrigeration equipment can be a great deal less efficient than the standard.

Clients should know what they can cope with. Before offering advice, listen to what they say. It is possible to get around almost every difficulty. The advice you would like to give may need to be modified to fit in with the particular nature of the client's fuel supply for cooking and refrigeration.

3.3   Helping clients with their planning for food

For many of us a shopping list is just a note to ourselves scribbled on a scrap of paper. A shopping list for a big shopping trip has to be more systematic. It is important in the same way that a periodic stock-taking is in a residential or day-care establishment. Everyone needs to be reminded occasionally of what is in the cupboard, to ensure that food does not go beyond its use-by date.

When making a shopping list for day-to-day items there is an assumption that there will be some basic ingredients in the larder or fridge. Items such as flour, salt, sugar, margarine, milk, tea, coffee, will be in most people's cupboards. Or will they? This needs to be checked. Others would expect to have much more in their store cupboard: dried fruit, rice, oats, flavourings, pulses, spaghetti, eggs, jams, syrup, tinned foods and perhaps some frozen items, too, if there's a freezer.

Food matters to people in a wide variety of different ways and people in care live in a wide variety of different circumstances. Planning food for them or helping them to plan meals and menus for themselves requires a good deal of thought and understanding. In order to provide everyday food, or food for a particular meal or special occasion, planning is essential. For many, this planning and organising is automatic. Making a shopping list, for example, will be the norm for most people and some can make the organisation of food look misleadingly easy. Others will need help.

ACTIVITY 3.5

What sort of planner are you? Do you have a store cupboard or do you buy meals or ingredients as you want them?

- Make a list of the food items that you usually have in a store cupboard at home, including those that you would usually keep for a few days in the refrigerator or vegetable rack (do not include frozen meals in this exercise). Could you make up a (balanced) meal from these items in an emergency? (Example: spaghetti with mixed vegetables; pizza with tinned tomato, onion and cheese; tuna, sweet-corn and rice; fruit crumble using tinned fruit.)

Whatever the type of meal or menu to be planned, there are a number of factors which have to be considered. Everything we know about food, people, caring, budgeting, food safety, planning food service, etc. comes to mind as we begin to draft a plan. Chapter 9 provides many tips and suggestions.

CASE STUDY 3.1

A busy care worker plans the meals for her family – husband and two teenage boys. They all help with the preparation but see it as a chore and are not very good at planning and organising meals unless she is there or leaves instructions.

On Thursday evening she is due to arrive home from work at 6.00 pm. Her husband will be late: coming in at 7.00 pm; one son will also come home at that time after playing football. The older son will be home at about 5.00 pm and probably help himself to the contents of the biscuit tin! Hopefully, he will read the note which asks him to start the preparation for the evening meal which is to be served at about 7.15 pm.

Our busy lady could rely on frozen, convenience foods or takeaways but these put a strain on the budget and can become boring after a while. She tries instead to plan meals for the week ahead in order to save money, time and having to think about it whilst she is at work.

The meal planned for this particular evening is:

- Fresh mince hamburgers – mince bought on the way home from work;
- Frozen broccoli, fresh carrots, jacket potatoes – son is asked to scrub potatoes and put them into the oven at 6.00 pm;
- Homemade apple pie with custard – son is asked to take pie out of the freezer when he gets in from school.

Considerations in her planning have been:

- not a lot of time for shopping;
- potatoes and other root vegetables will keep well;
- two hungry, active, teenage boys to feed;
- limited budget;
- homemade pies, cakes and biscuits can be cooked in bulk during a weekend baking session and either frozen or stored in tins.

It is easier to accommodate all these factors with a *planned* menu, which has been budgeted and shopped for.

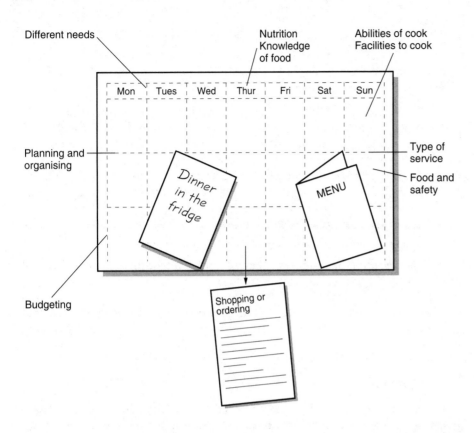

What sort of planner are you?

3.4 Keeping food safe

Food poisoning usually causes diarrhoea and vomiting, sometimes leading to dehydration. In the case of very vulnerable clients this can cause death. Due to recent media coverage, the food poisoning bacteria *Salmonella* and *Listeria* are well known.

It is not easy to advise clients who live independently about the dangers of illnesses caused by food which has become contaminated with food-poisoning bacteria. Clients can be helped to understand how to reduce the dangers of food poisoning once it is understood that food can be infected by other foods, unclean skin, hair and clothes and that bacteria will grow in the food if it is not stored properly. For some clients, however, even very basic standards may not be achievable due to poor living conditions.

Some simple guidelines to pass on to clients:

- always buy food as fresh as possible;
- try to keep storage and kitchen areas clean and in good repair;
- store foods correctly, for example dry goods must be kept dry; frozen foods must be kept below a certain temperature; high risk foods (see Chapter 8) must be refrigerated;
- never use food from a 'blown' tin;
- rotate stocks;
- don't let foods go beyond their use-by date;

- don't refreeze foods once they have thawed out;
- cook meat and poultry thoroughly (beware – some older clients may have been taught by their mothers to partly cook meat and poultry in order to keep it overnight. This practice is very dangerous);
- don't keep food hot for too long;
- follow the instructions on delivered meals and all prepacked and convenience foods;
- check refrigerator and freezer temperatures if possible.

Some guidelines for carers when helping clients with their food:

- wash hands thoroughly between tasks and especially after visiting the toilet;
- keep hair tied back;
- if in contact with food poisoning, notify the authorities (food poisoning is a notifiable disease)
- when going from house to house, use different protective covering in each; make use of disposable aprons but beware of using them near very hot ovens or hobs;
- keep all cuts and wounds covered; blue plasters are used by all food handlers;
- if you have a head cold, try not to handle food.

If a client is ill as a result of food that they have eaten, you must notify the local medical officer. (See Chapter 8 for more in-depth coverage.)

3.5 Community meals

It is generally recognised that there will always be the need for a hot meal service for some housebound and infirm clients. Meals-on-wheels is a familiar service to many. The scheme started during the second World War to enable housebound people to get a hot meal in the middle of the day. The service was coordinated by the Women's Voluntary Service (WVS) and has been under the care of the Women's Royal Voluntary Service (WRVS) since then. Today, meals-on-wheels provides 15 million meals per year through 70000 volunteers. Some meals are provided through lunch clubs and day centres. Meals are subsidised by local authorities and will be part of the total care package for the individual client. These may not necessarily be supervised by the traditional meals-on-wheels service.

The provision of a hot meal delivered to the door has its advantages and disadvantages. One of its main *advantages* is that a lonely and housebound person receives a daily visit from someone who cares. The person who delivers the meal can keep an eye open for problems and report back to the main care workers, if need be.

The *disadvantages* are that meals may come at odd times and, if the client is on the end of the run, the ingredients may have become mixed together and uniform in flavour and may be cold. Clients may not always have a choice although their likes and dislikes are usually taken into account and community meals have not always been successful in delivering adequate meals for therapeutic and cultural diets. The regular delivery of meals is especially important for a diabetic on insulin injections (see Chapter 5).

Sliced roast lamb
in gravy with vegetables and creamed potatoes

Normal Diet	Light Balanced Diet	Information for Diabetics	Calorie controlled	Cholesterol controlled

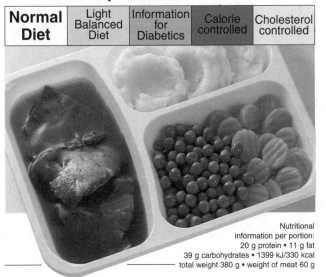

Nutritional
information per portion:
20 g protein • 11 g fat
39 g carbohydrates • 1399 kJ/330 kcal
total weight 380 g • weight of meat 60 g

One of many deep-frozen meals currently available from apetito (UK) Ltd

There is now the option of having deep-frozen meals delivered to clients once a week or once a fortnight. Although this scheme increases the variety of meals available to the client, this option could reduce the contact a lone, housebound client has with the outside world.

In addition to providing a shopping service, commercial companies, such as *apetito (UK) Ltd*, a German company, and Teleshop Services from Cheshire, deliver meals as chosen by clients and either sell or lease the freezers and even the cookers if necessary. Some companies are able to offer a range of special diets and meals for cultural needs. These meals are more expensive initially but the firms promise local authorities that they are able to make savings in the long term. They can be much more appetising and

a) Choosing a meal

b) Enjoying it . . . . and

c) stocking up the freezer

colourful although, over time, frozen, convenience meals can become as tedious as anything else. If possible clients need to be allowed to ring the changes.

Guidelines on the nutritional content of community meals have been set out by the Advisory Body for Social Services Catering (ABSSC) and also in the NAGE publication *'Eating through the 90's'* and the Caroline Walker Trust's *'Eating Well for Older People'*. Most meals supplied are to older people and the nutritional content is geared to their recommended intake of nutrients. Where meals are supplied to a younger person, the client should receive advice from the dietitian if necessary. The ABSSC guidelines lay down that the meal should provide one-third of the client's nutritional requirements and they also give portion sizes that will enable this provision for older people. For some local authorities (LAs) the guidelines, if adopted, may increase costs. If the LA buys in its community meals from a commercial supplier they may opt for a lower cost and ignore the nutritional standards.

Monitoring the total care package must include a regular check on a client's food intake and nutritional status. If there is doubt about the adequacy of a person's intake, steps must be taken to ensure that the client's overall health does not decline due to poor nutrition.

3.6 Monitoring and assessing food intake

It takes very careful monitoring to discover how much of a meal delivered to the client's home is actually eaten by the client. It is, however, necessary to assess a person's intake, as some commercial companies are not always able to achieve the levels of nutrients that they are contracted to provide.

Different approaches to monitoring will be needed for different situations. It may be easier to monitor a person's food intake in a residential situation than in a community care situation. Plate wastage, for instance, can be noted in a residential home whereas it is not always easy to assess what food is being thrown away by a client living at home.

In a paper *'Cost-effectiveness of nutritional support in the elderly'* presented to the Nutrition Society in February 1995, Dr S.P. Allison of the Queen's Medical Centre, Nottingham, comments '... for any treatment to be effective it must be appropriate to the patient's problem'. He goes on 'It seems almost absurd, therefore, to talk about the cost-effectiveness of a treatment when we are not collecting the information to make a simple diagnosis. Some centres are addressing this problem, with the introduction of simple, practical nutritional assessment protocols which form part of the medical and nursing admission process'. Such assessment systems can be adapted for use in any residential or community care situation.

Guidelines for monitoring food intake and what to look out for when assessing nutritional status are included in the Caroline Walker Trust's 1995 report *'Eating well for older people'*. The local dietetic department will also be able to help and refer you to the British Dietetic Association's NAGE document *Nutrition Assessment Checklist – Guidance Notes and Advice*.

An accurate assessment of food intake can be sought from the dietitian but good carers can pick up clues and will come to know when it is necessary to bring in expert help. Carers need to look out for signs and situations that cause them to suspect that a client might have a problem with food. Some of these are outlined in Table 3.1 overpage.

Table 3.1 *Factors that can affect food intake*

Sign or situation	Check it out
Bruising; wounds not healing	Are they able to eat fresh fruits and vegetables?
Unintentional weight gain or loss	Mention to the Health Visitor or Doctor; ask about swelling ankles; check waste bins if possible
False teeth taken out at meal times	False teeth become loose with weight loss
Feeling cold, even in the summer	May not be eating
Mental confusion	Cause or effect? May be forgetting to eat; lack of food may be causing mental lapses
Depression and loneliness	May need to be encouraged to eat properly
Housebound – little or no sunlight	Ask dietitian to check the diet for vitamin D intake
Cocktail of medicines	Sometimes drugs can cause problems with appetite, absorption, nausea
Little money for food	May need help with budgeting
Not able to shop	Ask about shopping services or help with transport etc.

Keep a checklist for each client. This could be with your client's record card or folder. It will need to include their favourite foods, dislikes, dietary restrictions, cultural or religious factors (special foods, fast and feast days),

---

NUTRITION ASSESSMENT CHART

Date of admission .... Height (actual/remembered) ....

Signature of nurse .... Weight (present) ....

Weight (remembered) .... (when) ....

Weight loss (kg) ....

Diet	Appearance	Swallowing	Ability to feed self	Condition of mouth	Action to be taken
1 Able to eat full hospital diet	Normal	No difficulty in swallowing	Independent in feeding	Mouth, tongue and gums healthy	Feed patient using appropriate hospital menu
2 Takes only half or less of diet	Unwell	No difficulty in swallowing	Can only use one hand. Needs food cutting up	Mouth dry or sore	Nursing help with feeding. Monitor dietary intake for 48 hours. ?Refer Dietitian
3 Very poor intake or soft diet/fluids only	Thin	Difficulties with swallowing	Needs verbal prompting	Poor teeth, ill fitting or no dentures. Sore mouth	Nursing help with feeding. Special diet or supplements. Advice from Dietitian
4 Unable or unwilling to take nutrition orally	Very thin	No swallow reflex or very delayed reflex	Dependent, needs feeding	Severe infection or ulceration of mouth, tongue and gums	Refer to Dietitian and/or Nutrition Team

	Week 1	Week 2	Week 3	Week 4	Week 5	Week 6
Weight						
Category						
Initial						

Source: Queen's Medical Centre Nottingham, University Hospital NHS Trust

special cooking methods, any food supplements, etc. Monitoring must be a continuous process. Keeping records can seem burdensome and routine; they may sometimes be completed in such a way as to be meaningless to others. Records should be designed to ensure that the individual client's needs are being met; they must be understood by all who read them. Computers are not always helpful here, as not everyone is computer literate.

Asking questions and keeping a check

Questions need to be designed according to the situation. You may be worried about a child in a family, a teenager with learning difficulties, an elderly person living alone. Their different needs, attitudes to food and their ability to determine what they eat will guide the way that questions are asked and determine when it is right to make enquiries. Some helpful hints are:

● frame questions broadly;
● look out for the answers that tell you what you want to know;
● people will often tell you what they think you want to hear;
● talk around the question or use conversation rather than questions;
● make sure that you understand what the client is saying (this is particularly important in multicultural communities);
● do not make judgements based on your own preferences and traditions.

Examples of simple questions to include in some way could be:

● What foods do you really enjoy? What do you most dislike?
● Which meals do you usually eat?
● What breakfast cereals do you eat most often? (cornflakes are low in fibre; porridge, muesli and All Bran are high in fibre)
● Have you lost or gained weight recently?
● Are you on a special diet? How long have you been on it? When was it last checked by the dietitian?
● Are you taking any food supplements?
● Are you taking any laxatives?
● What sort of fruits and vegetables do you eat? (carrots are low in vitamin C but high in vitamin A; peas contain moderate amounts of vitamins C and A; butter beans are low in vitamin C and A)
● Do you eat oily fish?
● How much milk, yoghurt, cheese do you eat? (to check calcium intake)
● Do you eat wholewheat bread, wholegrain cereal? (to check fibre intake)

As you ask the questions and chat with your clients, they will often want you to confirm that they are doing the right thing. They may punctuate their answers with 'Is that all right?' Try not to respond too quickly with unconsidered advice.

Ensuring the needs of particular clients are being met can be helped by:

● asking for the observations and opinions of relatives and others;
● regular discussions with those who prepare, cook and eat the food;
● tasting sessions;
● suggestion books;
● books of pictures of dishes;
● regular checks on the individual's health including weight and diet history where necessary;
● keeping a list of local interpreters and all religious leaders;
● locating a source of special implements and equipment to help those with disabilities.

ACTIVITY 3.6

Create a system for ensuring that the needs and likes of your clients are met. The system should allow for regular updating and should be understood by other members of the team. Your system could be based on a card-index system, a format similar to the one on page 67 'Keeping Track', a combination of the two or your own invention.

ACTIVITY 3.7

Consider how you would help a young mother to plan a week's food for her family. She lives on the top floor of a block of Council flats. She and her husband are on low income. She has a new baby and a three-year old child. (Note: she will not always be able to carry heavy shopping as well as the children up the stairs if the lift is out of order.)

ACTIVITY 3.8

Consider the needs of an elderly man (retired teacher) who has become very frail and thin and is not very mobile. He uses a walking frame. He lives alone with occasional visits from neighbours or relatives. He did not learn to cook until after his wife died. He gets meals-on-wheels three times a week.

As a community carer, how would you enable him to cope and to ensure that he gets all his nutritional requirements? What recipe books could you find to enable him to cook simple, interesting meals for one or two people?

ACTIVITY 3.9

1 Read case study 3.2.

How would you advise Dee?

2 Make a list of the details that you need to know before you give any advice. For example:

What is her benefit entitlement?
What does she like or dislike?
Are there any special considerations: cultural, religious, dietary factors, that have to be thought about?
Where are the shops?
Does she have family or other support?

Making a card-index system (Details decided by the care or work situation)

CASE STUDY 3.2

Dee, a young, unemployed girl of 17 is leaving care and going into a single person's Council flat. It has a kitchen alcove off the bed-sitting room with a small electric cooker.

She will have time to shop and cook. She may have learned to cook whilst in care or at school. (The NCH Action for Children's Leaving Care Project aims to give practical advice and support but there are very many other needs apart from food.)

Dee thinks she can spend about £2 per day out of her benefit on food. This will include stock items like milk, tea, coffee, bread, sugar, etc.

References and further reading

ABSSC 1990: *A Recommended Standard for Community Meals*

Allison, November 1995: *Cost-effectiveness of Nutritional Support in the Elderly*. The Proceedings of the Nutrition Society, Cambridge University Press

Lewis 1993: *Eating Well on a Budget*. Age Concern, England

MAFF 1991: *Food Safety*. A 'Food Sense' pamphlet

NAGE 1992: *Nutrition Assessment and Checklist – a Screening Tool*.

Orton and West 1991: *Working with Older People – a Guide to Services*. Open University

1989: *The 1989 Children's Act – a Resource Booklet*. Open University

1990: *Community Life – a Code of Practice for Community Care*. The Centre for Policy on Ageing

1991: *Working with Children and Young People*. Open University

1992: *Poverty and Nutrition Survey*. NCH Action for Children

1994: *A Lost Generation – a Survey of the Problems Faced by Vulnerable Young People Living on their Own*. NCH Action for Children

4 Different people – different needs

Labelling people is dangerous

It is sometimes useful to classify people within broad groups for convenience although there are very real dangers in giving people a label as they may not then be seen as individuals. It is vital to view all people as individuals, as it is also clear that the needs of children are different from the needs of older people; the needs of people within different cultural traditions vary; the needs of babies are different from those of teenagers. Children have a lot to learn, older people have a lot to teach; people from different backgrounds have a lot to share.

These different needs are not just in terms of food, diet and nutrition of course. Food intake is a reflection of several factors – emotional, physical, traditional, environmental. At all times it is important to remember that within groups, all people remain individual. No one can assume that because a man has reached the age of 80 he will not be active or that a small child does not know what he or she is talking about; blind people *can* cook and many people with physical disabilities find ingenious ways to cope.

Talk to each person about their food as far as possible.

ACTIVITY 4.1

1 Look back at Activity 1.5 on page 4 when your group compared notes about what is normal to you. If you are fortunate enough to work with people from different cultural backgrounds, some of the differences you listed may have been quite noticeable. Make a list of the differences you noted then.

2 Write down what you can remember about your own childhood. Try to recall the food you ate, the meal occasions, school dinners, what you didn't like. What happened when you refused to eat? How did your family react to sweets and chocolates?

3 Look back at Activity 1.8 on page 10 when you looked at the diet of an older client or relative using the biographical approach. If possible ask that person how his or her diet has changed in recent years, and why. If you are not able to ask the same person, talk with another older person about changes that have occurred in their diet. Make a list of these changes.

4 Using these three insights from different people into their food, diet, likes, dislikes and meal patterns, make a list of the many factors you might have to consider when planning or advising on food for others.

4.1 Caring for children and young people

Children are individuals. They can all expect to become responsible, caring members of the society into which they have been born. What they learn as young children, through example and experience or through formal teaching, will contribute to their ability to be full and fulfilled members of their community as they grow up.

When caring for children and young people, their individuality must be taken into account. Carers must try to see all situations from the point of view of their charges. Age differences can make it very difficult to understand the attitudes and behaviour of others.

Young children begin very early to explore and develop their individuality. They are entering a world of great variety and they are aiming to be independent of others. Rejecting food, like rejection of other things, is more likely to be a sign of independence than a genuine dislike.

Food is part of their learning about the world they live in and share with others. The food they are offered away from home may be very different to the meals they have with their family. Where family meals are thought to be inadequate, carers can have trouble encouraging children to eat what is considered to be more appropriate food.

Many situations involving food contribute to a child's learning, for better and for worse. Food can provide them with so much more than just nutrients:

- they can learn about adult superstitions and guilt feelings;
- they can pick up misunderstandings;
- they have access to television and other advertisements;
- they are influenced by teachers and other children at school;
- when a food is used as a bribe, a reward or a punishment it can affect the way the child views that food in the future.

Nutrition – the unseen essentials

The need for nutrients has to be appreciated by those who provide the food, as all children and young people must receive their nutritional requirements in order to achieve their full potential. It should, however, be treated like the foundations of a building – unseen but essential. An over-emphasis on nutrition and healthy eating can interfere with a child's learning and enjoyment of the great variety of foods available. It can also have the opposite effect to the one intended, as children will often do what they are told *not* to do to show their independence.

I'm me

One of the very few ways that small children have of expressing their independence is through food. When a toddler's favourite prune whip ends up all over the wallpaper it doesn't mean that it is no longer acceptable. It just means that he or she is expressing mood and authority. (This situation is in fact, encountered throughout life as people express their moods by complaining about food, cooking or catering. Hopefully, it has a less disastrous effect on the decorations as we grow up!)

Food and health

The future health of people is influenced by the diet in childhood, with the effects of diet and environment experienced during pregnancy and the first few months of life, also making a contribution. In fact, the future health of children probably begins whilst their parents are still growing as teenagers. At a time when boys and, more especially, girls are maturing and their reproductive capabilities developing, it is important that they receive adequate nutrition, in addition to other health measures, to ensure that the next generation has as good a start as possible.

The COMA report No. 41, *Dietary Reference Values*, assumes that women will have adequate stores of certain nutrients to pass on to the foetus during pregnancy. These stores are laid down during the teenage years, thus the health of children is dependent on the diet of the previous generation.

> *The diets of young people are crucial, as much for their own health as for the health of their future offspring.*

Nutrition and feeding for babies under one year old

Caring for babies, toddlers and young children involves a concern for their food in relation to health as well as to their future acceptance into society. It is usual in Britain to encourage mothers to breast-feed their babies for as long as possible. Breast milk will pass on to the child, all the nutrients required in a form that is designed for human babies and which can be readily absorbed (providing the mother's reserves have been maintained). It will also pass on long-lasting immunities and resistance to infections.

Dietary supplements

Any possible nutritional problem for the breast-fed baby should be addressed through the mother's diet. If there is some doubt about a mother's ability to provide adequate nutrition through her milk, her diet should be properly assessed by the dietitian. She may not be eating enough or taking enough fluid. If necessary, a vitamin and mineral supplement may be prescribed *for her*. The baby will then receive all its nutrients in the right proportions. Only if it is not possible for a mother to eat all the food that she needs for herself and her baby should there be a need for the baby's intake to be supplemented. This requires extremely careful monitoring as it is easy to cause problems by giving too much.

When a mother is unable to breast-feed her baby or is not able to make enough milk, use is made of one of the patent formula feeds which are designed to be as near to human milk as possible. A baby's digestive system will develop over time and at different rates and it may be necessary to try a different feed if a child reacts badly.

Weaning

The recommendations in the COMA report No. 46, *Weaning and the Weaning Diet*, suggest that:

- solid foods should not be introduced before the child reaches 4 months of age;
- pasteurised cow's milk should not be used as the main milk drink for children under 1 year of age;
- once a child starts weaning it is desirable to gradually introduce normal foods in a puréed form. It is preferable for these foods to be taken from the family's home-cooked food rather than purchased as a convenience food.

Great care needs to be taken when handling food to prevent food poisoning. All equipment should be sterilised thoroughly after each use. Chapter 8 provides more details.

During their early years, children in Western countries explore the wide variety of tastes, textures, and forms of food that is available. Later it can become more difficult to introduce new tastes and textures and different foods. Taste buds, sense of smell and the gastric system develop at different rates in different children. A child's refusal of a food does not mean that it will have a long-term dislike of it. It just means that the child hasn't reached that stage.

A number of assumptions have been made in the past about the acceptability of foods during weaning. Recent research from Birmingham University's Department of Psychology published in the British Food Journal in 1993, *Introducing the Infant's Solid Food*, by Gillian Harris, suggests that very young babies will be quite adventurous if their parents or carers allow them to be. It is only later, it seems, that they begin to prefer only what they have become accustomed to.

Allergies and sensitivities

Allergies are rare and reactions may be temporary and due to an immaturity in the baby's digestive or absorption system. Inborn intolerances to lactose (the sugar in milk), casein (a protein in milk), sucrose, or phenylalanine (an essential amino acid; see page 110) are usually diagnosed shortly after birth and dietary steps taken to compensate for them. An intolerance of gluten (a protein in certain cereal grains, see page 88) will often become apparent when weaning starts, but a diagnosis of gluten-sensitive disorders can also be made much later in life. A guide to foods during weaning is illustrated on pages 48 and 49.

Feeding the under-fives
Learning and playing

- Meal times are enjoyable events in a child's life.
- Food is instinctively desirable and children should be hungry.

It isn't, however, just a question of providing them with what they need or want. Around meal times and food, very young children can learn about:

- sharing and giving;
- counting – numbers of people, numbers of spoons, etc;
- concepts of division and fractions such as 'a half' and 'a quarter';
- different containers and implements;
- colours;
- laying a table;
- the difference between left and right hands.

Older children will learn about:

- living with other people;
- socially acceptable behaviour;
- traditions and customs.

Later, children can go on to learn about the foods themselves: where they grow, what they are and what can be done with them. This knowledge will be extended when they learn about cooking.

Eating habits, and their influence on later health, are developed in early childhood. A child that is over-fussy about food may be reflecting the parents' lack of self-confidence or sense of adventure with food and cooking. Carers of children need to encourage them to try as many foods as possible

Table 4.1 *A guide to foods during weaning*

Food groups	Examples	Major nutrients	4–6 months
Dairy products and substitutes	Breast milk, infant formula, cow's milk, lassi, yoghurt*, fromage frais*, cottage cheese, hard cheese Infant soya formula, tofu	Energy (Calories) and fat, protein, calcium, vitamin A, B vitamins, zinc Iron and vitamin D in breast and formula milks	MINIMUM 600 ml BREAST OR INFANT FORMULA DAILY Cow's milk products can be used in weaning after 4 months (*e.g. yoghurt, custard, cheese sauce*)
Starchy foods	Bread, rolls, pitta bread, chapatti, breakfast cereals, baby cereal, plain and savoury biscuits, noodles, spaghetti and other pasta, semolina, rice, oats, millet, potato, yam, plantain	Energy (Calories), protein, thiamin, niacin, folic acid, vitamin B$_6$, biotin, zinc Calcium, iron (*fortified cereal and bread*) Non–starch polysaccharide (*fibre*)	INTRODUCE AFTER 4 MONTHS Mix smooth cereal with milk: use low–fibre cereals (*e.g. rice based*) Mash or purée starchy vegetables
Vegetables and fruits	Leafy and green vegetables (*cabbage, green beans, peas, broccoli, leeks*) Root vegetables (*carrots, onion, turnip*) Salad vegetables (*tomato, cucumber*), mushrooms, sweetcorn, marrow Fruits (*apple, banana, peach, orange, melon*), fruit juices	Energy (Calories) and fat, protein, iron, zinc, B vitamins (*B$_{12}$ animal foods only*)	INTRODUCE AFTER 4 MONTHS Use soft-cooked vegetables and fruit as a smooth purée
Meat and meat alternatives	Lean lamb, beef, pork, chicken, turkey, fish, fish-fingers, egg, liver, kidney, sausages, burgers Lentils, dhal, peas, beans, baked beans, gram	Energy (Calories) and fat, protein, iron, zinc, B vitamins (*B$_{12}$ animal foods only*)	INTRODUCE AFTER 4 MONTHS Use soft-cooked meat/pulses Add no salt or sugar or minimum quantities to food during or after cooking
Occasional foods	Cakes, sweet biscuits, sweetened squash, sweetened desserts and milk drinks, ice cream, cream, sugar, jam, honey, etc., crisps, savoury snacks, fried and fatty foods	NONE OF THESE FOODS IS NECESSARY IN THE DIET They may contain a lot of fat, energy, sugar or salt Try not to use foods from this group every day	Choose low-sugar desserts; avoid high salt foods

*These products should preferably be unsweetened varieties.
**Includes breast milk, infant formula, follow-on formula and whole cow's milk

6–9 months	9–12 months	After 1 year	Extra information
500–600 ml BREAST MILK, INFANT FORMULA OR FOLLOW–ON FORMULA DAILY Also use any milk** to mix solids Hard cheese (e.g. Cheddar) can be cubed or grated and used as 'finger food'	500–600 ml BREAST MILK OR INFANT MILKS DAILY Also use any milk** to mix solids	MINMUM 350 ml MILK DAILY OR 2 SERVINGS DAIRY PRODUCT (e.g. yoghurt, cheese sauce) Whole milk can be used as a drink and soft cheeses included after 1 year. Lower fat milks can be used in cooking, but not as main drink	If milk drinks are rejected, use alternatives (e.g. cheese) and give water to drink Discourage large volumes of milk after 1 year (more than 600 ml) as it will reduce appetite for other foods Discourage feeding from a bottle after 1 year
2–3 SERVINGS DAILY Start to introduce some wholemeal bread and cereals Foods can be a more solid 'lumpier' texture. Begin to give 'finger foods' (e.g. toast)	3–4 SERVINGS DAILY Encourage wholemeal products; discourage foods with added sugar (biscuits, cakes, etc.) Starchy foods can be of normal adult texture	MINIMUM OF 4 SERVINGS DAILY At least one serving at each mealtime Discourage high fat foods (crisps, savoury snacks and pastry)	Most baby and breakfast cereals are fortified with iron and B vitamins Cereals and bread derived from wholemeals are a richer source of nutrients and fibre than refined cereals
2 SERVINGS DAILY Raw soft fruit and vegetables (e.g. banana, melon, tomato) may be used as 'finger foods' Cooked vegetables and fruit can be a coarser, mashed texture	3–4 SERVINGS DAILY Encourage lightly-cooked or raw foods Chopped or 'finger food' texture is suitable Unsweetened orange juice with meals especially if diet is meat-free	MINIMUM OF 4 SERVINGS DAILY Encourage unsweetened fruit if vegetables are rejected Food can be adult texture though some fibrous foods may be difficult (e.g. celery, radish)	Vegetables may be preferred raw (e.g. grated carrot, chopped tomato) or may need to be disguised in soups, pies and stews To improve iron absorption, give vitamin C (fruits and vegetables) with every meal
1 SERVING DAILY Soft-cooked minced or puréed meat/fish/pulses Chopped hard-cooked egg can be used as a 'finger food'	MINIMUM 1 SERVING DAILY FROM ANIMAL SOURCE OR 2 FROM VEGETABLE SOURCES In a vegetarian diet use a mixture of different vegetable and starchy foods (macaroni cheese, dhal and rice)	MINIMUM 1 SERVING DAILY OR 2 FROM VEGETABLE SOURCES Encourage low-fat meat and oily fish (sardine, herring, mackerel) Liver paté can be used after 1 year	Trim fat from meat Use little or no added fat when cooking foods such as meat which already contain fat
Encourage savoury foods rather than sweet ones Fruit juices are not necessary – try to restrict to meal times or alternatively offer water/milk	May use moderate amounts of butter, margarine. Small amounts of jam (if necessary) on bread Try to limit salty foods	Limit crisps and savoury snacks. Give bread or fruit if hungry between meals. Do not add sugar to drink. Try to limit soft drinks to mealtimes	Encourage a pattern of three main meals each day. Discourage frequent snacking on fatty or sugary foods

Table reproduced by permission of Department of Health from *Weaning and the Weaning Diet*, COMA Report No. 45, 1994

before they arrive at the age of two. After that, dietary tastes and patterns can become more difficult to alter and children may become the next generation of unadventurous eaters.

Children learn well if they are able to share in the variety of foods adults eat and, as soon as possible, eat with adults. Children have immature taste buds to begin with but their tastes develop and new flavours and textures can be introduced regularly. New foods may be rejected the first time they are tried but this does not mean that they will always be rejected. Try again later. The Birmingham research referred to earlier indicates that children would enjoy trying a wide variety of tastes and textures if only their grown-ups would be more adventurous. It is important that food does not become an issue. If a great deal of fuss is made because a child does not eat something, the child, parents and everyone else can become involved in an unnecessary battle of wills. Ask yourself: Did you eat your greens as a child?

ACTIVITY 4.2

Compile a list of four foods which can be given to a 1-year old child, under the three headings: taste, texture, colour. Plan three meals for young children which include some of your suggestions. (Foods can demonstrate different tastes: salt, sweet, tart, 'toasted'; different textures: bland, rough, crunchy, chewy; different colours: green, orange, white, brown, etc.)

Mealtimes – General principles and guidelines

Mealtimes should be relaxed, quiet and pleasant. However, it is also an ideal opportunity for learning. There is no other time of the day when an adult has the attention of a small group of children for up to three quarters of an hour. It is an ideal time for language development of the informal and spontaneous type and it is particularly important for adults to listen to children. The small group provides the opportunity for quiet children or those with English as a second language to talk, and they benefit from listening to other children and adults. Adults can also talk informally about themselves, their families, where they have been, etc.

Mealtimes can be beneficial for talking about foods. Many children do not know the names, where they come from, how they are grown, cooked, etc. Foods can be contrasted: mashed potato, roast potato, raw carrot, cooked carrot, etc. Many children are not aware of what we take for granted. Talk should be natural, not contrived, and we should remember that some children miss out on this relaxed and informal meal-time talk at home.

There are many incidental teaching points during this time. For example: big, little, middle-sized spoons; reflections in shiny spoons; sharp, blunt edges of knives; round biscuits, square pieces of cake; solid food and liquid food; green jelly, orange carrots, etc.

Emphasis should be on child independence. Evidence shows that independence and skill in everyday activities leads to greater confidence and skill in other areas of learning. Children should be encouraged to set the table, manage their own food using utensils properly, pour their own drink, scrape their own plate, help to clear the table, etc. Guidance or help should be given only when necessary.

Some Asian children may have used their fingers, rather than cutlery, at home. This is not a 'dirty' or primitive way of eating – it is a skill in itself and is particularly suited to eating Asian foods. Some young or new children are unable to choose and should be given a little of everything. The general principle is that a hungry child will eat. Never use food as a threat or punishment – you will always lose! ... those who are fussy or poor eaters are nearly always those children who have been nagged or threatened at home. Some children actually enjoy the attention of being cajoled and the ritual of saying 'No, I don't want to'. Such children generally eat well if ignored or given a different sort of attention.

Extract from one Nursery School's General Principles and
Guidelines on Mealtimes

The general principle is that a hungry child will eat (page 50.)

Some tastes and textures may not become acceptable until a child is older: bland, watery foods like cucumber, melon, lettuce, are examples. However, it is not usual for a child to reject well cooked, well presented foods that everyone else is eating, especially if they are hungry! For children, a colourful presentation can be the most important encouragement to eating well.

Healthy eating

The COMA report No. 45, *Nutritional Aspects of Cardiovascular Disease*, relates to adults in the UK and is not appropriate for children under five.

- Children need nutrient-dense foods, often in small, frequent amounts.
- Fibre intake should be part of the normal food as cooked for the family.
- Fats should not be over-restricted and 'low fat' products should be avoided. Children under 5 years should not be given skimmed milk and children under 2 years should not drink skimmed or semi-skimmed milk.
- Poly-unsaturated fatty acids in the form of margarines and oils should not be increased. The diet should include fats from a variety of sources.
- Salt should not be over-restricted after weaning, especially when children become very active.
- Some sugar and sugar products are acceptable, especially during periods of high activity.

Sugar and sweets

Sugar and sweets can be a problem, but they do have their uses in some situations. They are concentrated sources of readily available energy which active children often need. In order to maintain stores of readily available energy in the muscles during activity, a source of concentrated carbohydrate is essential. Starchy foods are too bulky and need prior digestion to release the energy. Giving sweets before or immediately after exercise is one way of getting around the problems created by the criticism that all sugar is bad.

Wherever possible, an alternative form of energy should be found, as sugary products have a very bad effect on teeth. The National Diet and Nutrition Survey on Children aged 1½–4½ conducted by Gregory *et al.* in 1992, included a dental survey. It was published by HMSO in 1995 and showed that 17 per cent of children under 5 had tooth decay. The survey looked at a wide range of factors which might contribute to dental problems, only one of which was sugar.

It is better if children do not acquire a taste for very sweet foods and this can be achieved by introducing a wide range of tastes and textures very early in the weaning programme. However, if parents or carers try too hard to condemn sweets they can have the reverse effect and create behavioural problems as well as toothache. Many advertisements and supermarket stands target children. It is not really fair to expect them to constantly resist such pressure.

Sugar and sweets must not be allowed to interfere with a child's intake of other foods. The overall diet must be nutritionally adequate. The rest of the day's food intake needs to contain enough vitamins of the B group (see page 120) to allow the energy in sugar and sweets to be released and properly utilised.

Bribes and rewards

Where sugar and sweets are used intelligently within a well-balanced adequate menu for all the family, they should not become the object of fuss and difficulty. Once a child has associated sweets or some other food with reward, mealtimes can become stressful occasions instead of a pleasure. Using sweets and desserts as a bribe can leave the child with the idea that these foods are to be prized above all others.

Children at school

The obligation to provide free school meals for secondary school children is no longer laid upon local authority education departments, although free meals are still part of the welfare provision for families in need. Local authorities provide meals for pre-secondary school children and special schools, while other provision is contracted out to private caterers. Meals eaten at school will vary from area to area and from school to school. Secondary school children may take their own meals and many will leave the grounds at lunchtime to buy what they choose in local shops.

The traditional school meals service has been the butt of much humour, but it has provided many children with a satisfying meal, covering a proportion of their nutritional requirements which they may not have received otherwise.

School dining rooms

Caring for children during mealtimes at school is important. Many young children find themselves in a very frightening situation when they first go into the school dining room with no familiar, reassuring adult accompanying them. Teachers or teachers' aides can help children at this time and perhaps also enable them to learn about food, sharing and other peoples' needs during their meal breaks.

How about school breakfast?

Research in the 1970s confirmed the observations of many teachers that children who go to school with little or no breakfast are less able to cope with lessons than those who have eaten adequately or nearer the time of their arrival at school. The recent practice of bussing children in to central schools from long distances, especially in rural areas, means that they are forced to eat breakfast very early, if at all.

Where school food provision is given with a 'whole-day' approach, the needs of modern children may be better addressed. The provision of breakfast for some children could be a very cost-effective way of enabling them to cope better with their studies.

Children and choice

Offering a menu with choice may not always be a wise move, especially if we want to help a child learn about different foods. In fact, choice is often limited by the menu planner's own judgements or constraints imposed by others. Local authority guidelines may be influenced by poorly-informed media coverage of an issue. Giving children a choice can be very confusing. Many carers in schools are questioning the wisdom of this practice. Good quality, well-cooked food, which is well-presented and appetising is a better way to provide children with their needs. It can also help them to resist appealing advertising by the food industry.

Children are influenced in their choice of food by many factors:

- They have access to all advertisements for food and hear adults talking about what is good and bad, often without understanding the discussion.
- Young children can be influenced by adults who care deeply about animal welfare. They may be too young to enter into the debate wisely and their long-term health can suffer if they are swept along without complete understanding.
- Schoolchildren, particularly at secondary age, are influenced by their peers and will often avoid the healthy choices on offer in school canteens because none of their friends choose them.

When choosing food, children need to be guided by adults who should be better able to understand which foods are appropriate. It is not fair to allow children a free choice whilst there is so much confusing media information.

- There is no need for a full-choice menu if the caterers and carers know their charges well and provide alternatives when necessary.
- With their classroom learning reinforced during meal times, children will come to know how to choose wisely.

Many groups are campaigning for more and better health education linked with food and suggest that there is a need for a more coordinated approach between classroom teaching, school meal provision and the school health service.

Health problems

The Diet and Nutrition Survey referred to on page 51 indicates that children are currently, on average, taller than a similar sample 25 years ago. However, some nutrient deficiencies were found including iron-deficiency anaemia and low vitamin D levels. Health problems associated with diet and nutrition will also include tooth decay, over- and under-weight, and sometimes rickets.

Dental problems

Most dental problems are caused by bacteria in the mouth which destroy the tooth enamel. The bacteria thrive on sugar, especially in an acid solution. Fruit squashes, soft drinks, fruit sweets and jams are examples of sugar in conjunction with acid.

Children need to understand the relationship between sugary foods and dental problems. It is important for them to get into the habit of regular teeth cleaning, especially after eating anything sugary. Acidity can be offset by using bicarbonate of soda in a toothpaste or as a mouthwash. Fluorine is a mineral known to help in the resistance of teeth to decay, although the Dental Survey referred to above showed that almost all of the children surveyed used fluoride toothpaste. Many water companies add fluorine to water supplies but as it is possible to take too much fluorine, which harms the teeth, each local situation is considered individually.

Overweight

Children need to gain fat at times during their growth. This is reflected by alternate phases of chubbiness and 'beanpole'. Fat is a very concentrated form of energy and immediately before a 'growth spurt', children often lay down fat as a store of energy for the subsequent growth period. This fat should not be 'slimmed off', however self-conscious the child (and especially if a teenage girl) may feel. The adult fashion for dieting and being slim can be passed on to even very young children and can badly affect health and growth. Disorders such as anorexia nervosa or bulimia nervosa may be exacerbated by an over-emphasis on 'slimming'.

Weight problems in children may be inherited or may have been introduced by unbalanced nutrition in the past as the child grew in the womb, or a poor diet in infancy. They may be physical or metabolic abnormalities.

Genuine obesity usually has a medical cause which is unrelated to the child's current intake of food. In some cases, however, emotional or psychological problems can cause a child to overeat. Childhood obesity is not easy to manage and it can be aggravated by an over-strict dietary regime. Overweight children can easily feel that they are being punished for something that they do not understand.

Some writers and workers in this field adopt a judgemental attitude: 'children, today, watch too much television'; 'children don't take enough exercise'; 'children eat too much junk food'. Such statements are far from scientific and often serve only to further disturb an already unhappy child. Many children have little opportunity or time for physical activity due to increasing restrictions on traditional play areas and the very considerable pressure of school work. Local provision and social circumstances make it difficult for many children to play out-of-doors. Many streets are regarded as unsafe; playgrounds may have been vandalised; school playing fields sold. The school curriculum is often too tight to allow for sufficient sporting activities and many teachers use television programmes as part of the teaching material.

The diet for all children must meet all the nutritional requirements. High energy needs, protein, vitamins and minerals are best covered by well-balanced regular meals. High-fibre, low-fat diets are not appropriate for growing, active children but may be prescribed if a child is persistently overweight. In this case the child must be under the supervision of a dietitian who will check that nutritional needs are being maintained as the child grows. Normal exercise will be encouraged.

Underweight

Underweight in children can usually be traced to poor diet. Several factors may be influential such as:

- feeding difficulties in infancy;
- financial poverty;
- ignorance about proper diet on the part of the parents;
- a variety of illnesses;
- a psychological need.

At times, though, it is genuinely very hard to provide enough food to satisfy the energy needs of a growing, active, child. When money is short, it can be very difficult to provide enough energy-rich foods and this often causes a great deal of worry to parents who are uncertain about the conflicting statements in respect of food. These energy needs are, in themselves, hard to assess and, especially for teenage boys entering a period of growth, the sky's the limit in terms of Calories. The biscuit tin needs to be the self-filling variety, it seems.

The eating disorder anorexia nervosa, which is characterised by extreme underweight, is a complex condition which should be under the supervision of medical and dietetic consultants. Carers coming into contact with this condition must carry out the advice given by the consultants.

The self-filling biscuit tin

NCH survey

Two key findings in the *NCH Action for Children's Poverty and Nutrition Survey, 1991*:

- One in five of the parents in the group had gone hungry in the previous month because of lack of money.
- One in ten of the children under five in the group had gone without food in the previous month.

Confirmation of the problems experienced by families on low incomes has been provided by the government's Low Income Project Team. The report of their survey, commissioned in 1994 and produced at the end of 1995, indicates that people on long-term state benefits and other low incomes in the UK are in great danger of malnutrition. Whereas an average family spends 17 per cent of its income on food, a family on a low income needs to spend 35–40 per cent of its income on food to maintain a near adequate intake of nutrients for everyone.

Rickets

This disease was very common in children in Britain at the beginning of this century. It is caused by a lack of vitamin D which is needed for the proper formation of bones. Vitamin D is made by the action of ultra-violet (uv) light from the sun on the skin. The sun does not have to be shining but the amount of uv rays that can be effective will be determined by the amount of cloud. In northern climates there is usually sufficient uv penetration to enable fair-skinned adults to make enough vitamin D for their needs.

The dietary requirements for vitamin D are very high when bones are being formed rapidly, as with growing children. They are also high for dark-skinned people, including very tanned people, in Britain where the skin pigment, melanin, can limit the ability of the uv rays to make the vitamin. Rickets may still occur in Britain if the supply of vitamin D in the diet is inadequate. During periods of rapid growth, some children experience back-ache and pains in other bones. This is not rickets but is nevertheless a good opportunity to check that vitamin D availability and intake is adequate.

Dietary sources of vitamin D are few, the best being oily fish. In order to compensate for this, all domestic margarines in Britain are fortified with vitamin D by law. The manufacturers of low-fat spreads also add vitamin D. It is good practice to use fortified margarine to make homemade cakes, biscuits and pastries for growing, active, hungry children.

Special diets

Special diets for children and young adults are considered in detail in Chapter 5. Some of these diets may be very specific and it is important to check that the diet is being monitored by the dietitian and regularly updated in line with changes in the child's nutritional needs, for example during growth periods. In the case of very young babies, this can mean weekly updates.

4.2 Diet during pregnancy

Pregnancy is the time when the foundations of the future health, intelligence and resistance to disease of the offspring are generally considered to be laid. Thus, diet during pregnancy is of fundamental importance. Making sure that a pregnant woman gets all her nutritional requirements, including Calories, can be difficult, especially where there are other children in the family and the amount of money to be spent on food is limited. A mother will naturally want to give the food to her other children. A Canadian project in the 1960s showed that where a mother's optimum nutrition is achieved, the child of that pregnancy will have a higher IQ, a greater resistance to infection and will be more likely to grow normally, than when her nutritional requirements were not achieved in earlier pregnancies.

For some nutrients the figures for the amounts required during pregnancy are based on the assumption that a woman will have adequate stores. However, her stores of these and other nutrients may have become depleted during earlier pregnancies or illnesses and it may be necessary to increase her intake of some nutrients above the suggested levels in order that the baby does not suffer. Taking a diet history will reveal some of the possible shortages if the carer has any doubts.

The nutrients that are assumed to be stored, to be passed on during pregnancy are protein, iron and vitamin A. Special attention is now focused on two vitamins in particular, folates and vitamin A.

- *Folates: a group of substances derived from folic acid* (see page 122). It is necessary to check the level of folic acid in the diet during pregnancy as part of the function of folic acid in the body is the correct replication of DNA, the chemical template that passes on information required by the cells. During periods of rapid cell division, as in pregnancy, any deficiency in folate in the diet can cause upsets in the process of cell replication. This can lead to abnormalities in the foetus which may be aborted as a result. Levels of folic acid in the blood will usually be checked at the health centre and may be supplemented if necessary.

ACTIVITY 4.3

If possible, talk with a friend or client who is pregnant. Write down any information they have been given by the doctor or clinic staff about diet. Do they understand it? Are they able to follow it?

- *Vitamin A* (see page 117). High levels of vitamin A can harm the growing foetus and it is recommended that eating foods high in vitamin A or its precursor, carotene, during pregnancy should be kept to a minimum. It is particularly recommended that foods rich in the vitamin should not be eaten together, for example liver and carrots.

During lactation (breast-feeding), all nutrient requirements become less as the amount of milk a mother makes is reduced. Care should be taken to ensure that stores which might have become depleted during the pregnancy and lactation period are replaced before returning to a normal diet and certainly before any future pregnancy is considered.

4.3 Caring for older people

Caring for older people calls for great skill and judgement in balancing individual needs with the needs of other clients, the staff or the neighbours and the community.

How old is old?

In a talk given in 1979 entitled *Food and Health from Conception to Extreme Old Age*, published by Chapman and Hall, one of the world's leading nutritionists, Dr Elsie Widdowson, suggested three groups of older people: old age, very old age and extreme old age, which is roughly equal to the 70's, the 80's and the 90's. Concern for older people can begin at an earlier age, especially if they suffer from a long-term disability or chronic illness. In the UK the official retirement age is 60 or 65; nutritionists have been heard to say that old age begins at 30!

Age is often a matter of perception. It is not uncommon for someone in their 80's to care about their elderly neighbours who are in their 60's. The basic principle of care is the same as for everyone else. Each person is an individual and all needs, ideals and circumstances have to be reviewed together and with discretion.

People who have reached retirement age will inevitably be older than those who care for them professionally. They have lived longer, gained experience, wisdom, lifestyles, customs and habits. Older people who are over 70 were born in the early years of the 20th century. People in their 80's will have lived through both World Wars and seen massive changes in the world. They have had a lot of time to develop their individuality. They are independent people with views and wishes which must be respected.

- Food has been an important aspect of life for older people, who have grown up without the choices and variety of different convenience foods that exist today.
- Food has been important in their family and social lives and in maintaining their health, well-being and comfort.
- Most will have experienced rationing and shortages.
- The women in particular will have learned to invent meals and 'stretch' expensive ingredients.

Carers can learn a great deal from their older clients.

Older people, both those in care and in their own homes, may feel abandoned even when they have relatives who visit often. They may have to face becoming less mobile, less fit and often more physically and mentally impaired. Arthritis is a particularly disabling condition common in Britain. Increasing loss of vision, hearing, mobility and memory can lead to frustration and anger at the corresponding loss of independence. In these circumstances older people may regard food as their only comfort and the only thing in their lives that they recognise. It is important, therefore, that their food is familiar and that they are not presented solely with the sort of food that pleases their carers. Some will not wish to be a nuisance and a bother to others. Because of this they will often deny themselves a great deal unless their needs are attended to with imagination and ingenuity.

Food for health

The summary of the COMA report No. 43, *Nutrition and the Elderly* recommends '....that the majority of people aged 65 and over should adopt, where possible, similar patterns of eating and lifestyle to those advised for maintaining health in younger adults. ...... A diet which provides an adequate intake of all nutrients can more easily be obtained if the energy intake remains at a level close to that recommended for younger adults'.

Nutritional status and history-taking

Assessment of nutritional status is an important routine aspect of history taking. Carers must be aware of the often inadequate food intake of older people. In order to assess the risk of diseases such as osteoporosis and iron-deficiency anaemia (see page 114), a system appropriate to the care setting for monitoring the intake of all nutrients needs to be devised by the care team.

Some ideas for beginning the monitoring process are given in Chapter 3 and more detailed examples are provided in the Caroline Walker Trust's document, *Eating Well for Older People* and the NAGE book *Eating through the 90's*. A chart used by a medical centre in Nottingham is shown on page 40.

Physical health

The idea used to be that people do not need to eat so much as they grow older because they are less active. It is now recognised that the body has to contend with the possibility of muscle wastage, less efficient repair mechanisms, increased likelihood of infection, increased disability and depression. To offset these, there is a definite need for energy and other nutrients. All nutrients must be in proportion and in adequate amounts to maintain optimum health.

As the incentive to prepare and eat food is often low, foods which are nutrient-dense should be encouraged. Those high in fibre or water will reduce total intake and may lead to too few nutrients being taken in for optimal health. It is wise, therefore, to:

● favour complex carbohydrates such as bread, potato, pasta, oatmeal;
● use fibre sparingly in order to concentrate the nutrients in the menu. Check with the dietitian if there is thought to be a need for extra fibre in the diet;
● keep the vitamin C intake high;
● monitor vitamin D intake. A high intake of vitamin D is now recommended for those who are unable to be in the sunlight for very

In 1979, Elsie Widdowson said:

Those who have reached extreme old age today were born in the last decades of the last century when times for many were hard, food was often inadequate in quality and quantity and growth during childhood was slow. .... Present day centenarians lived their childhood while Queen Victoria was on the throne and perhaps it is only the tough ones who have survived.

long. The figure of ten micrograms (10 µg) is the recommended daily amount and it may only be possible to attain this level with a vitamin supplement. Any use of synthetic vitamins must be part of the total menu plan if it is to be monitored properly.

Hypothermia

It is known that reducing Calorie intake at any time of life can increase the risk of hypothermia. In hypothermia, the body temperature falls below the acceptable range and many problems arise as a result. There may be an increase in the aging process (the body does not have the energy to repair itself and so cells die), a very low resistance to infection and thickening of the blood which can cause circulatory problems. In many cases, hypothermia in the elderly is caused by a low intake of food, especially those which stimulate the body to work.

Hypothermia can occur in other age groups and at other times as a result of prolonged exposure to the cold, for example. Many young people working in outdoor jobs can have very low body temperatures if their food intake is low.

Mental health and well-being

For many older people, especially those in residential care or those who are confined to their own homes, food is a major source of enjoyment and comfort. Their mental health depends on this enjoyment as much as their physical health will depend on its nutritional value. Food is one aspect of their new surroundings that most clients will find familiar when they move into residential care or start to attend a day care centre, so it is important that it *is* familiar and they *do* recognise it.

Catering for older people

The provision of food for older people must take into account all the factors that determine their view of a normal diet. This will often not be the same as the view of those who are caring for them, especially if the carers are very much younger. (Refer to Activity 4.1.)

Using the biographical approach outlined in Chapter 1, menu-planners can devise menus that suit the tastes as well as the needs of those in their care. Beware of changing fashions about what is 'good for you' and what is 'bad for you'. For example, who would dare to tell a sprightly 90-year old that he shouldn't have dripping toast for his tea because it is 'bad for him'?

Taste, texture, colour, presentation

As people get older, their taste buds become less sensitive and need extra stimulation. Food needs to be attractive and tasty. Where it is necessary for salt to be reduced, other flavourings can be used to add to the enjoyment of a meal (see Chapter 2). Reduced saliva production can make it difficult for some older people to chew and swallow. A drink with the meal will help and their food should not be overly dry. A jug of extra sauce can be provided, too, but beware of making everything sloppy and unappetising.

Chewing can be a problem for several reasons. Loss of weight can lead to ill-fitting dentures; debility may mean that the client hasn't the energy to

---

As one lady put it in an interview:

'I do not greet Chicken Fricassée with open arms, I must say. If I can just describe it to you: it looks a little bit like the sort of paste that you use for wallpaper – perhaps a bit more solid – and a few shreds of some indescribable animal substance floating around in it, you see. I must admit defeat – it's the look of it you see.'

ACTIVITY 4.4

Suggested intake of nutrients
Refer to the table on page 130. Write down and compare the Reference Nutrient Intake figure for energy for:

- teenage boys;
- pregnant women;
- older people over 75 years of age;
- yourself.

Compare your own day's intake of food (Activity 2.3) with that of an elderly client or relative. Are there any differences?

chew; a physical condition, such as a stroke, may leave the jaw very weak. Cutting food up, offering soft food or liquidising food may be necessary. If food is served in a liquidised form, the added water will reduce the nutritional content of the meals. When it is necessary to do this to food, the meals and snacks must be given frequently throughout the day to counteract this dilution (see page 95).

Colour and overall presentation can make the difference between simply eating a meal and really enjoying it. The art of garnish can be cultivated and contrasting colours used to make a dish most attractive.

> *Independence is important for all clients; receiving food that they recognise and can manage and maybe share with others is the first priority. It may be easy for carers to cut food up or liquidise it. This practice must not be encouraged if it is simply in order to speed up the meal time.*

Disabilities

Older people may find themselves becoming less able in a variety of ways. People may suffer impairment in their mobility, their vision or hearing, their mental agility and their desire to cope. Some disabilities can be severe, others are manageable. When disabilities increase slowly, people adapt and many invent ways which enable them to cope extremely well. On the other hand some may pretend that they can cope better than they really can rather than invite neighbourly 'interference'.

In Chapter 5 the section on Special Needs provides some guidance to carers involved with disabled clients.

Food in care

Food provision in residential care homes is monitored by the local authority's social services department and in nursing homes by the Regional Health Authority (RGA). Not all local authorities or RGAs employ a catering adviser or use the consultancy services of a dietitian. Food provision will thus be very varied across the country. The guidelines for nutritional content which have been issued by the Advisory Body for Social Service Catering (ABSSC), the British Dietetic Association's Nutrition Advisory Group for Elderly People (NAGE), 'Nutrition and the NHS' and the Caroline Walker Trust's *'Eating Well for Older People'* have been referred to in Chapter 3.

Nutrition is not the only aspect of catering for elderly people. Other important aspects need to be considered:

- food is part of social background;
- the giving and sharing of food is ingrained in our instincts;
- food is a major enjoyment for most people who are alone or in care.

Be careful when sitting people with others at the meal table. In a residential environment clients may find themselves eating at the same table as someone they may not wish to share with. One person may be intolerant of another's disability and, if that disability affects the way they eat, may become very distressed by it. Their comments and actions may then upset that person and others at the table. A great deal of sensitivity is needed when placing people at table and dealing with behavioural problems.

When feelings of loss of independence, increasing frailty and disability, depression and loneliness overcome people they may give vent to bouts of frustration and anger which will often be directed at the food. Frustration may cause people to throw food about, to refuse to eat, to try to gobble up everything in sight, to take food from someone else. We need to remember that this kind of behaviour can happen in many contexts in life, in restaurants, canteens, pubs, even hospital dining rooms. It is not a sign of senility. It is more a sign of anger and independence.

Such behaviour is a genuine cry for tender, loving care and can be controlled by remembering that familiar food is a great source of comfort. When frustration flares up it is important that something special is prepared and presented attractively to the client, preferably with the carer able to spend time alone with him or her.

4.4 Keeping track

ACTIVITY 4.5

Refer to Activity 3.6. Does the system you have compiled for keeping track work well? Modify your system if necessary to take account of the needs of children or older people in your care. The proforma on page 67 might be helpful.

It is part of the care plan for an individual that their food intake should be adequate for their needs and that they have appropriate access to the foods and meals that will achieve this. With all of the possible variations that carers and their clients might encounter, keeping track of a client's food intake can be difficult. The carer must watch for signs that could indicate a shortage of nutrients, even in the overweight, and notify the health professionals. The community dietitian can be asked to undertake any dietary assessment, including a diet history if there is any possibility of a problem. It may be necessary to alter the care package being offered.

4.5 Food and diet with cultural variations

Almost all cultural patterns and traditions, including the many western ones, have grown up around the religious practices of the region.

- For many, ' .... religious events are the main social events and religious observances are a normal part of day-to-day individual and community life'. (Alix Henley: *Caring for Muslims and their Families*)
- Food is often an important part of religious and cultural observances and people's attitudes to foods must be respected at all times.
- Not all members of a cultural or religious group maintain all the observances strictly and some do not practise them at all.
- As with all situations where food is being offered to people in care, it is essential to listen and learn from the client.
- All of the main religions have their specific holy days and festivals. The annual calendar is different for each of the main religious groups, often depending on the phases of the moon, and will be different each year. Cultures base their dates on different calendars which are not synchronised with each other.

Each year a calendar of religious festivals and other dates is published by the SHAP Working Party on World Religions in Education to enable everyone to fit in with holidays in our multicultural society. When caring for a mixed community it is wise where possible to discover the dates early in the calendar and help clients to take part in as many special events as possible.

- In the Christian tradition, Christmas is a fixed date while Easter and Whitsun are not. Sunday is still the week's main holy day;

- In the Jewish tradition there is Passover and Yom Kippur and Saturday is the week's main holy day;
- In the Sikh tradition 'new year' is in April and there is a Festival of Light and Deliverance in October or November;
- The Hindu tradition holds a Spring festival, Holi, and a Festival of Light, Diwali, on their new year's eve in October or November;
- The Muslim Festival of Ramadan ends a period of fasting and is similar to the Christian Christmas.

All of the Festivals involve special foods. Some of the observances involve fasting. It may not be desirable for a client to fast completely, even for a short time. Consultation with the family and religious leaders may allow for special dispensation to be granted.

Immigration

Taking up permanent residence in another country brings with it many problems as well as advantages. Where people have migrated from a very different culture and tradition there is always a conflict between maintaining the original culture and becoming part of the new one.

When people migrated to Britain a few years ago, many felt that they should change to the western diet and foods, believing that their own ways were inferior. Unfortunately, the modern western diet is not considered healthy, even for people born into the western culture, and even the traditional diet, which is more suited to the cold climates of the northern hemisphere, is not necessarily healthy for people who have come from other regions of the world.

Fortunately for everyone, many of the traditional ways are returning and all cultures are benefitting from a much wider variety of foods and dishes. Many children from all cultural backgrounds, however, prefer the convenience foods which are available and often their parents will provide them to save arguments.

ACTIVITY 4.6

Make a list of the meals that you enjoy eating that you first encountered:

- when travelling abroad;
- in a restaurant serving foods of a different culture;
- from a take-away or delicatessen;
- when trying recipes using ingredients available in the supermarkets.

How many of these dishes are now part of your normal diet? How have you adapted them to suit your own taste?

Variations in traditional dishes

In many cases, the same or similar ingredients are used in dishes from different regions. Differences in the final product often lie in the flavourings or in the cooking method. Sometimes fruits and vegetables will be used in ways which are unfamiliar to people of another cultural tradition.

Traditional recipes make use of ingredients which are readily available in the region from which they originate. Some of these will not travel well, so when making up a dish in another region the end product will not be the

BAHA'I

BUDDHIST

CHINESE

CHRISTIAN

HINDU

MUSLIM

JAIN

JAPANESE

JEWISH

NATIONAL

RASTAFARIAN

SIKH

ZOROASTRIAN
(PARSEE)

These illustrations are from the SHAP calendar. Try to find the main festivals for these religions for each month of the year

ACTIVITY 4.7

Visit your local library. Find recipe books from different regions and cultures. Compare recipes from the different regions which use much the same ingredients. See how many you can find which are similar.

ACTIVITY 4.8

Collect pictures of familiar dishes that you could use in a book of pictures. They may be from advertisements, recipe cards, magazine and newspaper articles, food wrappers, or your own drawings, for example.

same. Different countries make use of different types of fats and cooking oils which impart special flavours. Recipes are altered and made to suit the traditions and ingredients available in that area.

In many traditions there are some foods which are unacceptable. Some may be forbidden for religious reasons. Others may be rejected as unfamiliar or wrong within that society. The British, for instance, have never shared the French love of frogs or snails.

Language problems

Many people who have come to live in Britain are not able to speak or understand English. Often children translate for their parents. It is the second language for most first generation immigrants. Information about food, in particular that relating to special therapeutic diets such as diabetes, is translated into a number of languages including several from the Indian sub-continent. For people of whatever background who are unable to read, pictures of foods can be an invaluable means of communication.

Dietary considerations for some cultural groups

Hinduism is a way of life and a means of understanding the world. Its values cannot be separated. The Hindu caste system may determine who cooks the food and which crockery, etc. is used. People of the Hindu faith are mostly vegetarian (see page 96), although they may occasionally eat fish. Beef is forbidden. Eggs are a source of life and are not usually eaten, even in baked foods. They take no alcohol and periods of fasting are common. Older people withdraw from the concerns of the world and daily life, eat little and only those foods which are thought to be pure.

Sikhism is a branch of Hinduism. The only strict prohibition in the diet is against meat killed in the Muslim way, i.e. Halal meat. People of the Sikh faith do not usually eat beef and may not eat pork. Most are vegetarian and prefer to avoid eggs, viewing them as a source of life. They take no alcohol.

Pictures communicate in any language

Islam is a complete way of life with clear-cut rules. Devout Muslims are unlikely to adopt western culture and lifestyle where it conflicts with religious beliefs. People of the Muslim faith do not eat pork. Their meat is produced according to the Halal tradition. They take no alcohol or shellfish. They observe regular periods of fasting including one month of Ramadan.

Judaism People of the Jewish faith eat no pork. Other meat is produced according to the Kosher method. They eat no kidney, hindquarter meat, shellfish or gamebirds. Meat and dairy foods are not eaten together in the same meal and they are cooked in pans kept separate for the purpose. Members of the Jewish faith may obtain dispensation which allows them to relax these rules in some circumstances or emergencies, but they prefer not to.

Buddhism People of the Buddhist faith are usually vegetarians but will eat dairy products and eggs. They may eat some meat if it has not been killed specifically for the purpose of eating.

Rastafarian people eat no animal products except milk. Foods must be 'alive' so they eat no processed food, and all food should be 'organic'. Many prefer a strict vegan regime (see page 96). They take no salt, coffee or alcohol. Some cooking practices can lead to deficiencies in folate and vitamin C.

Baha'i Many people of this faith follow a strict vegan regime. The ultimate goal is a diet of fruit and grains only. Fasting is obligatory at specific times for those aged between 15 and 70 but not during pregnancy and lactation.

Confucianism and *Taoism* These Chinese religions are founded in the consciousness of concern for all human relationships with the world and all its animals and plants. Ask for information and guidance from individual clients and their relatives as practices in respect of food will vary.

Meeting needs

The best way to discover if you are meeting cultural and religious needs is to ask the client. If the client is not able to speak your language you may need to ask through a relative or friend. The next best way is to observe. Both asking and observing involve tact, respect and a non-judgemental approach. It is also necessary to ensure that you are all talking about the same thing. Even in a small country like the UK, the words we use to describe food and meals varies from region to region.

A checklist is suggested as part of the monitoring process in Chapter 3. This includes points to consider about:

● food restrictions;
● prayer times;
● meal times;
● particular cooking or processing needs;
● particular seating arrangements.

In multi-ethnic communities, carers will find it useful to have a list of names and addresses of interpreters, together with a file on foods and ingredients and where to buy them. Many large towns and cities have centres offering food services for different cultural groups and an appropriate religious leader can be called upon for advice in cases of genuine uncertainty.

ACTIVITY 4.9

Find out what facilities there are in your area or your nearest large town for advising and helping people from different cultural backgrounds and religions. Make a list of addresses of the local leaders of the Jewish, Hindu and Moslem communities and the different Christian denominations.

References and further reading

Children and young people

COMA Report No. 45 1994: *Weaning and the Weaning Diet*. HMSO

Francis 1986: *Nutrition for Children*. Blackwell Scientific Press

Hall 1984: *Feeding Your Children*. Judy Piatkus Ltd

Haslam 1985: *Eat It Up! – a Parent's Guide to Eating Problems*. Macdonald & Co

Karmel 1991: *The Complete Baby and Toddler Menu Planner*. Ebury Press

Lindon 1994: *Caring for Young Children*. Macmillan

Lindon 1993: *Caring for the Under 8-s*. Macmillan

Minett 1985: *Childcare and Development*. John Murray

National Diet and Nutrition Surveys (for children aged 1½ to 4½ years) 1985: Reports on the Diet and Nutrition Survey and the Dental survey, Volumes 1 and 2

Pay 1986: *Cooking for Kids the Healthy Way*. Macdonald Optima

1987: *Child's Diets and Change*. British Dietetic Association

1991: *Working for Children and Young People*. Open University

Pregnancy

1991: *While you are Pregnant – Safe Eating*. Department of Health

Older people

COMA Report No. 43 1992: *Nutrition and the Elderly*. HMSO

Eversole and Hess 1981: *Towards Healthy Aging – Human Needs and Nursing Response*. CV Mosby Co.

1995: *Eating Well for Older People*. Caroline Walker Trust

MAFF: *Healthy Eating for Older People* (A Food Sense Booklet)

NAGE 1993: *Eating through the 90's*. British Dietetic Association

NAGE 1992: *Food and Health Policies for Elderly People*. British Dietetic Association

Smyth 1992: *Caring for Older People*. Macmillan

1990: *Community Life – a Code of Practice for Community Care*. Centre for Policy on Aging

1995: *Budgeting for Food on Benefits*. National Consumer Council

Cultural and religious groups

Drummond and Wilbraham 1991: *The Englishman's Food – A History of Five Centuries of the English Diet*. Pimlico

Henley 1983: *Caring for Hindus and their Families*. National Extension College

Henley 1983: *Caring for Sikhs and their Families*. National Extension College

Henley 1983: *Caring for Muslims and their Families*. National Extension College

NAGE 1993: *In the Minority Through the 90s*. British Dietetic Association

Working Party on World Religions in Education: *The SHAP Calendar of Religious Festivals*. SHAP

1985: *Immigrant Foods* (Supplement to *The Composition of Foods*). HMSO

5 Special needs and special diets

5.1 Special needs

From time to time we will all have a special need for extra care and consideration. For some, though, the need is permanent. Helping clients with special needs to obtain a healthy diet that they enjoy eating is an essential part of a carer's task.

Start with the person

Each client is an individual, with individual likes, dislikes, habits, background, social place, capabilities and nutritional needs. The task for the carer is to design meals, menus and advice appropriate to that person. Caring includes being aware of each person's individual needs. He or she may have:

- physical disabilities which affect posture, mobility, manual dexterity, speech, coordination;
- a mental health condition or learning disability;
- a condition which affects memory or communication;
- difficulty with cutting up food;
- difficulty with chewing;
- a visual impairment;
- some internal disorder or a metabolic problem like diabetes;
- a special liking for a food which has been eaten regularly in the past;
- strong dislikes or aversions;
- restrictions for cultural or religious reasons.

In a residential home, nursing home, day-care centre, hospital, school or other place attended by regular clients, the group will be mixed, and will include perhaps only one or two of a variety of different special needs. Everyone must receive a well-balanced diet or their health will suffer. Each person is special and everyone's needs and likes have to be taken into account.

The record cards and documents outlined in Chapters 3 and 4 are especially helpful when trying to keep track of the very different special needs or dietary modifications of individual clients. When welcoming new people into the group, find out from them or their relatives what you need to know; other details will come out as time goes by.

It is tempting to plan and serve meals that are based on the lowest common denominator – the easiest ones to prepare that most people enjoy most of the time. Mince and mash comes to mind. Don't be tempted – it makes life very dull for everyone.

ACTIVITY 5.1

Think of ways whereby ordinary meals can be adapted. For example, if the dish is steak pie, how would you adapt it for:

- someone who has had a stroke and can only use one hand?
- someone whose false teeth no longer fit?
- someone who has to avoid salt?
- someone who has to reduce their fat intake?

Choice of foods

- *Nutritional requirements* – irrespective of a client's physical or mental ability, nutritional needs will always be determined by age, gender, activities and state of health.
- *Level of ability, disability or long-term ailment* – may determine whether the nutrient levels need to be modified.
- *Type of food* – will be determined by cultural background, religion, social habits, upbringing.
- *Modified foods* – any modifications of the foods offered will be determined by the level of ability/disability.
- *Understanding* – for some, ability to understand instructions or retain them may be impaired. Every effort must be made to ensure that clients receive a varied, interesting diet. Some clients may be unable to remember clearly the foods that are being offered and others may not like to be adventurous.
- *Other factors* – when advising people in their own homes, there are other factors which you must consider, for example income level, ability to shop, store food, cook food. Chapter 3 dealt with many of these factors in more detail.

Keeping track of individual needs and wants

Think in terms of an individual record or menu card for each person. Keep notes on individual likes, dislikes, special days, religious or other diets. Note, too, clients' ability to chew and cut up their food; their special needs, appetite, special favourites, and so on. Keep this sheet in a polythene pocket and keep the pockets in a loose leaf binder file for easy reference at meal times. Make sure that you use a binder and pockets that can be wiped clean with disinfectant to prevent bacteria from spreading. Always keep them spotlessly clean and away from food.

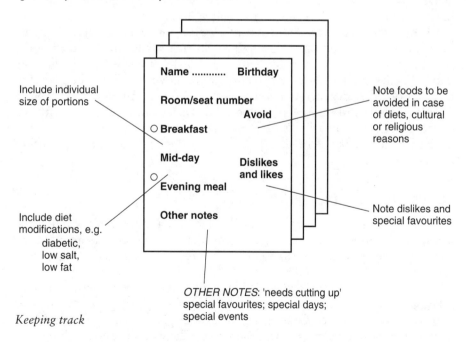

Keeping track

Use self-adhesive, removable labels for adding temporary notes to the out-side of the pocket, if necessary. For example, you might need to note:

- that someone is away for a meal or coming back later;
- a special meal time or fast for religious reasons;

- a need for a special diet dish that is different from the main menu;
- that someone is feeling unwell;
- that they are entertaining;
- that they have been given a gift of a special meal by a friend or neighbour.

Physical disabilities

Certain disabilities will determine a client's approach to buying, preparing and eating food.

- Mobility problems can arise from strokes, arthritis, degenerative disorders, accidents; these can interfere with a person's ability to shop and physically prepare food.
- Neurological disorders can impair the control of movement; this will include lifting food to the mouth.
- Conditions which affect joints can seriously impair a person's dexterity with cutlery and may interfere with chewing.

Physical disabilities can contribute to both weight gain and weight loss. Nutritional requirements remain the same as for a person of similar age and weight. Any alteration in the Calorie content of the diet must be on the advice of the dietitian.

Dietary modifications

A dietary modification for medical or cultural reasons must not be overlooked when giving advice to, or planning meals for, clients with disabilities. Food intake needs to be monitored (see pages 39 and 40) to ensure that all nutrient needs are being met. Where there is weight loss, the diet should be assessed accurately and modified to counteract this effect. It may be that the client is having difficulty with food and is not willing to admit to it.

Where there is severe reduction in physical movement, internal energy output can be increased by selecting protein-rich foods whilst reducing the concentration of fat and carbohydrate. This will help to offset muscle wastage and give clients a feeling of satisfaction and enjoyment. Some people with arthritis or other degenerative joint conditions have gained benefit from a mainly vegetarian diet. Any self-imposed diet needs to be checked with the client, the relatives and the dietitian. It must be shown to be effective within a reasonable period of time, especially if it creates difficulties for other diners or staff.

Independence and individuality

These are priorities. Everyone should be able to maintain their own lifestyle as far as possible and according to their wishes. Food can be adapted for clients that can only use one hand. It can be presented in a finger-buffet style, for example.

A wide variety of aids is available to help people cope with problems relating to food in their own particular situation. Across the country, 30 National Demonstration Centres will have on display much of the equipment available for use by clients with disabilities. Clients and carers will also be advised by Occupational Therapy departments within the local hospital or Social Services structure. As seen in Chapter 3 many supermarkets have taken to heart the criticism that they were not accessible to people with physical disabilities. Refer back to Activity 3.2 in which you assessed the shopping facilities available for disabled people in your area.

Information about special implements and modifications to buildings, equipment and furniture may be obtained through the Occupational Therapy Department at the nearest general or specialist hospital or from the National Centre for the Disabled.

Eating aids: a) modified cutlery,   *b) easy pouring,*   *c) cutlery and crockery*

Modified equipment: a) Kitchen tools with good grips,   *b) easy-to-carry tray*

Access for all

Visual impairment

Up to 3 per cent of people in the UK have some visual impairment, with partial sightedness being more common than total loss of sight. Carers will need to establish the extent and type of visual disability amongst clients within their care in order to make appropriate adjustments to service of food. Most visual impairment occurs as people grow older and many older people in care are coping with this in addition to other difficulties.

Visual impairment is often partial and the carer must try to determine the extent of the impairment in order to help unobtrusively with the presentation of food. For example, a person who has had a stroke may only be able to see half his plate and may thus only eat half his meal. Before taking away the plate, try turning it around. Others may not be able to see what is in the centre of the plate and may need a gentle hint that they have not yet eaten everything.

Helping people to cope

Sight can be lost gradually or very suddenly, causing mental distress leading to frustration and sometimes anger. This can affect not only a person's ability to cope with food, but also their attitude towards it. People who have been good cooks in the past can become frightened of trying, even with the many gadgets now available. They may be afraid to eat in public in case they make a mess or knock things over. Sometimes they will eat very unbalanced snacks rather than venture into a dining room or cafeteria.

- *Colour* – When thinking about food and its service, it is advisable to think about strong colours and contrast, especially in respect of the serving dishes, equipment and tables.
- *Touch* – Tactile surfaces, for example rough cloth, ridged edges, can also help. They enable people to judge things by feel, and can prevent embarrassing spillages.
- *Hearing* – When cooking, blind people need to have little background noise so they can listen to the sound of the food cooking. Together with the sense of smell, they can become very experienced in identifying different stages of cooking.
- *Finger foods* – These are easy to eat as they do not require cutting up or can be picked up in the fingers, for example sandwiches, sausages, chicken drumsticks, individual quiche, prepared fresh fruit or raw vegetable sticks.
- *Covering food* – Cling film is difficult to handle and can get most of us in a tangle from time to time. Cover food and dishes with a clean serviette or paper towel, if necessary.
- *Restricted movement* – Non-slip mats and trays, suction pads on certain items such as egg-cups, can make life easier, especially if the client is confined to bed.
- *Talking to people* – Always tell the client where the cup, glass, cruet, or extra dishes have been placed on the table or tray. If necessary guide the person's hand to them.

At home, many blind and partially sighted people have learned to cope very well with cooking and some will have invented their own techniques, like the blind chef who counts the number of 'glugs' as he pours the wine into the sauce. Pick up useful tips to pass on to others. The Royal National College for the Blind in Hereford offers courses geared towards helping blind people to cope in a sighted world. They also run courses for carers.

When describing to a client what he has on his plate, use the idea of the plate as a clock face. For example, the potatoes are at 2.00 o'clock; the meat at 11.0 o'clock; vegetables, towards you at 6.00 o'clock; and so on.

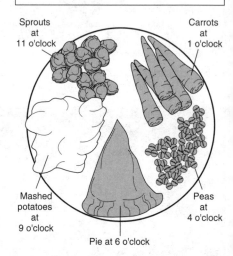

Using the clock face to describe items on a plate

Finger foods

A talking clock

Gadgets and modifications

There are many gadgets and modifications to standard equipment to help in the kitchen; some are used by sighted people, too. The RNIB has many of these available for sale and carers can usually assess them at their nearest National Demonstration Centre or Blind Institute centre. BBC Radio's 'In Touch' programme tests gadgets and reports on them in their programmes and in their annual book, *In Touch*. Talking weighing scales for measuring ingredients, a device for sensing when the tea cup is nearly full, a gadget for preventing the milk from boiling over – all are in regular use in the kitchens of visually impaired people. Ovens, hobs and timers are all available in a specially adapted range. Someone is even thinking up a talking microwave oven! Cookery books and recipe cards are available in large print and braille; some have been recorded on to audio-tape.

Many partially sighted people will need help with labels and instructions. These are not always easy to understand, even for people with normal vision. Manufacturers are being encouraged to improve them, but so far only bleach containers carry a notice in braille.

Dietary modifications

A partially sighted person may have other conditions which require some dietary modification and this must be adhered to. If a dietary modification has been prescribed, it is part of a person's treatment and their health will suffer if it is not maintained.

For example, a number of people with diabetes lose all or part of their sight as one of the complications of the condition. Their diabetic diet (page 81) must be followed. If a diabetic can no longer give his or her own injections of insulin, care must be taken to see that their usual routine and timing is maintained. Some will be relying on the district nurse for the injection and meals-on-wheels for their diet. These have to be coordinated.

ACTIVITY 5.2

Visit your nearest National Demonstration Centre or Occupational Therapy Department. Find out as much as possible about the adaptations to equipment that will help your clients. If possible arrange a visit for one or more of your clients with physical or visual impairment.

It is vital that insulin injections are given at the right times and that meals are provided at evenly spaced intervals.

This has to be written into the care plan for that person.

Hearing impairment

If the client is otherwise in good health, a hearing impairment need not interfere too much with the ability to cope with food and food issues. Some hearing defects are combined with speech and communication problems or conditions relating to the mouth, eating and swallowing.

Communication

The biggest problem is one of communication. Many hard-of-hearing and deaf people may not find shopping easy and may find it difficult to understand what is being offered on a menu. People whose first language is sign language may not find the written word as easy to understand as some hearing people might think. Pictures of dishes being served enable clients to point to what they would like.

In large crowded places such as a dining room, many people will turn off their hearing aids as they can cause confusion and disorientation. Shouting makes most hearing problems worse; slow speaking in a low pitched voice is usually more effective. If possible, face clients who are hard-of-hearing so that they can lip-read if they are able to.

In shops, clients may not be aware of special offers. One large supermarket chain has installed a minicom system in some of its larger stores and is also experimenting with an induction loop system to help those with hearing aids. Look out for the ear symbol which shows that the shop has taken part in the Sympathetic Hearing Scheme run by Hearing Concern and that there are staff available who can be of help. Some television advertisements carry sub-titles for the hard-of-hearing which can help with food shopping.

Memory loss and confusion

It is possible to trigger the memories of people suffering from amnesia by offering the type of foods that they used to eat when they were young. Using a book of pictures of foods may help them to choose what they like. Your book of pictures will also be useful where clients are confused or unable to communicate. Such confusion can give rise to a great deal of distress for the carer and client alike. Often a client will not understand what food is being offered or will not be able to say what they want.

Oral difficulties

Some clients have difficulties with chewing, swallowing or eating. Such difficulties may be short- or long-term, temporary or permanent. Temporary difficulties may be due to a passing problem such as teeth extraction, infection (e.g. severe tonsillitis), accident or surgical intervention. More permanent difficulties can be caused by carcinoma, deformity, muscular weakness following stroke, or a degenerative disease. In addition some drugs will cause saliva to dry up and loss of weight can cause false teeth to fit badly. In all these cases the food needs to be modified to suit the circumstances.

Whatever the situation, food should be presented attractively. It should taste well and be tempting. Watch out for foods such as lemon juice which can be very painful on a sore mouth. Some foods can increase the flow of saliva which can cause considerable discomfort if the salivary glands are affected.

ACTIVITY 5.3

1 Using the pictures that you collected in Activity 4.8, make a book of pictures that illustrate some of the meals on the menu that your clients are being offered.

2 Try out your book of pictures with some clients who have hearing impairment.

Ear symbol from the Deaf Awareness Project of Hearing Concern

Puréed or liquidised food for conditions of the mouth or throat will be largely water. Nutritional balance will suffer unless food is fortified with concentrated nutrients without altering its palatability. It must also be taken frequently. This may seem very time consuming for staff but the alternative is starvation for the patient.

The gentle art of garnishes

5.2 Therapeutic diets

KEY CONCEPT

Therapeutic diet: a food pattern that forms part of the patient's treatment plan.

Everyone has a diet of one sort or another because a diet is a daily intake of food, but some diets are called 'special'. Where special diets are designed to relieve or cure symptoms of a disease, they may be called *'therapeutic diets'* as they form part of a patient's treatment plan. A traditional western pattern of food intake may also be modified for non-therapeutic reasons. People may follow a religious or cultural food pattern; they may be vegetarian or vegan; or they may have a physical disability which needs to be considered. Most modifications can be achieved fairly easily by adapting items from the normal menu.

Clients may have a medical reason for a modification in their food intake, where the body is unable to cope with an ingredient in the normal diet, for example diabetes, heart disease, gall-bladder disease, coeliac disease (also referred to as gluten-induced or gluten-sensitive enteropathy). Therapeutic diets are also used in the treatment of a wide variety of other conditions. They are prescribed by the doctor to fit into the overall treatment plan for the patient. They may be needed for short periods of time to contain the effects of other treatments, following accidents or surgery, for example, or for longer periods of time where a long-term condition requires it.

Therapeutic diets are planned and monitored by dietitians (who are State Registered in the UK). Clients who claim to be 'on a diet' should have written instructions from the dietitian and carers need to ask to see them. Such instructions may not be available; where they are they may be quite old, may not seem appropriate for the client's present condition or may, indeed, not have been written for that client at all.

It is not always possible to arrange follow-up visits for all patients and some do not keep their arranged appointments. Unless the doctor refers someone back to the dietitian, their diet may never be monitored and altered as necessary. Quite a number of people take home a 'diet sheet' from the dietitian, put it carefully in a drawer, often well protected, and never refer to it again. They rely on memory, firmly believing they are following the advice they have been given. Carers have the unique opportunity to see that their clients' diets are checked properly. If appropriate instructions are not available or if the carer has some doubts about their usefulness, carers will need to contact the local dietitian who advises their Home or Social Services Department or the dietitian at the nearest General Hospital.

Terminology and basic principles

Over the past decades there have been many changes in the terms used by health workers and scientists to describe aspects of health-related nutrition. People who have been given advice and instructions in the past will often stick to the words they are used to, to help their understanding. It does not mean that because they do not use up-to-date language, they are ignorant or stupid.

Communication between carer and client is better if the carer is able to use words the other person understands and is able to translate specialist knowledge into laymans terms. You need to be sure of your clients' levels of understanding. Beware of talking down to clients and of 'blinding them with science'.

Nutritional balance

It is essential, for health and well-being, that everyone receives a well balanced intake of food. For a therapeutic diet to be effective, it is important for the right food to be delivered to the right client at the right time. The food should also be eaten by that client and enjoyed.

But what is normal? In this chapter a 'normal diet' is taken to mean the food eaten by most of the group for whom the menu has been planned. (What is 'normal' is also referred to in Chapter 1: Food and people, and in Chapter 9: Planning and serving meals and menus.) This normal diet can be modified:

- by altering the consistency of the food; or
- by being selective about certain ingredients.

An appropriate diet sheet may be obtained for a client from the dietitian. Diet sheets produced by food manufacturers do not relate to the special needs of individuals and their treatment and should not be relied upon. Always check with the dietitian.

The balance of nutrients is of special importance when catering for individual therapeutic diets. It is not desirable for a patient to develop extra health problems by neglecting to maintain normal nutritional balance, especially if their condition requires them to have extra nutrients. For normal nutritional balance, it is usual to divide the day's requirement for nutrients into three more-or-less equal parts and produce meals and snacks which cover each third, i.e. breakfast and mid-morning; midday and afternoon tea; evening meal and bedtime. Meal times can thus be seen to spread over about 16 hours which is another useful framework for balancing special diets.

When people say that they are 'on a diet' they often mean that they are trying to slim, which may not be for medical reasons.

For special therapeutic diets it is necessary to follow a specific regime designed by the dietitian.

Basics of a normal menu

It is useful to consider the concept of a normal menu in order to appreciate ways of adapting it. Daily meal patterns vary from country to country and within countries according to traditions, food supply, work patterns, etc. In Britain, in the early years of this century for example, it was usual for men working in local factories or on the land to go home for their midday meal. Other workplaces like shops, offices, schools and hospitals would have a staff canteen or restaurant which provided the midday meal (and possibly other meals, too). Taking diet histories from clients and patients shows how this pattern is changing and how, for many, the main meal is now eaten in the evening and quick, light meals are consumed during the working day.

Although meal patterns vary and the type of food eaten at each meal will differ between countries and regions, it is useful to adopt a standard framework from which menus can be constructed. In developed countries, it is still usual to consider a day's intake of food as consisting of three main meals (breakfast, midday and evening meal) with two or three between-meal snacks (mid-morning, afternoon tea and bedtime). The names given to these meals and breaks vary in different regions and this can cause confusion. Those used here are adopted throughout this book, particularly in the chapter on menu-planning, to avoid some of the confusion.

It is a useful framework, although not everyone adopts this pattern by any means: some people snack all the time; some eat one or two big meals only; some eat through the night, and so on.

Outline meal pattern basis for adaptation

Breakfast	Fruit, fruit juice and/or porridge or breakfast cereal
	(A cooked breakfast is not essential but some may like it. Yoghurt, cheese, ham or similar may be preferred by some)
	Bread, plain or toasted or crispbread or croissant or similar
	Butter or margarine; marmalade, jam or honey
	Tea or coffee
Mid-morning	Tea, coffee, milk or Bovril/Marmite-type drink
	Biscuit, crispbread or fruit – as desired
Midday (This meal pattern may be preferred in the evening)	Fruit, fruit juice, soup or starter
	Main cooked dish with meat, poultry, offal, fish, cheese, egg or pulses/nuts/vegetable dish
	Potatoes, rice or pasta
	Vegetables or salad
	Sauces and accompaniments as appropriate
	Pudding or dessert or fruit, biscuits and cheese, etc.
	Tea or coffee if desired
Mid-afternoon	Tea or coffee
	Biscuit, cake, scone, sandwich or fruit – as desired
Evening meal (This meal pattern may be preferred at midday)	Soup or fruit or fruit juice
	Sandwich, toasted snack or salad meal
	Salads or vegetables
	Cake, scone, biscuit and/or fruit or yoghurt, etc.
	Tea or coffee
Bedtime	Milk drink or tea/coffee, fruit drink or Marmite/Bovril-type drink
	Biscuit, scone, sandwich or fruit – as desired
Daily	Milk: whole/skimmed/sterilised, etc.
	Sugar: adding sugar to drinks is now less common

The outline meal pattern on page 75 uses the format of three main meals and three in-between meal snacks. The midday and evening meal patterns are interchangeable. It can be used as a basis for adaptation in special diets to ensure that all nutritional needs are met.

Some nutritional points to note:

- In a low-fat diet remember to replace the Calories lost by the reduction in fat;
- Make sure a low-salt diet is palatable so that it is eaten;
- In a diet for a diabetic, ensure that the meals are balanced and that Calories are adequate for the client's age, activities and state of health;
- In all cases refer to the client's own diet sheet, if there is one, or contact a registered dietitian. Each person is unique so each diet should be tailored to suit.

> *The diet, normal or modified, must **always** be nutritionally adequate, otherwise it will give rise to ill-health. It **must** be eaten by the person for whom it is intended otherwise their nutrition will not be adequate.*

Differences and similarities

Some people like to be different, feeling that their difference makes them noticed and gives them a sense of self-worth. Unfortunately this is not the case with all differences, particularly those which cause people to be dependent on others. Older people often play down difficulties they may be having with food (shopping, cooking, chewing, digesting, managing equipment, seeing). They may go without rather than make a fuss.

Picking up the clues calls for sensitivity and observation. Adapting meals and menus for those with special needs or who are on special diets calls for some ingenuity, if people are not to notice that they are being treated differently.

Therapeutic diets for children and young people

This age group comes under the carer's umbrella in many sectors: hospitals, home caring, schools. Where a modified diet is necessary, carers must follow the diet plan designed by the dietitan. As children are growing, active, developing resistance to diseases and, in some cases, recovering from illness, it is vital that their nutrition does not suffer in any way. Check that a child's diet is being monitored by a dietitian at the health clinic or hospital. Diets need to be reviewed and changed as a child's nutritional needs change. During growth periods this can be quite frequent.

The most common therapeutic diets required by children and young people are a gluten-free diet for coeliac disease (or gluten-induced enteropathy) and diets for diabetes (diabetic children always require injections of insulin, see page 77). Some children require quite complex diets for metabolic disorders such as cystic fibrosis and phenylketonuria (PKU):

- *Phenylketonuria* is a disease caused by the absence of an enzyme which breaks down the essential amino acid, phenylalanine (referred to on page 110). A breakdown product, phenylketone, collects in the brain causing mental retardation and sometimes very violent behaviour. Adhering to a strict diet, low in most normal protein foods but with a controlled amount of phenylalanine, enables the child to grow normally. Some adults who were not diagnosed as babies have spent many years in mental hospitals. Others have found a special diet helpful in controlling behaviour. Diets for all patients must be arranged in consultation with the dietitian.
- *Cystic fibrosis* is a disease caused by an abnormal gene which gives rise to several different malfunctions. It is usually characterised by serious

> **Metabolic disorder:** an inherited disorder of the way the body breaks down nutrients and builds up cells and tissues, etc. (metabolism).

lung problems, a deficiency in enzymes from the pancreas that digest food and an increased excretion of some minerals in the sweat. The diet has to compensate for poor absorption of some nutrients and the excess loss of others. Malnutrition can arise due to a low energy intake and absorption caused by lack of appetite and deficiency of enzymes, together with an increased energy demand to cope with the lung infections. The dietary management of cystic fibrosis will vary according to the way the condition affects the individual patient.

If vitamins and minerals need to be supplemented, the total intake must be monitored to avoid overdosing.

Food allergies, sensitivities and intolerances

Some children may have to avoid certain foods which produce allergic reactions. The most common is an allergy to milk and dairy products. This is a sensitivity to either the lactose (milk sugar) or the casein (milk protein) or both. Milk and whey powder (a milk product) are both widely used in manufactured food products. Many young children are thought to react to certain food additives and to become erratic in their behaviour as a result. Others have violent allergic reactions to ingredients like nuts (including nut oil, soya and soya products) and other specific items.

Generally, the programme for controlling the allergy entails removing the foods which contain the harmful ingredients from the diet and monitoring the results. This is not always easy as many processed foods contain ingredients which might not be obvious. Some food manufacturers and some supermarket chains provide leaflets and information packs about their own-name products as a guide for patients and their families. It is important to *check all labels* when buying foods for these children.

> *Check that a child's diet is being monitored by a dietitian and changed as the child's nutritional needs change during growth periods.*

Therapeutic diets for adults and older people

Adults will have developed likes, habits and patterns within their normal diet and many older people may find a 'special' diet very difficult. Great care needs to be taken to see that a diet does not seem to be a punishment. The most common special diets required by older people are for diabetics and for people requiring a low-Calorie, low-salt or low-fat diet. A high-protein/high-Calorie diet is required in all cases of debility (after illness, surgery, accident) and sometimes for the elderly. It is a very difficult diet to administer successfully as patients who need the food will often not want to take it. Sometimes a high-protein/high-Calorie/semi-soft diet is required for patients with difficulties in swallowing. The high water content dilutes the nutrient density and care is required to see that the patient does not suffer from starvation.

Diabetes

> **Insulin:** a hormone normally produced in the pancreas to control blood sugar.

Diabetes (diabetes mellitus) is a condition where the blood sugar level is high, sometimes dangerously so. This rise in blood sugar may be due to various underlying causes. For some it is a passing phase associated with another condition. Where it is permanent, it is usually due to the body's inability to make the hormone, *insulin*. In later life it is more likely to be due to the body's inability to efficiently utilise the insulin it makes. The sugar in blood, in the form of glucose, is the body's main energy source and comes mainly from starchy foods and sugars. The body normally controls the glucose level in the blood very accurately using the insulin made by the pancreas as required.

Insulin works by assisting the passage of glucose from the bloodstream across the cell membranes into the cells where it is used for energy. Insulin also helps the body to metabolise nutrients for energy. In some people the pancreas stops producing insulin and the resulting condition is known as *insulin-dependent diabetes* (some people may still refer to it as 'True' diabetes). People with this type of diabetes receive insulin by injection once, twice or three times a day.

In other cases the body is unable to use the insulin produced by the pancreas. The resulting rise in blood sugar can usually be treated by tablets or just diet. This condition is called *non-insulin-dependent diabetes* and may also be referred to as 'maturity-onset' diabetes. The tablets used do not contain insulin and do not have the same effect in the body. Some overweight people also have raised blood sugar levels and the symptoms of diabetes. They are usually treated as non-insulin-dependent diabetics, being prescribed tablets and a weight-reducing diet.

> **Type I** – Insulin-dependent diabetics: always treated with insulin injections;
> **Type II** – Non-insulin-dependent diabetics: treated with diet alone or diet and tablets which lower the blood sugar but which do not contain insulin.

Control of diabetes

Both insulin and carbohydrate levels in the blood fluctuate during any 24 hour period but the body's normal mechanisms for maintaining the blood sugar level are very accurate. People who are not diabetic maintain blood sugar levels within a very narrow range. It is the aim of good diabetic control to try to keep blood sugar levels within this narrow range most of the time. To achieve this, *the timing of meals is of the utmost importance*. Without good control, a diabetic is prone to complications caused by high blood glucose levels *(hyperglycaemia)*. Problems are also caused by too low a blood sugar level *(hypoglycaemia)* – described later.

Hyperglycaemia causes interference in circulation, with blockages occurring in the very small blood vessels such as those of the eyes, kidneys and toes. These blockages can lead to blindness, kidney failure and gangrene in the feet. Hyperglycaemia can also increase the risk and duration of bacterial infections as bacteria enjoy the high levels of sugar. It is the aim of good diabetic control to avoid such complications and ensure optimum health for clients.

High blood sugar levels can be detected by blood tests and many Type I diabetics perform regular pinprick tests using special kits. Excess sugar is excreted via the kidneys and this can also be detected in the urine using a simple kit. In both cases a chemical is used which changes colour in the presence of different concentrations of sugar. Used in conjunction with a daily diary of meal times, these tests help to prevent the fluctuations in blood sugar levels which can cause the complications.

> **Hyperglycaemia** or 'Hyper': too much sugar in the blood
>
> **Hypoglycaemia** or 'Hypo': too little sugar in the blood

Control of carbohydrate

The ingredient in the diet which is usually controlled in all types of diabetic diet is carbohydrate (sometimes written as 'CHO' or 'CH_2O'). Carbohydrate is found in all sugars and starches, including most fruits (as fructose), cereal grains, pulses and some root vegetables (as starch) and is also present in milk (as lactose). White refined sugar is sucrose and is found in all foods to which it has been added as an ingredient or sweetening agent. Sucrose is also found in some root vegetables like carrots and beetroot.

Diabetics are advised to obtain their carbohydrate from starches and natural 'intrinsic' sugars (i.e. sugars which have not been extracted and then added to other foods). This advice has been extended to all adults in the COMA Report No. 46: *Diet and Cardiovascular Disease*.

> ## ACTIVITY 5.4
>
> Read the section on carbohydrate in Chapter 6 and become familiar with the foods that supply most carbohydrate in the diet.

Most diet sheets for diabetics allow a specific amount of carbohydrate per day which is stated in grams (g). Balanced meals are built around this basis. The day's total is usually divided into a number of 10 g or 20 g portions which form a unit of *exchange*. Each region or clinic has its own preferred convention about the name given to a particular sized portion. They may be called 'lines', 'rations', 'portions', 'exchanges', for example. This can cause confusion if a client is accustomed to a different word from the one used by the care situation. It is important to check the carbohydrate value of the word used and the number of exchanges allowed at each meal or snack. Older diabetics may be confused and not give an accurate statement. The British Diabetic Association prefers the *10 g Exchange*.

The aim of this portioning scheme is to ensure that carbohydrate is eaten in a regular pattern throughout the day and that meals are evenly spaced. Carbohydrate is only one ingredient in a well-balanced meal or menu. It is not enough to just cover the exchanges and forget the other aspects of good menu balance. The diets for all diabetics must be nutritionally adequate in all respects and should be varied, appetising and acceptable.

The distribution of carbohydrate throughout the day will vary according to the type of diabetes, the type and times of insulin injection or tablets and sometimes according to the practice at the local diabetic clinic. Carbohydrate should never be restricted to a level lower than that required for a non-diabetic of similar age, weight and activity.

The inclusion of *fibre* in the diet of diabetics slows down the release of carbohydrate in the digestive system, allowing for a slow, more natural rise in blood sugar level. The soluble fibres found in fruit and some cereal brans have the added advantage of reducing the level of cholesterol in the blood (some diabetics have raised levels of cholesterol as part of their condition).

Type I: Insulin-dependent diabetes

The blood sugar level in this type of diabetes is controlled by injections of insulin. The insulin that is injected will often be bound with a substance that allows it to be released slowly into the bloodstream. Insulins may be fast-acting, intermediate, long-acting or mixtures. The client's doctor will prescribe the insulin that best suits the person.

Insulin injections may be given once, twice or three times a day, depending on the type of insulin. The injections are given *before* meals, not after, with the first injection usually 15–20 minutes before breakfast. Meals must not be delayed after injections are given.

The diet must be adequate in energy and all other nutrients to maintain health and normal weight for the person concerned. The proportions of energy that are derived from carbohydrate, fat and protein are similar to those recommended in Chapter 2. More complex carbohydrates like starch and complex sugars are recommended as they enable the blood sugar to rise more slowly. The diet for a Type I insulin-dependent diabetic is a normal well-balanced meal pattern suitable for a person of that age, weight, activity and general health. The differences lie in the regularity of the meal times to coincide with injections of insulin, the reduction of free added sugar and the preference for complex starches rather than simple sugars.

Meal times are important. Ideally, 2 to 3 hour intervals spread over 15–16 hours in the day give good control of blood sugar. For carers, it can sometimes be very difficult to achieve this regularity in injections and meals. It can be especially difficult when caring for someone in their own home who is dependent on community meals and a nurse calling in to give the injection. It is important for a regular routine to be established to help clients avoid the

---

Diabetic exchanges:
20 g of carbohydrate may be called '1 Ration'
or 10 g of carbohydrate may be called '1 Line',
so a day's total of 200 g of carbohydrate could be expressed as '10 Rations'
or '20 Lines'.

---

*If the food intake is **reduced** the blood sugar becomes difficult to control. If the food intake is **too high** the person may become overweight.*

Good diabetic control achieved through regularity must be an essential part of the care plan.

complications of diabetes mentioned earlier that lead to long-term suffering for the client and an increased need for care.

Stabilising

This is a process of establishing the right level, type and timing of insulin injections and the right level and timing of food intake. It initially takes place in hospital where sugar levels in blood and urine can be accurately monitored and the diet adjusted to suit the needs of the patient. There may be an initial period of re-adjustment when the person leaves hospital as the activity pattern, meal times and sometimes insulin timing may be different to the hospital routine. This can generally be overcome by timetabling meals and injections to suit the person's activities. The self-monitoring of blood and urine sugar levels and the daily diary are invaluable tools in the process of stabilisation.

Children may need periods of stabilising as they go through sudden growth spurts which require extra energy. As the amount of insulin is related to the number of active cells in the body, a child's need for insulin may fluctuate during a growing period.

Insulin reactions

For those diabetics on injections of insulin, it is occasionally necessary to give glucose or sugar to counteract an 'insulin reaction'. During an insulin reaction, blood sugar falls to a dangerous level giving rise to *hypoglycaemia* (sometimes called a 'hypo'). The person becomes confused and may lose consciousness. To avoid brain damage during unconsciousness, glucose or sugar must be given without delay or discussion (the reason for the reaction can be investigated later). Reasons for insulin reactions include:

- delay between injection and mealtime;
- sudden need for energy – e.g. infection, growth spurt;
- change in the diabetic condition.

Diabetics show a variety of signs of hypoglycaemia which their relatives or carers will come to recognise. They may act very strangely in their confusion and some can become quite violent as attempts are made to give them sugar or glucose. They will probably not remember this once the blood sugar has returned to normal. Many diabetics on insulin carry glucose tablets or sugar lumps with them and keep some by their bedside at night.

If a diabetic on insulin feels faint, confused or giddy, give **glucose** *or* **sugar** *in a warm drink, without delay or question.*

Type II: Non-insulin-dependent diabetes

The blood sugar level for non-insulin-dependent diabetics is controlled by tablets and diet or by diet alone. Many people in this group are normal or underweight. They need a diet similar to a non-diabetic of the same weight, age and activity, with meals spread out evenly throughout the day. The main ingredient in the meal which is absorbed as sugar is carbohydrate and this should be provided in small frequent amounts to maintain the person's energy and weight.

Non-insulin-dependent diabetics may have a raised level of fat in the bloodstream, so their diet may also include a fat restriction. If this is the case, carbohydrate in the form of starch and natural sugar must be increased to maintain a normal energy level. Fat-soluble vitamin intake will also need to be monitored to ensure that it is adequate. It is likely that fibre intake will also be increased.

The overweight diabetic

For an overweight person who has symptoms of diabetes, blood sugar level may be controlled by diet and tablets or by diet alone. The following points meed to be taken into account:

- overweight diabetics are usually above middle-age;
- they do not normally lose weight easily;
- drastic slimming measures can be dangerous;
- because the diet is probably 'for life', it is important to boost morale by allowing occasional treats and days off.

For diabetics who are also overweight, follow the guidelines given for low Calorie diets on page 84. The meal pattern will need to be modified to:

- give small, frequent meals;
- use large portions of lean meat, ham, poultry, offal, fish, cottage cheese or plain yoghurt;
- allow for a bedtime snack (this prevents the blood sugar from going down during the night).

In addition:

- use fruit squash sweetened with a no-Calorie sweetener;
- use low-Calorie sweeteners if necessary (note that sorbitol has the same Calorie value as sugar);
- avoid all foods labelled 'Diabetic' unless they are also low Calorie.

Meal patterns for diabetics

Controlled carbohydrate diets for diabetics who are not overweight should follow the guidelines outlined below:

- Diets should be planned individually by the dietitian. Where other conditions are involved, the diet needs to be monitored to ensure that nutritional balance is maintained.
- For all clients, the diet should be as near to a normal diet as possible, and should contain all the nutrients required for the age, weight and activity of the person concerned. Requirements usually rise during illness.
- Carbohydrate should not be restricted to a level lower than that required for a non-diabetic of similar age, weight and activity.
- Carbohydrate is best taken in the form of complex starches and natural sugars. Sugar and sweets are available for emergencies for those on insulin.
- Meal times should ideally run between 7.00–7.30 am and 10.00–10.30 pm in 2–3 hourly intervals. This meal pattern (together with the insulin injections, if required) can be moved forwards or backwards to suit shift work where necessary.
- The meal pattern outlined on page 83 should be followed whilst observing these ideals.

Meal patterns from all cultures can be adapted to fit into the needs and wishes of the client. The following guidelines for planning meals should help to provide good control.

Breakfast should, ideally, include:

- an appropriate protein dish, e.g. egg, bacon, fish, sausage, yoghurt, cheese;
- unsweetened fruit or fruit juice;
- cereal and/or bread, toast or crispbreads, according to the carbohydrate exchange;
- butter or margarine (or low fat spread if necessary).

Main meals should include:

- good-sized portions of lean protein, e.g. meat, poultry, fish, offal, cheese, eggs or vegetarian dish according to the menu;
- potatoes or bread, or exchange for rice, pasta, pastry or similar depending on cultural preferences; amounts according to carbohydrate exchange;
- vegetables or salad;
- a light pudding, fruit or cheese and biscuits or similar. Special recipes for diabetic dishes are available from diabetic clinics, dietitians and the British Diabetic Association.

Between Meal Snacks will usually include:

- a biscuit, scone, plain cake, crispbread, fruit or similar;
- tea or coffee or sugar-free squash.

Bedtime Snack – it is essential that diabetics on insulin should have a substantial snack before going to sleep at night to maintain good blood sugar control and prevent an insulin reaction occuring whilst they are asleep. This snack can take the form of:

- a milky drink and/or
- cheese and biscuit or fruit or a small sandwich.

Portion sizes will vary according to carbohydrate exchange and times of insulin injection.

For diabetics who do not require insulin, it may be better for meals to be more frequent and smaller to allow for a more even absorption of glucose into the bloodstream. For example, a gap can be left between the main course and sweet at main meal times.

Foods allowed, controlled and restricted for normal weight diabetics

a) *Foods allowed freely* (unless otherwise stated on the client's diet sheet):

- meat, poultry, offal, fish (all types);
- eggs, cheese, plain yoghurt, nuts;
- green vegetables, salads, berry fruits, melon, rhubarb;
- low Calorie fruit squash;
- no-Calorie sweeteners;
- tea, coffee, Marmite, Bovril, Oxo, etc.

All fats such as butter, margarine, oils, cooking fats and double cream are allowed to the same extent as in a normal diet; some diabetics have difficulty metabolising fats. Keep in mind the need for everyone to reduce their fat intake (see guidelines on page 20).

b) *Foods which need to be controlled or monitored* (refer to the individual's own diet sheet for carbohydrate exchanges):

- milk (all types), single cream, plain and flavoured yoghurt;
- bread, flour and flour products, pasta;
- rice, cereal grains, cornflour, porridge, breakfast cereals;
- pulses, root vegetables, potatoes;
- biscuits, scones, plain pastry;
- all products labelled 'Diabetic';
- fruits and fruit juices (dried fruits are much higher in carbohydrate than their fresh varieties as the sugar has been concentrated);

Diabetics, like everyone else, occasionally allow themselves a 'treat', usually on special occasions like Christmas (cake), Easter (chocolate egg), birthdays and anniversaries. Relatives and friends should be discouraged from regularly bringing in chocolates and biscuits, even 'diabetic' ones. Try to explain why, rather than just saying that they are 'not allowed'.

ACTIVITY 5.5

Following the example shown on page 91, copy and fill in the chart on page 92 in relation to a diabetic diet. Assess which items in the menus would be appropriate for a diabetic diet. Make suitable substitutes or adaptations to items which are not appropriate.

- some non-sugar sweetening agents which are used in products or meals prepared for diabetics. *Sorbitol* is a sweetening agent that is eventually metabolised as sugar. It has the same Calorie value as other carbohydrates. It releases slowly into the bloodstream and may be tolerated well by some diabetics. *Fructose* is a sugar which is very much sweeter than sucrose and is used in some 'diabetic' products such as jams, as it can be used in lower amounts. It is used by the body as sugar and should preferably only be used in its natural form, as fruit;
- some Diabetics find they do not tolerate alcohol well.

c) *Foods to be avoided*:

- sugar* (except in an emergency), all sugar products including jam, honey, marmalade, syrup, sweets; other refined sugars, e.g. lactose, fructose;
- powdered artificial sweeteners;
- cakes, biscuits, puddings; chocolate.

*Sometimes a standard recipe for a light pudding or cake which is made with sugar may be used as part of the carbohydrate exchanges in a diabetic's menu.

Outline meal pattern adapted for a diabetic on insulin
(assuming a standard day's activities and requiring 20 exchanges (200 g CHO)

The midday and evening meal patterns are interchangeable; meal times are specified but should be seen as approximates only; they should be kept to 2½–3 hour intervals but can start and end at different times according to the times of injections.

Early morning 7.00 am	Cup of tea if desired
Breakfast 7.30 am (or 15–20 mins after injection)	Fruit, fruit juice (no sugar) Porridge or breakfast cereal – two exchanges Egg or grilled bacon or yoghurt or similar; tomatoes or mushrooms if desired Bread, two small slices, plain or toasted or exchanged for crispbread or croissant or similar Butter or margarine or low-fat spread Tea or coffee
Mid-morning 10.30 am	Tea, coffee or sugar-free drink One semi-sweet biscuit or portion of fresh fruit
Midday 1.00 pm	Sandwich with two large slices of bread with butter, margarine or low fat spread; or exchange for large baked potato or rice or pasta dish Meat, poultry, offal, fish, cheese, egg or vegetarian dish Salad as desired Fresh fruit or plain yoghurt or cheese with crackers or small ice cream Tea or coffee if desired
Mid-afternoon 3.30 pm	Tea or coffee One semi-sweet biscuit or small scone or fruit
Evening meal (15–20 minutes after injection or keep to the 2½–3 hour intervals i.e. 6.30 pm)	Clear soup or grapefruit or melon or tomato juice Main course of meat, fish, cheese, egg or vegetarian dish Potatoes or pasta or rice or part exchange for pastry, Yorkshire pudding or similar Vegetables or salad Pudding equal to two exchanges or cake or fruit and yoghurt Tea or coffee
Bedtime 9.30 pm	Milk drink or tea or coffee Sandwich with two small slices of bread and cheese, egg, meat, fish or vegetarian filling or exchange for biscuit, scone, or fruit
Daily	One pint of milk (whole, skimmed or sterilised)

Low-Calorie diets for weight reduction (slimming diets)

An overweight client can pose problems for carers, especially if the person is not very mobile or requires to be lifted. Food is very important to most people, especially if someone is lonely, housebound or has little to do. Reducing food intake can give rise to a great deal of misery in addition to the normal depression that goes with 'slimming'. It is important not to adopt the attitude of meting out a punishment.

Losing weight is usually difficult and should only be undertaken with supervision from a doctor and a dietitian (gimmick diets are often unbalanced and can lead to ill-health).

It is often necessary to continue a weight reducing regime for many months. In order to boost morale, 'treats' and 'days off' are necessary as part of a long-term regime. If a client does not appear to be losing weight on a prescribed slimming diet, check that they are not retaining water (oedema):

- water shows up on the scales as weight and may not be noticed at first;
- water cannot be 'slimmed' off and a low-Calorie diet may be dangerous if excess weight is water not fat.

A low-salt diet (see pages 85–86) may be prescribed to remove excess water.

Meal pattern for low-Calorie diets

Meals should be small, frequent and varied, whilst at the same time being nutritionally adequate. Weight loss is achieved most successfully where the day's food intake is divided into five or six small meals spaced evenly throughout the day. Allow for a 'bite' to eat at bedtime and between other mealtimes if possible.

Try to ensure that meals are tasty, attractive and interesting – if the diet has to continue for a long time it would be a pity for people to stop enjoying their food. Allow for occasional treats on 'special' days. Remember also that where fat intake is reduced, the fat-soluble vitamins may need to be supplemented.

Breakfast should include:

- egg, bacon (grilled), fish or ham; or plain yoghurt with a sugar-free muesli or cereal in place of the bread;
- bread (toasted or plain) or crispbread;
- thin scrape of butter or margarine or low-fat spread.

Main meals should include:

- good portions of lean meat, poultry, offal, fish or low-fat vegetarian dish;
- a good variety of vegetables or salads;
- a portion of pasta, rice, bread or potato;
- a dessert which makes use of low Calorie ingredients such as skimmed milk – fresh or dried, half-fat evaporated milk, low-fat yoghurt, fruit and fruit juices, tinned fruit in natural juice, egg white, jelly, no Calorie sweeteners. For example egg custard, junket, fruit fool, jelly whip, fruit in jelly.

Foods allowed, controlled and restricted for weight reduction diets

a) *Foods allowed freely:*

- lean meat, poultry, offal, ham*, white fish (fresh or smoked*);
- vegetables, salads; clear soup, Oxo, Bovril, Marmite*;

Example recipe:
Low-Calorie 'Cream' soup Serves 4–6

1 pint stock without fat
10 oz mixed vegetables: onion, celery,
    leeks, tomato, carrot, swede, turnip,
    mushroom, etc.
Herbs and seasoning as desired

Method: Cook together until the vegetables
are tender. Purée the mixture in a blender
or through a sieve. Reheat. Season to taste.
Before serving, stir in 1–2 tablespoons of
low-fat plain yogurt.

Other sweetening agents

- *Sorbitol* has the same Calorific value as sugar and starch;
- *Cyclamate* is 30 times as sweet as sugar. It is banned in foods for sale in the UK as it may be linked with some diseases;
- *Aspartame* (sold as 'Candarel' and 'Nutrasweet' in the UK) is 180 times as sweet as sugar. It is approved for use in the UK but with some restrictions.

Other agents have been tried: some leave an aftertaste and some have delayed reaction which is not very helpful!

ACTIVITY 5.6

Following the example shown on page 91, copy and fill in the chart on page 92 in relation to a low-Calorie diet. Assess which items in the menus would be appropriate for a low-Calorie diet. Make suitable substitutes or adaptations to items which are not appropriate.

- tomato juice, fresh grapefruit, lemons, melon, rhubarb, plums, gooseberries (all without sugar);
- dietetic fruit squash, tea, coffee;
- no-Calorie sweeteners.

b) *Controlled foods*

- oily fish, cheese*, eggs, plain yoghurt;
- milk – all types, including synthetic and filled milks (see page 17);
- bread, crispbreads, pasta, potatoes;
- rice, breakfast cereals, porridge;
- butter, margarine, low-fat spreads;
- fruit, fruit juice, tinned fruit in unsweetened fruit juice;
- pulses, nuts (vegetarian dishes will make use of these for protein instead of meat and fish);
- low Calorie puddings.

*Clients requiring salt restriction should also avoid ham, bacon, sausage, smoked fish, tinned meat and fish, cheese, Oxo, Bovril, Marmite.

c) *Foods to be avoided*

- fats, oils, fried foods, cream, ice cream, sweet yoghurt;
- biscuits, cakes, pastry;
- sugar, jam, honey, syrup, sweets, chocolate;
- roast nuts, crisps;
- dried fruit, tinned fruit in syrup, fruit squash;
- alcohol.

Sweeteners

If possible clients should try to curb their taste for sweet foods. This is not all that easy, especially for older people. Saccharine is a tried and tested artificial sweetener. It is 400 times as sweet as sugar. When used for sweetening desserts it should be added last as it becomes bitter if heated. Liquid saccharine, for example Sweetex liquid, is easy to control as it can be added drop-by-drop.

Low-salt diets (low-sodium diets)

Salt (sodium chloride) is found in most foods, although natural foods are generally low in salt. The amount in natural foods varies depending on where the plants were grown or where the animals grazed (some parts of the world have a high salt content in the soil).

In developed countries, salt is normally added to food during cooking. It is also used as a preservative during processing. Further salt may then be added at table. In the body, salt is kept in a specific dilution with water. In conditions where the body does not eliminate salt properly, water can build up. This increases pressure in the arteries, veins and all the organs, especially the heart and kidneys. In these conditions salt intake is reduced in order to reduce the excess amount of fluids in the body. Alternatively a person may be prescribed diuretics (drugs in tablet form to help them excrete more water (sometimes called 'water tablets'). These clients may need to increase their potassium intake either by eating more fruit and vegetables or by taking a potassium supplement.

A low salt diet may also be prescribed for disorders of the heart, kidneys and liver, for blood pressure and sometimes for ear diseases such as Ménière's disease. In addition, other nutrients may be modified, e.g. fat.

Salt restriction may vary from minimal ('no added salt', i.e. no highly salted foods and no salt at table) to a very strict 'low sodium diet'.

Meal pattern for a low-salt diet

A no-added-salt diet will consist of a normal intake of ordinary foods with no salt at table and no very salty foods. For greater restriction it is necessary to cook without salt. Remember that the meals must be eaten by the person for whom they are intended so the food must be tasty, attractive and 'normal'.

Foods allowed, controlled and restricted for low-salt diets

a)   *Foods allowed freely* (unless there are other factors to consider):

- unsalted meat, white or oily fish, poultry, offal, eggs;
- potato, rice, pasta, flour, cornflour;
- vegetables, salad, fruit, fruit juice, squash;
- double cream, ice cream; unsalted butter or margarine, lard, oils, vegetable fat, unsalted dripping;
- sugar, syrup, honey, jam, marmalade, boiled sweets;
- tea, coffee;
- herbs, pepper, vinegar;
- homemade salt-free cakes, pastries, biscuits, soups, sweets;
- unsalted nuts and crisps;
- unsalted breakfast cereal, e.g shredded wheat, puffed wheat, some mueslis, porridge oats, porridge.

b)   *Controlled foods:*

- milk, single cream, yoghurt;
- bread, plain biscuits, crispbreads, bought baked goods;
- most breakfast cereals, salt-free Marmite;
- chocolate and cocoa powder.

c)   *Foods to be avoided:*
(For 'no added salt' diets a little salt is allowed in cooking)

- salt, some salt substitutes;
- salted meats (e.g. ham, bacon, corned beef), tinned meat;
- smoked and cured fish, tinned fish;
- tinned and packet soups and sauces;
- Oxo, Bovril, Marmite;
- salted butter and margarine, cheese;
- salted nuts, crisps and peanuts, dried fruit;
- all foods prepared or preserved with salt.

Remember to *check all labels* for added salt.

Cooking without salt

Thought has to be given to making foods palatable without using salt. Suggested ways of reducing salt in the diet can be used for all menus since it is now recommended that everyone reduces the salt content of their diet (see page 20). Cooking methods which add flavour include grilling, roasting, toasting and shallow frying. Deep-fat frying is also useful but keeping a check on fat in the diet is now recommended for everyone in the UK. Flavours which can be used in a low salt diet include herbs, spices (including curry powder,

> **Low-salt pastry** (short crust)
>
> 8 oz flour
> 2 oz lard or unsalted vegetable fat
> 2oz unsalted butter or margarine
> 5 tablespoons of cold water
>
> *Method*: Make up and use as for ordinary shortcrust pastry.

ACTIVITY 5.7

Following the example shown on page 91, copy and fill in the chart on page 92 in relation to a low-salt diet. Assess which items in the menus would be appropriate for a low-salt diet. Make suitable substitutes or adaptations to items which are not appropriate.

> **Low fat sponge** (standard Swiss roll recipe)
>
> 2 eggs or 1 egg and 2 egg whites
> 3 oz caster sugar
> 3 oz self-raising flour
>
> *Method*: Make up as for ordinary fatless sponge.
>
> Use for sponge cakes, Swiss roll, sponge drops or trifle base. Use a jam filling for low-fat diets. (Add a little low-fat chocolate powder or some instant coffee as an occasional change of flavour.)
>
> This recipe is low in salt. If it is divided into eight, each portion will contain approximately 2 g of fat, and 20 g carbohydrate so can be used as an exchange in a diabetic diet.
>
> Other recipes containing fat can often be adapted with a little thought and ingenuity.

ginger); certain vegetables e.g. onion, green or red pepper, garlic; acid flavours such as vinegar, lemon juice, tomato, yoghurt.

Unsalted bread can be toasted and made into breadcrumbs. Unsalted butter can be used in cakes, pastry, etc. It adds flavour to sauces and can be used in shallow frying and grilling. Unsalted breakfast cereals can be used in cooking as well as at breakfast. Flapjack using unsalted butter, unsalted muesli and sugar is a very acceptable snack for anyone.

Some suggestions for low-salt cooking:

- use standard baking recipes, substituting unsalted fat for the ordinary variety. Omit the 'pinch of salt' (unsalted bread is not recommended as it isn't very nice and doesn't keep well);
- soak bacon before grilling or frying in unsalted butter or oil;
- use sage and onion stuffing with grilled, fried or roast meats;
- use herbs and spices in other meat dishes;
- shallow fry or grill fish, or bake or poach with pepper, lemon and bayleaf. Use unsalted raspings or crumble as a topping;
- use herbs and spices, where appropriate, in vegetables, for example mint in potatoes and peas, rosemary in carrots, chives and pepper with tomatoes, thyme with courgettes;
- sauces can include lemon and parsley, hollandaise, tomato, onion and mixed herbs, yoghurt;
- Salads can be dressed with a vinaigrette dressing, yoghurt, citrated cream or lemon juice. For example, try sliced cucumber and onion in vinegar, sliced tomato and chives, cucumber and orange in citrated cream, beetroot in vinegar with celery.

Low-fat diets

People may have an intolerance of fat for a variety of reasons. It may be due to a disorder of the gall bladder, the liver or the small bowel. Other people just find fat hard to digest. A standard low-fat diet is not suitable for people with heart disease, coeliac disease or for those who want to lose weight. *For all diets that are low in fat, the Calories must be replaced.*

Fat provides at least one third of the day's energy. If it is reduced, there is a danger of unnecessary weight loss and lowered resistance to infections and disease. To replace Calories, increase the intake of foods which are high in protein and carbohydrate (especially starch) but low in fat (see page 88). Fat-soluble Vitamins A and D are found in all dairy fats and eggs as well as in oily fish. They can become deficient in a low-fat diet. A Vitamin supplement is the easiest way to replace the fat-soluble vitamins but this needs to be controlled.

Foods allowed, controlled and restricted for low-fat diets

a) *Foods allowed freely* (unless other factors need to be considered):

- lean meat, ham, offal, poultry, low-fat vegetarian meals;
- white fish, (fresh or smoked);
- low-fat cottage cheese, yoghurt, skimmed milk; egg white, meringue;
- potatoes, vegetables, salads, fruit, fruit juice, squash;
- sugar, syrup, jam, honey, marmalade, boiled sweets;
- bread and flour products made without fat; pasta, semolina, rice, cereal grains, cornflour, custard powder, breakfast cereals, porridge;
- tea, coffee, Oxo, Bovril, Marmite.

b)   *Controlled foods:*

- some butter or margarine, oil, fats, dripping may be allowed if tolerated;
- low-fat convenience foods, low-fat instant chocolate if tolerated;
- low-fat spread may be used in place of butter or margarine;
- low-fat evaporated milk may be used instead of cream;
- fatless sponge.

c)   *Foods to be avoided:*

- fried foods, fatty meats, pork, sausages, tinned meats and pastes;
- some convenience vegetarian meals, full-fat soya products;
- butter, margarine, oil, vegetable and animal fats, nut butters (except a small amount if allowed on the diet sheet);
- oily fish, tinned fish;
- egg yolk, mayonnaise, salad cream (low-fat yoghurt can be used for salad dressing with added vinegar or lemon juice if desired);
- cheese, whole milk, evaporated milk, cream, 'filled' milks and creams*, ice cream;
- nuts, peanuts, crisps, other packet snacks;
- chocolate, cocoa, toffee;
- Horlicks, Ovaltine;
- cream crackers, biscuits, cakes, pastry.

*'Filled' milks and creams are made with skimmed milk and vegetable oils to substitute for full cream milk or cream. They may be liquid, dried or canned.

Remember to *check all labels* for the fat content of foods.

Foods which are *high in protein but low in fat* include white fish (fresh and smoked), chicken, turkey, liver, kidney, gammon, cottage cheese, low-fat yoghurt, egg white, skimmed milk, low-fat soya products and pulses.

Foods which *contain carbohydrate but are low in fat* include bread, cereals, pasta, rice, crispbreads, cereal grains and the flours made from them, potatoes, root vegetables, pulses, fruit (fresh, stewed, tinned, dried), sugar and sugar products.

Low-fat desserts can incorporate meringue, fatless sponge, skimmed-milk puddings and custards, fruit, jelly and egg white. Some examples are trifle, fruit conde, jelly whip, fruit charlotte, summer pudding and Queen's pudding.

ACTIVITY 5.9

Following the example shown on page 91, copy and fill in the chart on page 92 in relation to a low-fat diet. Assess which items in the menus would be appropriate for a low-fat diet. Make suitable substitutes or adaptations to items which are not appropriate.

ACTIVITY 5.8

1   Using a standard recipe book, write out the recipes for the following menu:

　　Chicken casserole and rice
　　Cauliflower in sauce
　　Fruit trifle

2   Adapt these recipes to provide a low-fat menu. Where possible add extra low-fat protein to supplement the meal. If possible cook the meal for yourself and see what it tastes like.

Gluten-free diets

Gluten-free diets are prescribed for people who are sensitive to the protein, *gluten*. This sensitivity, called gluten-sensitive enteropathy or gluten-induced enteropathy, causes the lining of the small intestine to change in such a way

---

Gluten: an elastic protein formed when water is added to the flours made from wheat and rye.

Gluten-free recipe books and an up-to-date list of brand-name foods guaranteed to be gluten-free are available from The Coeliac Society.

Some supermarket and chemists' chains produce a list of their own-brand products which they guarantee to be gluten free.

Always check the list of ingredients on labels of packets and tins and all processed foods.

ACTIVITY 5.10

Imagine that you have been diagnosed as sensitive to gluten. Ask the main supermarket chains if they have any information about their own-brand products' suitability for your diet (some of them do). Ask also for help and advice at local branches of national pharmacy chains.

that it is unable to absorb nutrients from the diet. Patients suffer from malabsorption, loss of weight and diarrhoea. Removing gluten from the diet reverses the condition and people are able to lead a perfectly normal and healthy life.

Gluten sensitivity can be diagnosed at any age and many adults with bowel problems may be advised to avoid gluten during periods of inflammation and pain. Gluten comes from wheat and rye flour, therefore all products made from these flours should be avoided. Most people with coeliac disease or gluten-sensitive enteropathy are advised to avoid oats and barley too.

As gluten is the substance which enables baked goods like cakes, bread, pastry, Yorkshire puddings, to hold their shape, their gluten-free equivalents are noticeably different in taste, texture, shape and shelf-life. Gluten-free flour and gluten-free bread are obtainable from chemists and some health-food stores. Pure starch, e.g. pure cornflour can be used as a substitute for wheat flour in many recipes. Some gluten-free products are available on NHS prescription. This is particularly useful for those who are exempt from prescription charges.

Foods allowed, controlled and restricted for gluten-free diets

a) *Foods allowed freely:*

- rice and rice products, e.g. rice crispies;
- corn (maize) and corn products, e.g. cornflakes, cornflour, custard powder*;
- special gluten-free flour and commercial gluten-free bread, cakes and biscuits, gluten-free pasta;
- potatoes, yam, pulses, nuts, seeds, e.g. sesame, sunflower;
- all fruits, fruit juice, fruit squash;
- vegetables, salads;
- fresh meat, offal, poultry, ham, bacon, fish;
- eggs, cheese, milk, milk products, yoghurt, cream;
- butter, margarine, all oils, fats;
- sugar, boiled sweets, jam, honey, marmalade;
- Oxo, Bovril, Marmite, tea, coffee, etc.
- homemade gluten-free soups, sauces, cakes, biscuits, pastry, bread, puddings, etc. made with gluten-free ingredients;
- some snack foods, e.g. salted nuts, crisps.

Foods made using gluten-free mixes

*'Corn' is often used to refer to other cereal grains in the UK agricultural business and some brands of cornflour and custard powder include starch from other grains. Check with the list of guaranteed foods supplied by the Coeliac Society.

b) *Foods to be avoided:*

- all foods which contain gluten, i.e. made from wheat and rye;
- semolina and pasta made from wheat semolinas;
- barley, oats and products made from them, e.g. barley water, Scotch broth, oatmeal, flapjack.

Avoid all foods which have not been guaranteed as gluten free.

Outline meal pattern adapted for a gluten free diet

The meal pattern for a gluten-free diet is completely normal apart from the use of gluten-free substitutes. The midday and evening meal patterns are interchangeable.

Breakfast:	Fruit, fruit juice and/or Corn or rice-based breakfast cereal with sugar and milk if desired Cooked breakfast if desired Gluten-free bread (plain or toasted) or rice crispbread Butter or margarine; marmalade, jam or honey Tea or coffee
Mid-morning	Tea, coffee, milk or Bovril/Marmite-type drink Gluten-free biscuit, crispbread or fruit, nuts, crisps as desired
Midday (This meal pattern may be preferred in the evening)	Fruit, fruit juice, clear soup or gluten-free starter Main cooked dish with meat, poultry, offal, fish, cheese, egg or pulses/nuts/ vegetable dish Potatoes, rice or gluten-free pasta Vegetables or salad Gluten-free sauces and accompaniments as appropriate Gluten-free pudding or dessert or fruit; gluten-free biscuits and cheese, etc. Tea or coffee if desired
Mid-afternoon	Tea or coffee Gluten-free biscuit, cake, scone, sandwich or fruit as desired
Evening meal (This meal pattern may be preferred at midday)	Gluten-free soup or fruit or fruit juice Gluten-free sandwich, toasted snack or salad meal Salad or vegetables. Gluten-free cake, scone, biscuit and/or fruit or yoghurt, etc. Tea or coffee
Bedtime	Milk drink or tea, coffee or fruit drink or Marmite/Bovril-type drink Gluten-free biscuit, scone, sandwich or fruit as desired
Daily	Milk: whole, skimmed, sterilised, etc. Sugar: adding sugar to drinks is now less common

Cooking without gluten

- Use cornflour (check that it is gluten-free) or potato or rice flour for thickening sauces;
- Adapt standard recipes for cakes, pastry, scones, puddings, etc. Substitute gluten-free flour for ordinary wheat-based flour;
- Use gluten-free breadcrumbs or raspings as a topping for savoury dishes served 'au gratin';
- All vegetables are gluten-free including potatoes
- Gluten-free puddings include rice pudding, custard (made with gluten-free custard powder) and cornflour-based sauce, homemade sponges, crumbles, pastry (using gluten-free flour); charlotte, bread and butter pudding, Queen's pudding and summer pudding using gluten-free bread; trifle using gluten-free sponge; jelly, fruit (fresh, tinned, stewed); yoghurt, cream and some makes of ice cream.

'Universal' shortbread (gluten-free, low-salt, low-protein and may be suitable for a diabetic)

3 oz cornflour
3 oz rice flour
2 oz caster sugar
4 oz unsalted butter

Make and use as for ordinary shortbread. It can also be used as a sweet crumble topping.

This Recipe will make 15×10 g or 8×20 g carbohydrate exchange biscuits for use in a diabetic menu.

ACTIVITY 5.11

Following the example shown on page 91, fill in the chart on page 92 in relation to a gluten-free diet. Assess which items in the menus would be appropriate for a gluten-free diet. Make suitable substitutes or adaptations to items which are not appropriate.

Example of an exercise to assess a menu to cope with special diets
Items which are suitable for each diet without too much adaptation have been ticked.

Adaptations are suggested for this midday meal menu from a residential home for the retired to enable one or more of the items at each course to be suitable for the special diets listed.

Menu	*Diabetic*	*Low-Cal.*	*Low-fat*	*Low-salt*	*Gluten-free*	*Vegetarian*
Chicken and leek soup	thin	thin	no fat	not salted	gluten-free	leek only
Boiled beef (not salt)	✓	lean	lean	✓	✓	–
or Vegetable lasagne	#		low fat	not salted	*	✓
or Grilled fish and parsley sauce	✓	✓ / –	✓ / L. fat	✓ / ✓	✓ / Gl. free	–
Mashed or	✓	✓	✓	✓	✓	✓
sauté potatoes	✓	–	–	✓	✓	✓
Roast parsnips	✓	boiled	boiled	✓	✓	✓
Green beans	✓	✓	✓	✓	✓	✓
Rice pudding and jam	no sugar	– / –	L. fat / ✓	✓ / ✓	✓ / ✓	✓ / ✓
or Fruit salad and cream	fresh / ✓	fresh / –	✓ / –	✓ / ✓	✓ / ✓	✓ / ✓
or Cheese and biscuits	✓ / #	✓ / fruit	L. fat / fruit	– / –	✓ / Gl. free	✓ / ✓

* Gluten-free pasta is very popular.
# The diabetic client's preferences will determine which carbohydrate exchanges to include in the meal.

Copy this chart and use it for Activities 5.5, 5.6, 5.7, 5.9, 5.11 and 5.12.

	Diab-etic	Low-Cal.	Low-fat	Low-salt	Gluten-free	Vege-tarian
Menu One						
Steak and kidney pie and gravy						
Boiled potato						
Cabbage Carrots						
Stewed apple and custard						
Menu Two						
Chicken curry						
Rice						
Accompaniments: – banana – apple/lemon juice – peanuts – mango chutney						
Tropical fruit salad Cream						
Menu Three						
Cheese and tomato pizza						
Side salad						
Crisps						
Creme caramel						
Menu Four						
Fish pie (potato topping)						
Peas Tinned tomato						
Pear and ginger upside-down cake						

High-protein diet (must also be high in Calories)

This can be the most difficult of all diets to achieve successfully. It is typically needed for people who are ill. They may be wasted, debilitated, depressed, not interested in their food and are likely to lack the energy to cope with eating. For these reasons, the food has to be very palatable and attractive, easy to handle (clients will have difficulty cutting up anything that is tough or awkward), easy to chew and digest, offered frequently and in very small portions.

For this dietary regime to be successful:

● energy intake must be very high, above the normal requirement for that individual;
● a Calorie source is necessary before a main meal as part of this pattern. Glucose in a drink is a useful supplement; some clients may prefer a sherry or other aperitif;
● a vitamin supplement might be useful initially.

Remember: small is manageable; frequent is essential.

Small is manageable

Frequent is essential

To achieve a high-Calorie, high-protein intake, especially in the weak and ill, it is usual to give some food about every hour. This is time-consuming but worth it. As clients become more robust, the same meal pattern can be followed but larger amounts are acceptable.

- Concentrate on foods which contain protein, such as lean meats, ham, offal, poultry, fish, cheese, eggs, yoghurt, milk; but not to the exclusion of other foods. To ensure a high energy intake include fats, oils (of which the easiest to digest is butter) and cream; starchy foods, sugar and glucose.
- Avoid meals which are cloying, always soft, bland and colourless, but remember that chewing may be tiring for the very weak.
- Ordinary dishes such as soup, potato, porridge, etc. may need to be 'fortified' to add extra protein and energy in a small helping.
- To increase protein and Calories, powdered milk can be added as a paste to foods such as porridge, potatoes, milk puddings, soups and sauces; or as a powder to pastry, batter or bread mix.
- Yoghurt, eggs and cheese can also be used as an added ingredient in some dishes. Avoid making the food too sickly or unpalatable.

Commercial high-protein/high-Calorie drinks can be over-sweet and even the savoury ones can be cloying to the mouth. They may interfere with a patient's appetite and reduce overall food consumption. Be careful not to give a high protein drink just before a main meal. It will interfere with the client's enjoyment of their meal. Some commercial 'high-Calorie only' supplements are available, e.g. 'Caloreen' and 'Maxim'. Such products are made from starch and help increase Calories where required. They have no taste and can be added to sweet and savoury dishes alike. they have the same Calorie value as sugar and starch. 'Caloreen' is manufactured by Clinitec and is available on prescription. 'Maxim' is manufactured by Iams Ltd.

Some ways and means of increasing nutrients include:

- adding butter and cream to many sweet and savoury dishes, which also provide vitamins A and D;
- adding sucrose, glucose and other sugars to fruit and fruit drinks. They may make sweet sauces and puddings too sickly if used in excess (sugar can also lead to diarrhoea if used in excess). The sugars will provide extra Calories but no other nutrients;
- adding cheese to sauces, egg, potato, etc. It will provide vitamins A and D as well as extra protein and Calories.
- adding alcohol, which is very high in Calories but no other nutrients. For example, sherry can enhance egg flips, milk shakes, trifles and sauces; brandy and rum can also be used in egg flips and chocolate drinks, sauces, poached fruit and fruit cake or mince pies; white wine can be used in sauces, soups, fish and meat dishes; some clients might enjoy a Gaelic coffee with cream, sugar and whiskey.

> *Alcohol is a very potent and addictive drug so great caution is needed when suggesting its use. It should only be offered with the approval of the client and the doctor (who will need to consider the other drugs the client is taking); and will need the permission of the client's relatives where appropriate.*

Salads and vegetables are necessary to make meals attractive, clean the palate and maintain balance. These can be used as a garnish and make an acceptable sandwich filling if cut up very finely. Remove very hard parts, tough skins and pips, if possible. Fruit and fruit juices, if tolerated, can be used as vehicles for extra Calories in the form of sugar or cream.

Semi-soft and puréed diets

It is not always necessary to liquidise everything in the meal. Clients may be able to cope with some items and not others. Try a variety of different approaches but always make sure that the food is tempting, attractive and tasty.

A semi-soft diet should aim to provide a high-protein, high-Calorie intake, as above. It will, however, contain more water and because of this, small amounts of food and fortified drinks should be offered at very frequent intervals, in some cases half-hourly. If small amounts are given only at main meal times the diet will be very low in Calories and all nutrients.

Where food needs to be puréed or liquidised, remember that *much of the meal will be water*. Nutritional balance will suffer unless food is offered frequently and concentrated sources of Calories and other nutrients are included where appropriate, without altering the palatability of the food.

Meal pattern for high-protein/high-Calorie diets
(Food should be liquidised only if necessary)

7.30 am	Cup of tea with milk and sugar
8.00 am	"glass fruit juice with glucose Porridge or Semolina made with milk and Caloreen with butter or cream, sugar and extra skimmed milk powder
9.00 am	1 wineglass egg flip or milk shake. See recipes below or use commercial products for a change
10.00 am	"glass fruit juice with glucose
11.00 am	Coffee with milk and sugar; biscuit
12.00 noon	"glass fruit juice with glucose
12.30 pm *Lunch*	Soft meat or fish or egg or cheese dish Cream potatoes with butter and dried skimmed milk with Caloreen added Small helping of vegetables for colour, texture or garnish
1.00 pm	Sweet – as chosen. Try to add some extra Calories and/or protein (the client may prefer to have something refreshing)
1.30 pm	Tea or coffee with milk and sugar
2.30 pm	1 wineglass egg flip or milk shake (see recipes)
3.00 pm	"glass fruit juice with glucose
3.30 pm	Tea with milk and sugar Biscuit, or small sandwich or scone or cake
4.30 pm	1 wineglass egg flip or milk shake (see recipes)
5.00 pm	"glass fruit juice with glucose
5.30 pm	As at 12.30 (lunch) or sandwich/snack-type meal
6.00 pm	As at 1.00 – (sweet)
6.30 pm	Tea or coffee with milk and sugar
7.30 pm	1 wineglass milk shake or egg flip (see recipe)
8.30 pm	Milk drink, as desired

High Calorie drink (see recipe) throughout the day

Recipes for use with high-protein/high-Calorie diets

Cream of vegetable soup (high-protein, high-Calorie)

This recipe can be adapted to produce a variety of different soups: cream of mushroom, cream of tomato, for example.

	Paste ingredients:
10 oz mixed vegetables	1 oz cornflour
"pint stock	1 oz skimmed milk powder
Seasoning to taste	1 oz Caloreen

Method: Cook vegetables in the stock until tender. Purée and strain if necessary (some clients may find pips and skins hard to swallow and may choke). Season.

Mix the paste ingredients together with a little water. Add to the soup and bring back to the boil and cook for 2–3 minutes, stirring. Before serving top with a spoonful of double cream, or full-fat natural yoghurt or some grated cheese. Toast or bread served alongside will soften if dipped into the soup.

High-calorie drink

¢pint boiling water
1 oz glucose
1 oz Caloreen   ⎫
pinch of citric acid ⎬ dissolve in the water
2 drops yellow or green colouring ⎭

Method: Allow to cool. Make up to 1 pint with cold water, soda water, tonic or spring water as desired. 1–2 pints may be drunk throughout the day.

Milk shake

"pint full cream milk
1 oz glucose
1oz Caloreen
1oz dried skimmed milk
Flavour: coffee, chocolate, fruit flavourings as desired.

Method: Mix all ingredients together in a blender. Strain; cool; serve topped with a scoop of ice cream or some whipped cream, if desired.

Egg flip

"pint full cream milk
1 egg
1 oz glucose
1 oz Caloreen
1 oz dried skimmed milk

Method: Mix all ingredients together in a blender. Strain; cool; serve with sherry or brandy as desired.

5.3 Dietary considerations for vegetarians and vegans

There are a number of diets described as vegetarian. Check with the client, who may have religious or cultural preferences, too.

Partial vegetarian:

- some avoid red meat;
- some will eat fish but not meat;
- some will avoid only certain meats, e.g. chicken or pork.

Lacto-ovo-vegetarian:

- no meat, fish or poultry or their products including lard, suet, gelatine;
- will take milk, eggs and other dairy produce but may prefer to avoid the rennet in cheese.

Lacto-vegetarian:

- no animal foods except milk and milk products.

Total vegetarian (vegan):

- no animal products at all including rennet, gelatine, etc;
- avoid supplements derived from animal products e.g. whey powder derived from milk;

ACTIVITY 5.12

Following the example shown on page 91, copy and fill in the chart on page 92 in relation to a vegetarian diet. Assess which items in the menus would be appropriate for a vegetarian diet. Make suitable substitutes or adaptations to items which are not appropriate.

- use only margarines that contain no milk products. Vegetable fats, solid and liquid are available for cooking;

In addition, vegans may need dietary supplements, for example to boost vitamin D, folate and vitamin B_{12} (see page 121).

Fruitarian:

- will eat fruits, nuts and seeds, usually uncooked.
- will often avoid cereals and pulses, unless sprouting, in addition to all animal products.

Macrobiotic:

- strict vegetarian regime which is based on whole foods, organically grown.

Planning meals for lacto-ovo-vegetarians

Most Vegetarians and Vegans prefer their cereals and sugars unrefined and their vegetables and fruit to include the skins. Use egg and cheese dishes very sparingly and preferably when on the main menu only. Too many can be boring and off-putting. Soya products such as 'milk', yoghurt, cheese, curd are available for use in recipes, as are vegetarian 'lard', 'suet', and all vegetable margarines.

Foods allowed, controlled and restricted for vegetarian diets

a) *Foods that can be included:*
- all vegetables, potatoes, fruits, salads;
- pulses, nuts, cereal grains, flour and flour products, pasta;
- vegetable oils and fats, nut butters;
- sugar, honey, jam, etc.
- Marmite, tea, coffee, cocoa, chocolate, soya products,
- commercial vegetarian meals.

Always check with the client about what they will and will not eat.

b) *Foods to be avoided* (unless asked for):

- all meat, poultry, offal, ham, bacon, sausage, fish;
- fish oils, dripping, lard, suet;
- gelatine, rennet;
- margarine, except vegetable margarine.

Check with the client about the acceptability of cheese, eggs, butter and margarine.

5.4 Planning meals and menus for special diets

The choice of foods must take into account the following:

- *Nutritional requirements:* these are always determined by age, gender, activities, state of health;
- *Level of ability/disability or long-term ailment:* this will determine whether the nutrient levels need to be modified and may determine whether the foods themselves need to be modified;
- *Cultural background, religion, social habits, upbringing:* this will determine the type of food to offer.

When advising people in their own homes, other factors need to be considered. For example: their income level, their ability to shop, the amount and type of storage space for food, cooking facilities and their ability to cook. For some clients, ability to understand instructions or retain them may be impaired.

Refer back to the diagram on page 27.

Always try to use ordinary recipes and adapt them for the special diet you are dealing with. Keep the balance of the meal by altering as little as possible. A well planned menu will usually accommodate several special diets and often it is only necessary to alter one part of the meal or modify one recipe in order to accommodate other diets. Above all, remember that all menus for special diets must be *nutritionally adequate* for the person for whom they have been prescribed.

References and further reading

Annually: *In Touch.* (a guide to services for people with a visual handicap) BBC Broadcast Support Services

Rawcliffe and Rolph 1985: *The Gluten-free Diet Book.* Martin Dunitz

The Coeliac Handbook. The Coeliac Society

Thomas 1994: *The Manual of Dietetic Practice.* Blackwell Science

1990: *Countdown.* The British Diabetic Association

ACTIVITY 5.13

1 Think of three dishes for sweet courses for someone on a low-fat diet who needs to maintain a normal Calorie intake. Use foods which contain protein and/or carbohydrate but are low in fat.

2 For a person on a low salt diet, suggest ways to improve the flavour of:

- fish;
- potatoes;
- vegetables.

6 Nutrients and nutrition

The aim of this chapter is to explore in more detail some of the subjects covered in Chapter 2.

6.1 Introduction

Food and health

Food is often said to be either 'good' or 'bad' for you. The UK government has issued guidelines on 'healthy eating' (as some foods seem to contribute to ill-health); there are 'Health-Food' shops in the High Street; advertisers of health foods promise great energy and vigour if we eat their product. How can this be? What is the connection between food and health?

What is 'health'?

The *Oxford Concise Dictionary* defines health as 'soundness of body or mind'. It defines food as 'substance to be taken into the body to maintain life and growth'.

Food affects our physical and mental health in several ways:

- The relationship between food and physical health is usually reviewed in the context of the nutrients in food or its *nutritional value*.
- Other factors that might be affecting physical and mental health are reviewed by scientists looking at environmental factors, including chemical residues in crops and animals and such things as the appropriate processing and packaging of foods.
- Some of these factors may well affect the individual's nutritional requirements, but research is still limited, confused and often conflicting.
- Carers should keep in mind the effect food has on mental state and well-being as outlined in Chapter 1.

Nutrition and dietetics

Nutrition is very important in determining a body's response to factors which can cause disease if not resisted. No amount of other treatment will be totally effective if the nutritional state of the patient is inadequate or unbalanced. Our *choice* of food determines the *diet* (i.e. food eaten) which provides the *nutrients* which determine the *nutritional balance* which is fundamental to *health*.

Nutrition is the study of the varying needs of living cells; knowledge about the way they work and are governed is increasing. *Human nutrition* is the study of the human body's needs for nutrients. The sciences studied by nutritionists include physiology, biochemistry and *metabolism*.

These studies can seem complex as substances which may be nutrients are investigated; various drugs and chemicals are used which may affect health or alter nutritional requirements; 'food' alone is a very diverse subject.

Dietetics (i.e. applied nutrition) is the study of food, diet and nutrition as applied to humans. Dietitians apply the principles of nutrition to food and people. Where dietitians are applying the principles to the treatment of diseases, etc. using therapeutic diets, they must be State Registered in the UK, to protect people from unqualified practitioners.

The latest research on nutrition can be found in the nutrition journals including *The Proceedings of the Nutrition Society* and *The Journal of Human Nutrition*. Some of the basic textbooks for nutritionists, dietitians and health professionals include new knowledge and understandings. However, they cannot include all the most recent knowledge. The most up-to-date findings are often first highlighted in the media (television, radio, newspapers and magazines). Information gleaned in this way should not be used without first discussing its accuracy with a dietitian or clinical nutritionist. Many media channels are simply using items of information as an entertainment or to create a discussion. They are not obliged to be wholly accurate or to present the whole picture within its context.

> **KEY CONCEPT**
> **Metabolism** – the process in an organism or living cell by which nutritive material is built up into living matter or is broken down into simpler substances for special functions

The living cell

Living cells are the building blocks of healthy systems. Our bodies are made up of many millions of living cells, all of which need certain materials to function and survive. In complex bodies like the human body, they work together and provide each other with some of these materials. All materials, however, originate from the nutrients in the food we eat, together with water and oxygen.

The nutrients, which are all described later in this chapter, are chemical compounds which are used by living cells to renew themselves, reproduce (by dividing into two) and produce substances for other cells to use. Any upset in the supply of nutrients can affect the cell's ability to reproduce properly and function effectively, ultimately producing symptoms of ill-health. A body's total need for nutrients will be affected by:

- illness;
- drugs;
- surgery;
- disability;
- ageing;
- inherited metabolic disorders;
- environmental pollution.

All living cells – from single-celled microorganisms to those found in complex, multi-celled organisms like the human – are similar in structure and function (although there are some fundamental differences between animal and plant cells). Differences between our cells are determined by the genetic template, DNA, which is specific to each type of cell. This chemical pattern enables cells to reproduce and operate accurately, provided the appropriate nutrients are available. The specific needs of individual cells are decided by their particular function.

The main parts of a cell

Semi(partially)-permeable membrane: protects the cell, gives it shape and allows small micro-particles to cross it. It contains lipids, including essential fatty acids (EFAs), and proteins. Within higher animals, nutrients travel to the cells in the bloodstream and the cell's products, including waste products, are carried away by the blood. Larger particles of nutrients have to be helped through the pores in the cell membrane. Glucose, for example, is helped by insulin.

Nucleus: the part of living cells in higher organisms which contains all the controlling mechanisms for that cell. (Some very simple organisms do not have a recognisable nucleus.) It contains the genetic material, DNA, which determines the cell's characteristics and the way it functions. The genetic material itself is dependent on the supply of nutrients in the diet to enable cells to reproduce and function accurately.

Cytoplasm: a jelly-like substance which contains all the ingredients that the cell needs to perform its function, remain healthy and replicate when required.

> *Any deficiencies in nutrients, including Calories, will affect the cell's ability to reproduce accurately or function properly. Even quite small deficiencies in some nutrients can result in disease, cell death or abnormal cells.*

Food is fundamental to the healthy functioning of *all* cells in the body. The amino acids (small units of proteins), the chemicals in the cell environment and the energy to carry out all processes, must all come from the nutrients in food. The most important of these requirements is for *energy*. Any reduction in Calorie intake can lead to the death or malfunctioning of body cells. The cells will metabolise protein for energy rather than go without; they are then not able to repair themselves or operate properly.

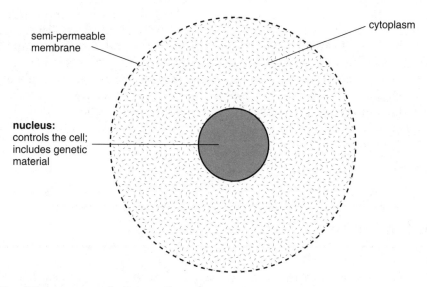

Simplified structure of a living cell

Nutrition and nutrients

As we have seen, the word 'nutrition' means supplying or receiving nourishment or food. 'Nourish' is defined as *'to sustain with food'*. In fact the words 'nourish' and 'nurse' come from the same root.

You are probably already familiar with the five main groups of nutrients in food:

- *Carbohydrate and fat* – these are the two main sources of energy (measured in Calories or kilocalories (kcals) or kilojoules (kJ));
- *Protein* – the building material of all living tissue;
- *Vitamins* – vital regulating substances;
- *Minerals* – essential elements which include the trace elements.

These nutrients are discussed in detail on the following pages.

Energy

The body's main requirement is for energy. Energy is needed for most body functions and activities, including:

- growth, repair and replacement of cells;
- resistance to infection, warmth, insulation;
- digestion of food and absorption of nutrients;
- metabolism of nutrients;
- breathing, heartbeat and circulation, muscle tone;
- physical activity;
- brain activity.

The two main sources of energy in the diet are carbohydrate and fat. In humans, the amount of energy required by an individual is dependent on that person's *metabolic rate* (MR).

Metabolic rate

The differences in the rate at which different bodies operate is like the gear ratio in an engine. Some bodies operate at a fast speed but inefficiently. Others are slower and use little energy to achieve the same results. The basal metabolic rate (BMR) is the amount of energy that a body uses to maintain the basics for survival – heartbeat, circulation, breathing, body temperature and muscle tone. The metabolic rate is controlled by the thyroid gland, although other factors also affect it, for example age, sex, body size, hormones, drugs, pollution, physical activity and level of food intake. Other nutrient requirements can be equally dependent on individual metabolism and circumstances.

6.2 Carbohydrate

Carbohydrate provides the main source of energy in the traditional diets of most countries. The majority of staple foods (page 12) are high in carbohydrate. Its name stems from its chemical nature which is hydrated carbon, i.e. carbon to which water has been linked. (Carbon is the one element found in all living things or those which have lived.)

Carbohydrate is a substance made in all green plants by the process of *photosynthesis*. By this process the energy from the sun is harnessed and made available to be used to support life on this planet.

Photosynthesis

In order to make carbohydrate, the plant takes in *carbon dioxide* (CO_2) from the air and *water* (H_2O) from the soil and, in the presence of the green pigment, chlorophyll, converts them into *glucose*, a simple sugar. The energy from the sun is used to enable the process to take place. *Oxygen* (O_2) is also produced and given off into the air.

This process can be diagramatically represented:

$$\text{Sun's energy}$$
$$\downarrow$$
$$\text{carbon dioxide} + \text{water} \rightarrow \text{glucose} + \text{oxygen}$$
$$CO_2 + H_2O \rightarrow CH_2O + O_2$$
$$\text{(Chlorophyll)}$$

When the plant, or animals that have eaten the plant, want to obtain energy from the glucose, the process is reversed. Glucose is 'burnt' with oxygen to produce carbon dioxide and water. Energy is released.

This process, which is called *respiration*, can be diagramatically represented:

$$\text{glucose} + \text{oxygen} \rightarrow \text{carbon dioxide} + \text{water}$$
$$CH_2O + O_2 \rightarrow CO_2 + H_2O$$
$$\downarrow$$
$$\text{energy}$$

Storing the energy

Having made the glucose, which is a simple sugar, plants store it in other forms. Glucose is a single sugar or *monosaccharide*. The plant can convert it into other single sugars and into double sugars or *di*saccharides. It can also join several hundreds of glucose units together to form starch, a *polysaccharide* or join several thousand glucose units together to form cellulose and other substances referred to as *non-starch polysaccharides (NSP)*.

Monosaccharides (single sugars):

- Glucose – made in plants but not obtainable from them. Glucose can be made in the laboratory for use in the diet.
- Fructose – a mirror image of glucose – found in fruit, honey (fruit sugar).
- Galactose – found alone in seaweed, for example, and with glucose in the milk of mammals including humans.

Disaccharides (double sugars) are formed by joining together two single sugars:

- Lactose – is the sugar in mammalian milk (and is the only animal source of carbohydrate in the diet).
- Sucrose – is the sugar in beet, cane, maple, honey (together with fructose) and is the one which is normally refined to provide 'sugar' and 'sugar products'.
- Maltose – is normally only to be found when starch is broken down during fermentation e.g. by the action of yeast during breadmaking or brewing ('malting').

Polysaccharides:

- Starch consists of many units of glucose packed together for convenient storage. Starch has to be converted back to glucose during digestion in order that we can use it for energy. Starch is found in parts of plants where there is a need for concentrated stores of energy, especially seeds, roots, tubers. (Some seeds, pulses and nuts store their concentrated energy in the form of fat rather than starch.)

- Liquid glucose and other glucose polymers (e.g. 'Caloreen', 'Maxim') are used in many manufactured products. They are a mixture of glucose, maltose and some short-chain polysaccharides, made by breaking down starch in a controlled manufacturing process.

Non-starch-polysaccharide (NSP):

- Pectin is the gelling agent found in some fruits and vegetables (e.g. apples, turnips).
- Gums such as agar (a gelling agent extracted from seaweeds) and guar gum.
- Cellulose makes up the fibrous structure of different parts of plants. It is insoluble and undigestible. It is of particular importance in the human diet as it provides the main source of fibre (see page 124) which gives bulk to the faeces. Cellulose is made of glucose units which are woven together into very complex structures. Some animals are able to digest and release the energy from the glucose in them.

Pectins and gums are soluble and digestible. There is evidence that they may reduce levels of cholesterol (see page 108) in the bloodstream.

Functions of digestible carbohydrate

The main function of digestible carbohydrate in the diet is to provide a supply of energy. Sugars provide energy more quickly than starches because they are simpler in structure and easier to digest and absorb. If we absorb excess energy the body converts it into fat.

Carbohydrate is metabolised to give approximately 4 kilocalories per gram. The guidelines on healthy eating given in Chapter 2 recommend that we obtain 60 per cent of our energy from this source. So in a diet of 2000 kilocalories, 1200 kilocalories would be expected to come from 300 grams of carbohydrate (60% × 2000 = 1200; 1200 ÷ 4 = 300).

Sources of carbohydrate

With the exception of milk, all dietary carbohydrate comes from vegetable sources. Animals do not store carbohydrate except for some readily available energy (glycogen) in the muscles and liver (which disperses after death). The milk of mammals contains a sugar, lactose (a disaccharide).

Carbohydrate is best obtained from starches and unrefined, natural sugars.

Starches are found in:

- plant roots, e.g. potatoes, yams, cassava (tapioca);
- cereal grains and products made from their starch content, e.g. wheat (flour products, bread, semolina, pasta, etc.), rice (all types including ground rice, rice flour), corn (including cornflour, custard powder), barley (pearl barley, barley water), rye (rye flour products, bread, crisp-bread), oats (oatmeal, rolled oats, porridge);
- breakfast cereals;
- sago;
- pulses – peas, beans, lentils.

Natural sugars include:

- fructose: found in fruit (especially dried fruit), honey, maple;

Starch can be accidentally converted into glucose during some cooking processes. For example, when the thickening in a tomato or other acidic sauce suddenly goes thin again, it's because the starch has been broken down to glucose by the acid.

ACTIVITY 6.2

Set up a tasting session with a group of people from work or college, to taste a variety of sugars. The local pharmacists will usually stock glucose, fructose and lactose. Sucrose (sugar) can be found in most kitchens. Maltose can be tasted in the glue on stamps and the browned (but not burnt) part of toast.

- sucrose: found in root vegetables, e.g. beetroot, carrots, parsnips;
- lactose: found in milk (no lactose is found in cheese and much of the lactose in milk is converted to lactic acid during the making of natural yoghurt).

Refined sugar is found in sugar, syrup, treacle and all products sweetened with them. Refined sugar and sugar products should not form a large part of the daily intake of carbohydrate.

6.3 Fat

Fat can be found in solid or liquid form (oil) and is a much more concentrated source of energy than carbohydrate. Certain plants convert some of the energy they make into fats for convenient storage. They store the fat in their seeds (e.g. nuts) and occasionally in the fruit (e.g. olives and avocado pears). Animals store all of their energy in the form of fat; distributed throughout the flesh as well as in layers within specialised fat cells. Most white fish store fat in the liver, while in oily fish the fat is distributed throughout the flesh.

Functions of fat

The main function of fat in the body is to provide a store of concentrated energy and heat. It also insulates the body, protects vital organs and acts as a buffer against injury. Fat can prevent hunger by delaying the emptying of the stomach. Essential fatty acids found in some fats form part of the cell membranes.

Fat is metabolised to give 9 kilocalories per gram. If we obtain 30 per cent of our energy from fats and oils, as recommended in the guidelines on healthy eating, we would expect a diet of 2000 kilocalories to provide 600 kilocalories from 67 grams of fat [$30\% \times 2000 = 600$; $600 \div 9 = 66.66$ (= approx 67)].

Sources of fat

These include all foods which contain or are cooked with fats or oils. Animal fats are usually solid with the exception of fish oils. Meat fats include lard, dripping and suet. Invisible fat is found throughout the flesh of many meats, especially red meats. Breeders of animals are trying to reduce this fat content, although it usually drains away during cooking. Red meat that does not contain a marbling of fat will not roast or grill well and will have a different taste and texture. Milk fats include butter, cream, cheese, egg yolk and ghee. Fish oils are mainly found in oily fish such as herring, sardine, mackerel and salmon.

Vegetable fats are usually oils and are derived from nuts, e.g. almond oil; seeds, e.g. sesame seed oil, sunflower seed oil; the germ of cereal grains, e.g. wheat germ oil, corn oil; some pulses, e.g. peanut oil. Coconuts and the cocoa bean are high in fat. These two fats are solid at room temperature.

Margarines and spreads may be made from animal fats, vegetable oils or a mixture of both. Margarine must not contain more than 10 per cent water so 'low fat' substitutes are referred to as 'spreads'. Liquid fats used in margarines have to be hardened by hydrogenation (see page 107).

The chemical structure of fats

To understand the current discussion about healthy/unhealthy fats in the diet it is useful to understand something of their chemical nature. The following explanation is not a 'scientific' representation and is intended to be a simple guide only.

Edible fats are called *triglycerides*. They are made up of three fatty acids linked to a unit of glycerol (glycerine):

1 Triglyceride

A *fatty acid* is a chain of carbon and hydrogen atoms attached to the glycerol at one end and to an oxygen-containing group at the other. The fatty acid chain can be short chain, medium chain or long chain. In the chain, carbon atoms can make four links with other atoms or groups:

2 Carbon atom

In a fatty acid, these links are joined on two sides to other carbon atoms while the other two links join with two hydrogen atoms (except at each end where they link with other groups). Where all the available links are attached to hydrogen atoms, the fatty acid is said to be *saturated*:

$$\text{glycerol} - \overset{\overset{\displaystyle H}{|}}{\underset{\underset{\displaystyle H}{|}}{C}} - \overset{\overset{\displaystyle H}{|}}{\underset{\underset{\displaystyle H}{|}}{C}} - \overset{\overset{\displaystyle H}{|}}{\underset{\underset{\displaystyle H}{|}}{C}} - \overset{\overset{\displaystyle H}{|}}{\underset{\underset{\displaystyle H}{|}}{C}} - \text{contains oxygen}$$

3 Saturated fatty acid

Many longer chain fatty acids do not have all of the carbon links attached to hydrogen atoms. The spare links form double bonds with neighbouring carbon atoms. These fatty acids are said to be *unsaturated*. Where a fatty acid contains one such double bond it is called a *monounsaturated fatty acid*:

$$\text{glycerol} - \overset{\overset{H}{|}}{\underset{\underset{H}{|}}{C}} - \overset{\overset{H}{|}}{\underset{\underset{H}{|}}{C}} - \overset{\overset{H}{|}}{\underset{\underset{H}{|}}{C}} - \overset{\overset{H}{|}}{\underset{\underset{H}{|}}{C}} - C = C - \overset{\overset{H}{|}}{\underset{\underset{H}{|}}{C}} - \overset{\overset{H}{|}}{\underset{\underset{H}{|}}{C}} - \overset{\overset{H}{|}}{\underset{\underset{H}{|}}{C}} - \overset{\overset{H}{|}}{\underset{\underset{H}{|}}{C}} - \text{contains oxygen}$$

4 Monounsaturated fatty acid

A fatty acid containing more than one double bond is called a *polyunsaturated fatty acid*:

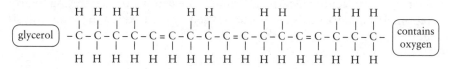

5 Polyunsaturated fatty acid

All edible fats contain mixtures of fatty acids of different lengths and degrees of saturation. Fats containing a high proportion of saturated fatty acids are usually solid at room temperature, e.g suet, lard and some pastry margarines. Fats containing a high proportion of monounsaturated fatty acids are liquid at room temperature but will begin to solidify if left in a refrigerator, e.g. olive oil. Fats containing a high proportion of polyunsaturated fatty acids are liquid at room temperature and will not solidify even in a freezer, e.g. most vegetable oils and fish oils.

Essential fatty acids

A few polyunsaturated fatty acids cannot be made by the body. They have to be provided by the diet and they are called *essential fatty acids (EFAs)*. The traditional UK diet is usually adequate in EFAs as only small amounts are needed.

Functions

Mono- and polyunsaturated fatty acids have been shown to have beneficial properties in reducing the incidence of heart disease and other problems associated with the circulation of the blood. EFAs are found in cell membranes.

Good sources of EFAs include wheatgerm oil (thus they are found in wholewheat products), corn oil and sunflower seed oil.

Problems associated with fatty acids in cooking and processing

Hydrogenation

The list of ingredients given on a packet or tin of a manufactured food product may include the words 'hydrogenated vegetable fat'. In order for the liquid fat containing polyunsaturated fatty acids to become solid and be suitable for use in certain food stuffs, or for spreading on bread, hydrogen is introduced to break the double bonds and saturate the fatty acid. Thus diagram 5 becomes the same as diagram 3 only longer. Any useful properties that the mono- or polyunsaturated fatty acids may have had will be lost in this process.

- Margarine is a mixture of hydrogenated fatty acids with varying amounts of liquid fat, depending on the texture the manufacturer wants to achieve.
- Special margarines and fats are manufactured for specific uses in the food industry and at home.
- Hardened (hydrogenated) vegetable oil is available in the domestic market for use instead of lard. It has no advantage over lard and does not produce the same texture in baked products.

Trans-fatty acids

Trans-fatty acids are mirror images of, largely, monounsaturated fatty acids. Some trans-fatty acids exist naturally but more can be formed during hydrogenation. Trans-fatty acids appear to be used by the body in the same way as saturated fatty acids and may be harmful.

Oxidation

The double bond in an unsaturated fatty acid can be broken by oxygen. The two carbon atoms link with one molecule of oxygen. This destroys any useful properties the unsaturated fatty acid may have had, and imparts an unpleasant taste. The fat is said to be 'rancid'. *Anti-oxidants* are added to some products to prevent this happening. Vitamin E (see page 120) is a natural anti-oxidant and is often found in the same oils as the polyunsaturated fatty acids.

Double bonds are weak links

When taken to high temperatures, in a deep-fat fryer for example, the unsaturated fatty acid chain can break across the double bond. The fragments of fatty acids left are hard to define and the body has difficulty recognising them in order to digest them or detoxify them. They have been thought to cause diarrhoea and may be harmful in other ways. The fat in the deep-fat fryer will solidify in time and a sticky residue will be left on pans and tins.

Cholesterol

Fat in the diet (triglycerides) is one of a group of substances in nature called *lipids*. Another lipid in the body and in the diet is cholesterol. Cholesterol is a substance essential in animal metabolism. It is involved in the way energy is released and used. It also forms the basis of a number of hormones and is part of vitamin D.

Cholesterol cannot be called a nutrient as the body manufactures most of it. It is a breakdown product from energy metabolism (especially fat) and is normally excreted via the gall bladder and the large bowel. In the past it appears that people living in cold climates were better able to metabolise fats, including the ones high in saturated fatty acids, as they produced heat to maintain body temperature. With the increased use of central heating and other means of maintaining body heat, there is less need for dietary fat to produce heat. Some products from both fat and carbohydrate are not broken down beyond the stage of cholesterol, which can build up and cause problems.

Excess cholesterol can replace other lipids in the membranes of arteries causing damage and blockage. Arterial blockages give rise to a number of fatal and disabling diseases such as strokes, high blood pressure and loss of limbs. Coronary heart disease (CHD) has become a major killer in the past 50 years in western countries. The guidelines on healthy eating incorporated in the COMA Report No. 46 recommend a reduction in the intake of saturated fatty acids.

For those suffering from arterial diseases, both the fat content of the diet and the cholesterol content are reviewed and may be modified. Bowel contents need to be moved along efficiently to prevent cholesterol being reabsorbed. Insoluble fibre (cellulose) is effective in achieving this and some types of soluble fibre are thought to reduce cholesterol levels in the blood.

KEY CONCEPT

Anti-oxidant: a substance which prevents oxidation.

Oxidation: a destructive process which happens in all tissues. It is normally controlled well but certain diseases increase it. Anti-oxidants reduce the damage caused.

Some vitamins and minerals, as well as some enzymes, act as anti-oxidants. They are useful in reducing damage in heart and vascular diseases.

6.4 Protein

Unlike carbohydrates and fats, protein contains nitrogen in addition to carbon, hydrogen and oxygen. Whereas carbohydrate and fat can be made from each other and from protein, protein cannot be made from them. Proteins are made up of small units called *amino acids*.

Functions of protein

All cells are made from protein, thus it is the main nutrient in the diet that is used for the growth, repair and maintenance of cells. It is required:

- to replace and repair body cells as they wear out;
- to build new cells during growth (pregnancy, childhood, adolescence) or after major surgery or accident (including strokes);
- during illness and fevers;
- to make all the controlling substances which the body needs to maintain itself in a healthy state.

The body is able to recycle much of the protein from worn out cells and tissues when it is in equilibrium. Where there is wasting or loss of tissue during periods of immobility or following accident or surgery, protein is lost from the body and must be replaced as quickly as possible.

The energy value of protein

The body's first call on all its food is for energy; the protein in a meal will be used for energy at the expense of growth and repair if other energy sources in the diet are low. When energy intake is adequate, protein will be used to replace and repair cells. Excess and replaced protein can then be used for energy.

Protein should not be expected to provide much energy during periods of growth, severe illness, immediately after accidents, strokes or surgery, as very little will be available. Protein yields approximately 4 kilocalories per gram when it is used for energy and should provide about 10 per cent of the day's energy needs for healthy adults. In a diet of 2000 kilocalories, 200 kilocalories would be expected to come from 50 grams of protein ($10\% \times 2000 = 200$; $200 \div 4 = 50$).

Sources of dietary protein

Protein is found in all living cells and material used for growth in plants and animals. All such material will provide protein, although some cell structures contain too much water or fat for them to be useful sources of protein in the human diet (lettuce or lard, for example).

Good food sources include:

- meat, including offal, poultry, game;
- fish, including white fish, shellfish, molluscs;
- eggs;
- milk, including skimmed, semi-skimmed, sterilised, tinned, homogenised, 'filled'. (Dried and evaporated milks of all types have a higher concentration of all the nutrients);
- cheese and yoghurt;
- seeds, nuts;
- whole cereal grains and the flours made from them, e.g. wheat flour and bread;

- potatoes;
- pulses, e.g. peas, beans, lentils (and including peanuts, cashew nuts and soya bean). Soya beans are used as a meat substitute in the manufacture of many processed foods for vegetarian diets and for those allergic to cows' milk products.

Amino acids

Amino acids are the small units that make up proteins. There are about 20 different amino acids. As the letters of the alphabet are put together in different ways to make different words, these amino acid units can be combined to make hundreds of different proteins. Proteins do not usually contain all the amino acids and may use one or more amino acids more than once in their structure.

The differences between animals and plants, between species of animals and plants and between the different cells within each depends on the way these amino acids are combined together. It is possible to discover the origin even of very ancient fossils by the proportions and patterning of the amino acids within it.

The chemical template, DNA

The pattern of amino acids in human protein is as specific as it is in all other species. This pattern is determined by the chemical template, DNA. The DNA is programmed to enable the correct amino acids to be picked up in a specific sequence in order to create a unique protein. If any amino acids are missing for some reason, the DNA may pick up the wrong one or not create the protein at all. In this way cells may die or disease processes may begin.

Essential or indispensable amino acids

The human body needs all of the amino acids but it can make most of them out of recycled body tissue as it is repaired or replaced, and out of any excess intake. However, *eight* amino acids cannot be made in the body. These are called *essential* or *indispensable amino acids (EAA or IAA)*, and must be provided in the diet. Where the body is building tissue very rapidly, for example during growth or following massive trauma, a further *two* need to be supplied in the diet.

Biological value of protein

Human diets are usually very varied as we consume food from many sources, both animal and vegetable. The amount of protein in a food that can be converted to human protein is called its *biological value (BV)* and is dependent on its amino acid content and pattern. It is expressed as a percentage.

When assessing the BV of a protein in food, it is usual to compare only its essential amino acid content with human needs. A purely arithmetical model has been formulated, called reference protein, and it is against this model that the biological value of a food protein is determined. Where the amino acid content and pattern of a food protein is quite similar to human protein, a high proportion of it can be converted. Such proteins are said to have a *high biological value (HBV)*. Most proteins from foods of animal origin, except gelatine, have a high biological value.

Proteins of *low biological value (LBV)* contain the amino acids needed but some of them are in such small amounts that they limit the amount of human protein that can be made from them. Most proteins from foods of vegetable origin, except soya, are of low biological value.

ACTIVITY 6.3

Look back to page 107. Write down the meaning of the word 'essential' in nutrition.

The complementation of proteins in foods

For a food to be completely convertible into human tissue it would have to come from a human source. Short of becoming cannibals, the only time when this will happen is when a human baby takes milk from its mother. The biological value of the milk will be 100 per cent.

The BV of foods that we eat is often limited by just one of its IAAs being lower than that required by humans. This applies to both proteins from animal as well as vegetable sources. Often, though, the amino acid that is limited in an animal protein is present in excess in a vegetable protein. Eating the two together at the same meal ensures that the combined intake of amino acids provides a much higher biological value to the body.

This type of complementary action is seen more effectively when two or three proteins of vegetable origin are eaten together. The amino acids that limit the BV of one source are made up by an excess in the others and vice versa. Some traditional dishes combine proteins of high and low biological value, for example:

- Yorkshire pudding with beef;
- Cornish pastie;
- Lancashire hot-pot;
- spaghetti bolognaise;
- risotto;
- fish and chips.

Where cereal grain flour, pulses and perhaps potatoes are eaten together, a very high biological value can be achieved as the limiting amino acids will be different in each protein. This is a very effective way of producing good quality meals, often quite cheaply. For example:

- vegetable lasagne with baked potato;
- lentil and potato soup with croutons;
- baked beans on toast.

When a soup is made from good quality bone stock and includes pulses, other vegetables, potatoes and cereal thickening, the missing amino acid in the gelatine (from the bones) can be made up. Such a soup can be further enhanced by a topping of plain yoghurt or grated cheese before serving, providing a cheap, nourishing meal with a high biological value.

Animal or vegetable?

Protein from vegetable sources has, in the past, been referred to as *second class protein*. This gave the impression that it was inferior and not useful. In fact, most people obtain a considerable amount of protein from vegetable foods in their traditional diet and when two or three vegetable proteins are eaten together, the body can select amino acids from a larger pool. Far from being inferior or useless, this approach to meals and menus is very efficient and can certainly be very cost effective.

Most staple foods contain protein. Traditionally, this vegetable source is supplemented with only a small amount of animal protein or other vegetables. For example:

- Lancashire hot-pot used potato, turnip and mutton bones;
- Cornish pastie used potato, turnip and beef scraps in pastry;
- Irish stew used potato, vegetables and mutton bones;
- Scotch broth used barley, vegetables and mutton bones;

- traditional pasta and rice dishes from Europe and Asia used fish and meat very sparingly.

Table 6.1 gives the amino acids by name. It is not usually necessary for us to know these names but they crop up sometimes in a variety of contexts so it is useful to have a list to refer to.

Table 6.1 *Amino acids relevant to the human diet*

Essential/indispensable amino acids (EAA/IAA)	Others
isoleucine	alanine
leucine	arginine
lysine	asparagine
methionine	aspartic acid
phenylalanine	cysteine
threonine	glutamic acid
tryptophan	glutamine
valine	glycine
	*histidine
	proline
	serine
	tyrosine

*Histidine is an IAA for growing infants.

Some of the names in the table may seem familiar:

- *'Aspartame'* is a sweetening agent used in foods. It is derived from the two amino acids, aspartic acid and phenylalanine.
- Phenylalanine is the amino acid that has to be regulated in the management of the condition, *phenylketonuria* (PKU) referred to on page 76.
- Salts of the amino acid, glutamic acid, are used as flavourings in savoury foods. The most common is *monosodium glutamate* which occurs naturally in such products as soy sauce.
- *Tryptophan* can be converted to one of the B vitamins, nicotinic acid.

You will come across references to the amino acids by name in other contexts. For example, some vitamins are linked with specific amino acids.

The rest of the Activities in this chapter link with Activity 7.4 on page 140, which is a series of exercises based around your own intake of food.

ACTIVITY 6.4

1   Write down one day's intake of food from your own diet. Select a day when you ate well and with variety. You can refer to the diary you began to keep in Activity 2.3. Include beverages such as tea/coffee/alcoholic/soft drinks. Keep all your sheets that relate to these exercises together as they will be needed for later activities.

2   At this stage, all you have to do is to look at your day's intake of food and write down which of the foods you *think* provided good sources of:

total carbohydrate	total fat
starch	saturated fat
natural sugars	unsaturated fat
refined sugar	total protein

Do not attempt to calculate anything at this stage. (On page 141 you will find an example of how to lay out your day's food intake for calculation purposes. When you come to calculate your intake in the next chapter, follow the suggested layout and the tips and guidance given in Activity 7.4.)

6.5 Minerals

There are many inorganic elements (minerals) in the human body of which about 15 are known to be essential (major minerals). An inorganic element is one which has not been part of any living tissue.

Minerals have three main functions in the human body:

- as the hardening constituents of bones and teeth, for example calcium, phosphorus and magnesium;
- as soluble constituents of blood and body fluids which help to control their composition and balance, for example sodium, potassium and chlorine;
- as essential parts or carriers of enzymes, hormones and proteins such as the blood constituent, haemoglobin, for example iron and zinc.

Out of all the essential elements, these eight are most common in the body and thus need to be supplied by the diet in the greatest amounts. Sulphur is also an essential mineral. It is found in two of the amino acids, methionine and cysteine, and one of the B vitamins. Sulphur is unlikely to be deficient in a diet adequate in protein.

The remaining minerals are referred to as *trace elements*. They are equally important but are needed in very much smaller amounts. These include chromium, cobalt, copper, fluorine, iodine, manganese, molybdenum and selenium. They may be toxic if taken in excess so it is not advisable to take them in the form of dietary supplements advocated by some 'health and fitness' advisers. Other minerals found in the body are there by accident. Some may be found to have a useful function while others may be toxic.

The effects of cooking and processing

Inorganic elements are not affected by normal cooking methods. Some heat processes may break down substances holding minerals and release the mineral into the product. For example in the canning of fish, bones may be softened and release calcium into the fish and canning liquor. Water-soluble minerals such as salt may be dissolved out of foods intentionally by soaking and discarded unless required.

The major minerals

Iron

The average adult human body contains about 3–4 g of iron, over half of which is in the red blood cells in the form of haemoglobin. (Iron = 'haem'; protein = 'globin'.) Haemoglobin transports oxygen from the lungs around the body. Other iron-containing compounds help the cells to utilise the oxygen. Oxygen is needed by all body cells to metabolise the fuel (carbohydrates and fats) to provide energy and heat. During this metabolism, carbon dioxide is produced. Haemoglobin also carries the carbon dioxide back from the cells to the lungs to be excreted.

Storage

Some iron is stored in the liver and some is found in muscle protein. Babies are born with a store in the liver (which can deplete the mother's reserves if not compensated for) which should be enough to see them through the first six months of life as milk is a very poor source of iron.

Sources

Iron in food comes in two main forms: *haem* iron and *non-haem* iron. Haem iron is similar to the haem in red blood cells and is easier to absorb. The best sources of haem iron are red meat and offal, such as liver, kidney and heart (white meats and fish are fairly poor sources of iron). Non-haem iron sources include egg yolk, bread and wheat flour (In the UK, iron is added by law to refined flours and breads made from them), potatoes, chocolate, some tinned fish and pulses. Some breakfast cereal manufacturers also add iron to some of their products.

About half of the average UK intake of iron comes from cereals and products made from them. About one fifth comes from red meat and offal.

Absorption

Iron is a very insoluble metal which the body finds very hard to absorb. Haem iron is more readily absorbed than non-haem iron. Other factors in the diet can help or hinder its absorption:

- vitamin C eaten at the same time helps absorption;
- phytic acid in cereal grains, and tannins in tea and some fruits, bind with iron and make it difficult to absorb;
- oxalic acid in some fruits and vegetables binds with iron and makes it unabsorbable. The iron in some green vegetables (e.g. spinach and watercress) is therefore not available to the body. These vegetables are no longer regarded as good sources. (Don't tell Pop-Eye!)

Deficiency

Iron is not usually lost from the body except during bleeding or following injury. During menstruation, women lose some iron and their extra dietary requirements need to be allowed for. Some iron is lost via the digestive system. Loss of blood through internal bleeding may go undetected for a long time.

Iron deficiency anaemia will occur if losses due to bleeding are not replaced. This deficiency causes a lack of haemoglobin in the red blood cells. Sufferers feel tired as there is a lack of oxygen for metabolism of fuel into energy. They look pale and are very prone to infections. Other types of anaemia (see pages 121 and 122) produce similar symptoms but are caused by other factors. They do not respond to an increase in iron intake.

Calcium

The average adult human body contains about 1 kg (just over 2 lbs) of calcium. All but 5–10 g is combined with phosphorus in the bones and teeth. The amounts of calcium and phosphorus in the bloodstream are kept in a well-controlled balance as the skeleton acts as a store.

Functions

Calcium and phosphorus (as calcium phosphate) form the hardening substance of bones. (Bones are made of collagen, a jelly-like protein which needs to be made hard before the bones can bear any weight.) Calcium is also

ACTIVITY 6.5

As a continuation of Activity 6.4, say which foods you *think* provided good sources of iron in your one day's meals.

required for the normal clotting of blood, for the normal contraction of muscles including the heart muscles (it prevents the muscle cramp – tetany), for nerve function and for the activity of several enzymes.

Sources

The best sources of calcium are milk, cheese, yoghurt, tinned fish (more is obtained if the bones are eaten, too), flour and bread in the UK (Calcium is added by law to all refined flours and the breads made from them). Hard water can also provide calcium for some people.

Absorption

Calcium, like iron, is difficult to absorb as it is insoluble in water. The presence of vitamin D (page 118) in the body enables calcium to be absorbed from the intestines. In fact, little calcium would be absorbed if vitamin D was not present. (Vitamin D is also required for the correct use of calcium and phosphorus by the body.) Phytic acid in the bran of wholegrain cereals, and oxalic acid in some green vegetables and rhubarb, bind with calcium and prevent its absorption.

Deficiency

A deficiency of calcium in the body causes bones to become weak, resulting in the disease, *rickets*. Vitamin D, in addition to extra calcium, is required to prevent this condition from occurring. Adults, especially older people, can suffer from a similar disease called *osteomalacia*. The bones lose their substance and can become deformed. Extra calcium and a vitamin D supplement will help to overcome this.

   Osteoporosis is a different disease which affects many post-menopausal women and some men. Bones become brittle and break easily as they lose their substance. This is caused by the loss of the protein, *collagen* from the bones which is, in part, due to hormonal changes although its exact cause is unknown. Young people are advised to take plenty of exercise as well as a good balanced diet to build up their bone strength. Calcium and vitamin D can help in treating the condition but, as it is the bone volume that has decreased, they cannot be the complete answer to the problem. Osteoporosis is often treated with hormone replacement therapy (HRT).

Phosphorus

This mineral is combined with calcium to harden the bones and teeth. It is the second most abundant mineral in the body. Phosphorus is also essential for the release and use of energy, the functioning of many enzymes and, by combining with some of the B vitamins (page 120), enables them to be activated. It is widely distributed throughout the foods we eat and is not known to be deficient in any human diet.

Sodium

Most sodium in the body is in the form of salt (sodium chloride). The chloride part shifts between sodium outside the body cells and potassium within them. This maintains an essential balance in the body fluids which controls the flow of vital elements throughout the body. In all body fluids, salt and water are maintained in the same ratio. Requirements for salt are closely linked with those for water.

ACTIVITY 6.6

As a continuation of Activity 6.4, say which foods you *think* provided good sources of calcium in your one day's meals.

Sources

Sodium is normally eaten as common salt added at table or in cooking. It is also taken in the form of sodium bicarbonate and the flavouring agent, monosodium glutamate. Many foods naturally contain some salt; the amount being determined by the levels in the soil in which crops are grown or on which animals are reared. Salt is used as a preservative in foods such as kippers, bacon and cheese. Most savoury, and many sweet, convenience foods include salt, while snacks such as salted crisps and nuts are high in salt.

Excess salt is excreted via the kidneys and some is lost in sweat and in faeces. Very young infants are not able to excrete salt via the kidneys so it should not be added to their feed. In very hot weather and during diarrhoea and vomiting, excess salt can be lost from the body. This leads to dehydration and in extreme cases can lead to death.

Potassium

Potassium is found in the fluids within cells and the total amount in the body is related to the amount of lean tissue. It acts with sodium to balance the contents of all body fluids across the cell membranes. It is widespread throughout the foods we eat, in particular those with a cellular structure, e.g. fruit, vegetables, meat and fish.

Potassium plays an important role in maintaining muscle contractions, particularly in the heart muscle. Both excesses and deficiencies can cause the heart muscle to contract abnormally and can lead to heart failure.

Deficiency is rare and usually associated with injury, tissue wasting or other diseases where there is tissue loss. Excess potassium can also be lost due to diuretic treatment, during diarrhoea and vomiting or through abnormal sweating. Because it is found within the cells, deficiency is hard to diagnose by simple blood tests.

Table 6.2 *Trace elements and other minerals*

Element	Functions	Sources
Chlorine	Maintains balance in the body's fluids with sodium and potassium. Found in association with other elements, e.g with hydrogen as hydrochloric acid	Usually taken in with sodium as sodium chloride (common salt)
Chromium	Helps the body to use glucose	Found in most foods. Good sources are meat, nuts, cereal grains
Cobalt	Forms part of the structure of vitamin B_{12}	Found in foods which are good sources of vitamin B_{12} (see page 121)
Copper	Takes part in a number of enzyme reactions and the synthesis of protein fragments	Good sources are meat, shellfish, cereals, vegetables. Deficiency is rare
Flourine	As fluoride: part of bones; helps teeth to resist decay	Naturally found in tea and the edible bones of some seafoods. Added to some water supplies and toothpastes
Iodine	An essential part of hormones made by the thyroid gland in the neck which control metabolic rate	Found in the sea and soil in most areas. Crops and animals reared in iodine-rich areas are good food sources
Magnesium	An essential constituent of bones. Takes part in the release of energy from foods and other enzyme reactions	Part of the green pigment, chlorophyll (see page 103) so is found in all green-leaf vegetables
Manganese	Facilitates a number of enzyme reactions	Tea is a good source; also nuts, cereals and spices

Table 6.2 (continued)

Element	Functions	Sources
Molybdenum	Takes part in a number of essential enzyme reactions in relation to the activity of DNA	Widely found in foods. Natural deficiency is rare
Selenium	Helps to prevent the breakdown of and damage to cells	Good sources include meat, fish, cereals
Sulphur	An integral part of many body proteins; takes part in some essential processes. Deficiency is not assessible	Forms part of the structure of two amino acids, methionine and cysteine; also part of vitamin B_1 (thiamin). Found in all proteins and foods containing vitamin B_1
Zinc	Part of a large number of enzymes which regulate or trigger processes. Also bound with insulin during secretion from the pancreas	Main sources are milk and milk products, meat, bread and cereals. Whole grain cereals can interfere with absorption

6.6 Vitamins

At the beginning of the 20th century it was discovered that foods contained minute traces of substances found to be vital for life. It was thought at first, that they were amines (similar to amino acids). They were called *'vital amines'* hence the term *vitamins*. They were originally grouped as fat-soluble (A) and water-soluble (B). Later, it was discovered that there was more than one substance in each group. In addition to vitamin A, vitamins D, E and K are fat-soluble. Vitamin C is water-soluble and vitamin B is now known to be a wide-ranging group of substances, some of which have similar functions and sources whilst others are very different.

Vitamins are vital substances required for regulating all body processes. In children, a prolonged deficiency of any vitamin will affect growth, overall health and survival rates. Deficiencies during pregnancy will also affect the health of the child of that pregnancy.

Fat-soluble vitamins

These vitamins are soluble in fat and fat-dissolving fluids. They are not, however, found in all fatty foods. They are stored in the body (mostly in the liver) and can become toxic if taken in excess.

Vitamin A (retinol)

Retinol is found in a few fatty foods of animal origin and also in animal liver, where it is stored. It can be formed in the body from a pre-cursor, *carotene*. Carotene is a yellow/orange pigment found in many fruits and vegetables. In green vegetables its colour is masked by the green pigment, chlorophyll.

Functions

Retinol plays a part in resistance to bacterial infection, being part of the fluid that keeps skin and membranes free from infection. It is also part of the substance in the retina at the back of the eye which helps the eye to adjust to dim light, and so is important for night vision. Both the pre-formed retinol and its precursor, carotene, are important anti-oxidants (page 108).

Sources

Sources of the precursor, carotene:

- carrots, oranges, tomatoes, apricots, green-leaf vegetables (cabbage, sprouts, peas, beans, etc.);
- domestic margarine in the UK is required to provide a similar vitamin A value to that of butter. Carotene may be added to margarines for colour and as a contribution to the vitamin A content;
- low-fat spreads may be coloured and fortified with carotene.

Sources of the pre-formed vitamin, retinol:

- liver, kidney;
- oily fish and fish liver oils;
- eggs, full-cream milk, cream, butter, cheese (carotene in the grass and animal feed gives the fat in these foods their yellow or orange colouring).

The pre-formed vitamin (retinol) is not found in any vegetable oil or fat.

Toxicity

Because it is stored and can become toxic, it is not advisable to give several foods which are very high in the vitamin together in the same meal.

Losses during cooking and processing

Neither retinol nor carotene are destroyed during cooking. They may be discarded if they have dissolved into cooking fat or canning oil. This will be noticeable in the case of carotene as the fat will turn orange or red.

Vitamin D

This is the name given to a group of substances derived from cholesterol. Two forms are cholecalciferol (vitamin D_3) and ergocalciferol (vitamin D_2). Although vitamin D is fat soluble, it is only found in a very few fats. Vitamin D_3 is found naturally in some fats from animal sources. Vitamin D_2 can be manufactured from plant material and is used to fortify processed foods for vegetarian and vegan diets, as there are no naturally occurring sources of vitamin D from vegetable sources.

Functions

The functions of this vitamin relate almost entirely to bone structure and health. When bones form, their shape is partly controlled by vitamin D acting through a hormone. Vitamin D is vital during pregnancy and lactation to ensure that the baby's bones are formed properly. When bones are hardened, the laying down of calcium and phosphorus is controlled by vitamin D, which also helps the absorption of both minerals from the intestines.

High levels of vitamin A can affect the development of a growing foetus. As liver contains very large amounts of the vitamin, it is recommended that it should be avoided during pregnancy.

ACTIVITY 6.7

As a continuation of Activity 6.4, say which foods you *think* provided good sources of pre-formed vitamin A and of carotene in your one day's meals.

Sources

All vitamin D comes directly or indirectly from the sun. The sun's rays acting on the skin begin a process whereby the body makes vitamin D. This is absorbed and used or stored until required. Other animals make it in the same way. Vitamin D is also stored in the liver.

Good food sources of vitamin D:

- liver, kidney;
- cheese, butter, full-cream milk;
- oily fish and fish-liver oils;
- vitamin D is added to domestic, household margarines in the UK. Using domestic margarine in homemade cakes, pastries, sauces and other cooking will help to boost the level of vitamin D intake.

Fat in the diet is required to absorb dietary vitamin D. There are no vegetable sources of vitamin D.

Losses during cooking and processing

Vitamin D is not destroyed during cooking, but may be discarded if it has dissolved into cooking fat or canning oil.

Toxicity

Vitamin D is stored in the liver and can become toxic if taken in excess. Excess vitamin D can cause calcium and phosphorus to leech out of bones and be deposited as stones elsewhere in the body.

Necessity in the diet

In the latest figures for nutrient intakes (see Chapter 7) no level of requirement for vitamin D is given for healthy adults. It is assumed that healthy, active people will get all the vitamin D they need from the sun. A certain level is recommended for children, the elderly and for pregnant and lactating mothers, people who might be vulnerable in terms of bone structure and substance.

For those who are unable to spend time out of doors on a regular basis or for those regions where the climate is more cloudy than sunny, an adequate intake of vitamin D in the diet needs to be ensured. Estimating requirements is difficult as it is hard to assess how much people are making for themselves, how much they need as individuals and how much they are storing. The pigment in the skin, melanin, protects the body from the sun's harmful ultra-violet rays by turning brown. It then interferes with the making of vitamin D. In northern climates, all but very fair skinned people can suffer from bone problems if their dietary intake of vitamin D does not compensate for the lack of ultra-violet light.

For young children, the elderly, during pregnancy and lactation and for the housebound, a figure of 10 micrograms (µg) is suggested to ensure healthy bones. This is a very high figure as natural food sources are few and do not contain large amounts. To ensure an adequate intake, use should be made of domestic margarines in cooking and, if possible, oily fish. Vitamin supplements are sometimes prescribed to boost the dietary intake. It is important to monitor the vitamin D intake from both the menu and the supplement and for the total amount to be controlled to prevent an excess intake.

ACTIVITY 6.8

As a continuation of Activity 6.4, say which foods you *think* provided good sources of vitamin D in your one day's meals.

Vitamin E

This is the name given to the tocopherols, a group of fat-soluble substances which have specific functions in animals, although their precise function in humans is yet to be determined. The requirement for this vitamin appears to be determined by the body's need for essential fatty acids.

Vitamin E is an anti-oxidant. Its main function is to prevent the EFAs from losing their properties through oxidation. It is often added to domestic margarine, other fats or products containing fat to prevent the fat oxidising (becoming rancid).

The traditional UK diet usually contains enough vitamin E for normal needs. It is found in the same food sources as the EFAs – the oils of wheat-germ, sunflower seeds, sesame seeds and corn (see page 107). It is not, however, found in refined vegetable cooking oils unless it has been added as an anti-oxidant.

Vitamin K

This vitamin plays a part in the way the blood coagulates. It is not normally deficient in the traditional UK diet. Green leaf vegetables are a particularly good source – the darker green the leaf, the more vitamin K is present. The human body is able to make some vitamin K by the action of bacteria in the intestine.

Water-soluble vitamins

Vitamins of the B group

There are several vitamins in this group. The names are quite well known as they appear on most packets of breakfast cereals:

- vitamin B_1 – thiamin;
- vitamin B_2 – riboflavin;
- vitamin B_6 – pyridoxine;
- vitamin B_7 – nicotinic acid (niacin is the American name and includes nicotinic acid and nicotinamide);
- pantothenic acid;
- biotin;
- vitamin B_{12};
- folic acid.

Functions

The functions described here relate to all B vitamins with the exception of B_{12} and folic acid. These have a different role in the body and are described later. All of the main group of B vitamins are involved in many enzyme systems in the body. They take part in the way the body metabolises fat and carbohydrate for energy. In effect, they form part of the substances that together provide the 'match that sets light to the fire'. Requirements for these B vitamins are calculated in relation to energy need. They vary as energy requirement varies, for example, thiamin requirements may be expressed as 0.3–0.4 mg per 1000 kcals.

Pyridoxine (vitamin B_6) function specifically relates to reactions linked with the body's use of amino acids. It takes part in the conversion of the essential amino acid, tryptophan, to nicotinic acid.

ACTIVITY 6.9

Write down what you can remember about the essential fatty acids (EFAs). What factors make them lose their beneficial properties? Check your memory by referring back to page 107.

Sources

The main B vitamins are all found in the same foods which, in themselves, are good, natural sources of energy including:

- meat, fish, milk, natural yoghurt, eggs;
- pulses, potatoes, fruit;
- cereal grains, especially whole grain; flour and flour products (In the UK, vitamin B_1 and nicotinic acid are added to refined flours and breads made from them);

Some B vitamins are produced in the bowel by the action of bacteria on fibre. Some nicotinic acid can be made in the body from the essential amino acid, tryptophan.

Vitamins of the B group will be adequately supplied by a balanced day's meals along with other nutrients, provided the menu uses mainly fresh foods.

Losses during cooking and processing

Being soluble in water, B vitamins can be thrown away with washing and cooking liquid. Vitamin B_1 (thiamin) and B_2 (riboflavin) may be destroyed by heat and by alkalis (e.g. bicarbonate of soda) used in cooking and processing. Vitamin B_2 (riboflavin) is destroyed by ultra-violet rays from the sun. Milk contains a high content of riboflavine which will be reduced if it is allowed to stand in bottles on a sunny doorstep.

The vitamin B content of natural foods is reduced by refining and processing; some will be refined out and some will be lost through heat or chemical treatment. Thus processed, convenience foods usually contain less of these vitamins than the fresh foods they replace. Manufacturers will often seek to replace vitamins lost in processing with synthetic supplements. Breakfast cereal manufacturers, in particular, add a wide range of extra nutrients, some of which were not in the original material. They may not add all that are lost and they may not be able to assess the right proportions.

Vitamin B_{12}

Functions

This vitamin comprises a group of related substances, all of which contain the mineral, cobalt. It plays a part in the accurate formation of rapidly dividing cells, particularly those in the bone marrow which form red blood cells. It is also required for the correct formation of nerve sheaths. Deficiency of vitamin B_{12} leads to *pernicious anaemia*, a type of anaemia in which the blood cells are not properly formed even though they may contain enough iron. Prolonged deficiency can lead to irreversible damage to the nerve sheaths.

Sources

B_{12} is found in most natural animal products, especially red meat and liver (it is not found in the fats). It may also be obtained from eggs, milk and cheese. Some breakfast cereal products have added B_{12}, and it is found in some microorganisms, such as yeast. There are no natural vegetable sources except some seaweeds.

Deficiency can occur in vegan diets unless a supplement is taken. Some patients are unable to absorb the vitamin due to a missing factor in the

---

Problems of the balance between B vitamins and carbohydrate energy can be seen in the case of packet cake and pudding mixes and their made-up convenience equivalents. The flour is extra refined to hold more sugar and it does not contain the added vitamins that household flours are required to have.

Other examples of possible imbalance:

- frozen chips will not contain the same level of B vitamins as fresh if the potatoes are peeled in strong alkali;

- other long-life 'fresh' potato products for use in the catering industry may be stored in a preservative which destroys these vitamins.

ACTIVITY 6.10

As a continuation of Activity 6.4, say which foods you *think* provided good sources of the B vitamins in your one day's meals.

gastric juices. Patients who have had a total gastrectomy will probably need to take a B_{12} supplement.

Vitamin B_{12} is water-soluble and can be destroyed by heat.

Folate (folic acid and its derivatives)

Functions

Together with vitamin B_{12}, the folates are required for the accuracy of cell division. They also take part in the making of some amino acid-containing molecules. Deficiency leads to a characteristic type of anaemia *(megaloblastic anaemia)*. Deficiency can result from an inadequate intake and also when needs are increased, for example during pregnancy and certain medical conditions in older people. Folic acid is closely monitored during pregnancy as a deficiency can cause defects in the development of some nerve cells leading to conditions such as spina bifida. If possible, folate intake should be supplemented before pregnancy and during its early stages.

Sources

Folic acid is found in green-leaf vegetables, some cereal grains, liver and yeast. The folate content of foods from intensive growing methods has been shown to be much lower than their organically grown equivalents. A diet rich in other B vitamins and vitamin C will usually be rich in folates.

Folates can be lost during cooking and processing, either by leaching into the cooking water or by oxidation.

Vitamin C (ascorbic acid)

Ascorbic acid is a very water-soluble crystal which is readily oxidised, i.e. destroyed by air. It is not stored in the body and is excreted through the kidneys.

Functions

Vitamin C forms a major part of the connective tissue which binds all cells together. Without it these tissues, including skin and blood vessels, would fall apart. The disease which results is called *scurvy*. It is characterised by skin lesions, internal bleeding, bruising, loss of hair and poor wound healing.

Vitamin C is vital for wound healing and at all times during growth or repair of cells. It helps the cells to resist virus infections, is an anti-oxidant, and enables iron to be absorbed more easily from the intestines (it is advisable to include vitamin C in meals which contain iron in order to ensure absorption).

Deficiency

Prolonged deficiency can lead to death due to internal bleeding and the inability of cells to function together. An inadequate intake can lead to wounds not healing and becoming septic, excess loss of blood, bruising and a low resistance to infections. A higher than average intake should therefore be encouraged for all people who are vulnerable to these conditions.

For any person awaiting surgery or a major treatment project, it is advisable to check vitamin C intake and boost it if necessary during the waiting period. Following major surgery, accident or trauma, vitamin C will need to be increased above the recommended intake for a healthy adult, to encourage proper healing.

Large doses of synthetic ascorbic acid taken over long periods of time may be harmful and should only be considered in the case of repeated infections or where there is a need to boost intake quickly.

Sources

In the 17th century, Captain Cook discovered that citrus fruits (oranges, lemons, limes, grapefruit) cured the scurvy that sailors developed on long voyages. He didn't know about vitamins of course, but all citrus fruits contain large amounts of vitamin C. Good sources are:

- citrus fruits (lemons, limes, oranges, grapefruit);
- berry fruits (strawberries, gooseberries, blackberries);
- black-, red- and white-currants;
- tomatoes, fresh pineapple;
- rose-hips (rose-hip syrup made from wild hips is made up for babies);
- fresh green vegetables and salads;
- potatoes (these provide many people in the UK with much of their vitamin C as they are generally eaten frequently and in large amounts);
- sprouting onions and pulses, e.g. bean sprouts (normally these vegetables are low in vitamin C but the content increases rapidly as they sprout);
- synthetic ascorbic acid (added to many commercial bottled drinks and obtainable in tablet form).

Cooking freshly peeled potatoes in a deep-fat fryer, where there is no water or air, may in fact preserve more vitamin C than boiling them in water.

Losses during cooking and processing

Vitamin C is easily lost or destroyed for the following reasons:

- It is very soluble in water and will be thrown away if vegetables are soaked or cooking liquid is discarded.
- It is destroyed by air, i.e. oxidation and heat increases this destruction. (Heat alone does not destroy very much vitamin C, so cooking vegetables with a lid on the pan, for example, can preserve vitamin C.) Some metals also increase oxidation, e.g. copper.
- It is destroyed by alkalis, e.g. bicarbonate of soda used in cooking and caustic soda, which may be used in the large-scale processing of foods, such as the peeling of root vegetables for the food industry.

ACTIVITY 6.12

As a continuation of Activity 6.4, say which natural foods and which supplemented foods you *think* provided good sources of vitamin C in your one day's meals.

Necessity in the diet

Estimates of the requirements for ascorbic acid have always been based on the amount needed to prevent scurvy. Over the years the suggested intake has been gradually increased. Some countries base their estimates on other factors, for example amounts needed to resist viral infections. The figures suggested for requirements vary from country to country and in some places are much higher than in the UK.

The suggested intake of vitamin C for healthy adults in the UK is 40 mg, however many people consume more than this. Vulnerable groups will need to aim for a higher intake.

6.7 Other dietary constituents

Fibre (non-starch polysaccharide)

Fibre consists of cellulose and other non-starch polysaccharides (see page 104). It may be referred to as roughage by older people. Fibre is not regarded as a nutrient as most of it is not absorbed. It is, however, vital for health as it provides the stimulus for the digestive tract to operate efficiently.

Functions

Fibre increases muscle tone in the digestive tract. Good tone ensures that food, waste products and digestive juices are moved along properly. This is important as digestive juices are very potent and could cause damage to the digestive tract itself, if they were not moved along. Other toxic substances could also cause problems if not excreted efficiently. Fibre also encourages chewing (probably the best cure of all for indigestion) as the sorts of foods which contain fibre need to be chewed. Bacteria in the large bowel soften the fibre as it moves along. They produce B vitamins in the process which are absorbed.

> **CAUTION:** *Fibre reduces the nutrient density of the diet.*

Deficiency

Signs of deficiency include constipation and indigestion. Lack of dietary fibre is linked with diseases such as bowel cancer and diverticular disease (the muscle walls in the large bowel become weak and form pockets in which bowel contents can become trapped and set up painful inflammations).

Sources

Fibre makes up the hard indigestible parts of plants including stalks, leaves, pips, skins, bran and peel. Good food sources include:

- whole cereals (wheat, oatmeal, barley, rye, rice, corn, etc.), wholegrain breakfast cereals, porridge, bran flakes, etc;
- fruit (raw, dried, stewed);
- vegetables, salads;
- nuts, pulses, seeds.

Ideally, fibre should come from natural foods. A fibre-enriched food or a supplement in the form of raw bran is not usually necessary nor advisable. Ways of increasing fibre in the diet for those who need it are given on page 22.

Effects of cooking and processing

Cellulose is softened by normal cooking methods but remains indigestible and therefore still provides fibre in the diet. Some commercial methods of food preparation, such as high pressure heat treatments, do break down some cellulose into sugars; such foods will not provide as much fibre. Examples are canned celery, peaches, carrots, etc.

> ### ACTIVITY 6.13
>
> As a continuation of Activity 6.4, say which foods you *think* provided good sources of fibre in your one day's meals.

Water

Approximately two thirds of the body's weight is water. It is the main transport system as almost all body processes, both inside and outside the cells, take place in solution or suspension in water. Water is found in solid foods as well as liquid. In addition, carbohydrates, fats and proteins produce water as they are metabolised.

Water and salt are maintained at a specific level in the body which is balanced by the kidneys. Water is lost via urine, sweat, exhaled air and some through bleeding and in the faeces. Excess losses in diarrhoea and vomiting, and during heavy manual work in hot weather, can lead to dehydration if not replaced.

Under normal circumstances, healthy adults should drink about 2 pints of water-based liquid daily. Water is absorbed readily through the membranes of the digestive tract.

Alcohol

An alcoholic: one who has become dependent on the effects of alcohol and who regularly consumes a large amount.

There are a number of different alcohols in nature. The type that is usually referred to as 'alcohol' and is found in alcoholic drinks is *ethyl alcohol* or *ethanol*. Some alcohols are very poisonous, methyl alcohol or methlated spirits, for example. Alcohol is potentially a very addictive drug. It has an immediate effect of raising blood temperature (which can be dangerous in cold conditions). It relaxes inhibitions, impairs judgement and 'loosens the tongue'. A person who has consumed alcohol can become increasingly cheerful in company or increasingly depressed if alone. Excess intake can lead to loss of self-control, accidents involving innocent parties and death.

Alcohol is metabolised to produce heat and energy (7 kcal per gram). This energy source cannot be converted to body fat but releases other sources for storage as fat. Alcoholics who obtain a large part of their energy requirement from alcohol are usually underweight. They may also suffer from general malnutrition or a deficiency of one or more of the specific nutrients.

The body has natural mechanisms for breaking down alcohol but the ability to do this effectively varies between men and women and between different races. Alcohol is detoxified in the liver; liver damage is a common cause of death in alcoholics.

6.8 Digestion, absorption and metabolism

Digestion

Digestion is the process by which food is broken down into the smallest parts that can be absorbed through the walls of the intestines:

- carbohydrates are broken down into glucose;
- fats are broken down into fatty acids and glycerol;
- proteins are broken down into amino acids.

Many of these substances, as well as other nutrients, are broken down further or built up in the body during metabolic processes, i.e. after digestion and absorption have taken place. For a detailed explanation of the digestive process, the enzymes and their action, refer to *The Manual of Nutrition* (see References and further reading) or any good biology textbook.

Digestion takes place mainly in the stomach and small intestines by the action of digestive juices. These are secreted by the lining of the stomach, the pancreas and the linings of the different parts of the small intestine. Several litres of digestive juices are secreted every day. They have to be made on site, as and when they are required. They are all very potent chemicals and would cause great harm to the tissues if they were around all the time. Most digestive juices are themselves digested and thus the water and other chemicals in them can be reabsorbed as they pass along the digestive tract.

Good nutrition depends on allowing time for the food to be digested and the nutrients to be absorbed. This happens most efficiently when meals are eaten slowly, when there is no rush or stress and when there is little muscular activity after the meal. Digestive juices, including saliva in the mouth, begin to flow at the sight or aroma of food. The body can also be conditioned to produce juices at particular times of the day when it is normal for that person to eat. Regular meal times, attractive food, appetising smells and good presentation are all essential to good digestion and absorption of nutrients. Eating on the move is not recommended for efficient processing of food.

Absorption

The nutrients derived from the digestive process are absorbed through the walls of the small intestine into the bloodstream or lymphatic system. Some nutrients may be absorbed through the walls of the stomach: glucose, some minerals and vitamins, for example. The residue of the food, including fibre, bacteria from the gut, other undigested material and some digestive juices, are excreted through the large bowel.

The processes of digestion and absorption of a meal will take 24 to 36 hours. Rhythmic muscle contraction along the digestive tract is called peristalsis. It begins with the swallowing reflex and ends with the evacuation of the bowels. Bowel action is often stimulated by the first swallowing reflex of the day, i.e. shortly after breakfast. The digestive tract, however, is very sensitive to stress and normal rhythms can be upset in different ways under different circumstances. The residue to be excreted will, naturally, be less when food intake goes down. Many older people become bothered by this but they should be encouraged to relax as their stress is probably aggravating what they see as a problem.

Metabolism

Absorbed nutrients are transported around the body in the bloodstream and are either used immediately or stored. The body builds up its own tissue and substances, regulates its internal environment and maintains its health and well-being. This is *metabolism* (see page 100). Metabolism occurs at different rates in different people .

The liver is the site of a great number of metabolic processes, involving the manufacturing of material for use by other parts of the body. The liver also stores material and detoxifies poisons and other unwanted substances. Many of these unwanted substances are excreted by the kidneys which act as a filter as the blood passes through them. Some minerals may be excreted through the skin.

The processes of digestion, absorption and metabolism all involve the body in work of some description. In order to achieve this the heart rate goes up, the breathing rate goes up, the blood flows faster and the body temperature rises. One advertisement used to refer to its breakfast product as 'central heating for kids'. In fact, most food has the effect of increasing metabolic rate and warming up the body. The effects of these processes can be beneficial:

- For clients who are immobile, food intake can be designed to maximise their internal energy output through digestion and absorption. Protein metabolism uses the most energy so a diet which is high in protein and relatively low in other Calorie sources can help an overweight, sedentary person to lose weight and remain happy.
- Because of the effect on body temperature, food is a good way of ensuring that people, especially older people, keep warm and are less suceptible to hypothermia.

It is important, however, to be aware of the uncomfortable and possibly harmful effects for some clients:

- For clients with heart or breathing problems, a large intake of food at one sitting can cause severe distress and occasionally death.
- For the weak and debilitated, there may not be enough energy circulating to enable them to chew the meal, make the digestive juices or deal with the end products of absorption and metabolism. An energy source is needed prior to a meal.
- Posture is important to enable food to be swallowed and digested efficiently. Sitting upright with an appropriate back rest if necessary is the most useful position.
- Where a person does not *chew* or has difficulties with *chewing*, quite severe problems can arise in other parts of the digestive tract as a result. Check that clients with dentures are wearing them for eating and that they fit. When there has been loss of weight, dentures may fit badly and the resulting problems with eating and digestion can lead to further loss of weight.

References and further reading

Garrow and James 1993: *Human Nutrition and Dietetics*. Churchill Livingstone
MAFF 1995: *The Manual of Nutrition*, 10th edition. HMSO

7 Food figures

So far in this book, the emphasis has been on facts, ideas and good practice. This chapter considers the figures that are necessary for the application of some of those facts related to food in care. In order to achieve balance in the diet, calculations, often quite rough ones, have to be made and the role of different sets of figures has to be understood. In the past the picture has been confused for many people who care for others as well as themselves, by misunderstandings and misconceptions about food figures. The nutrients in food in particular have often been misrepresented.

Figures that relate to food, diet and nutrition include the daily nutrient intakes, currently referred to as *dietary reference values*, food composition tables and nutrition information on food labelling. Food portion sizes are also relevant. In addition, the annual National Food Surveys provide sets of tables relating to the average food consumption for the UK.

7.1 Daily nutrient intakes

A number of misconceptions have arisen over the years about nutrient requirements. Many of them relate to the body's use of energy (Calories) and have sprung up around fashionable so-called 'slimming' diets.

Nutrient intakes

Guidance is needed to determine what constitutes a balanced diet with adequate amounts of energy and other nutrients for individuals and groups of people. Most developed countries have been producing such guidance for several decades. The figures given differ from country to country and have changed over the years. This change has come about for several reasons:

- Knowledge of the harmful effects of excess as well as shortage of nutrients has increased.
- Life styles have altered with people in the developed world taking less exercise and more drugs, eating more processed food, and being exposed to more pollution.
- People in western countries are living longer.
- People need less food to maintain body heat as more homes and work places are centrally heated. The balance of nutritional need has altered.

The human body is not a machine. It does not operate according to the laws of arithmetic, especially in relation to energy. In the past, some health care professionals as well as unqualified practitioners have tried to equate energy intake with specific gains or losses in body fat.

The idea is that, if fat burns to provide 9 kcal per gram, arithmetically speaking, an intake of 100 kcal per day in excess of needs would result in a weight gain of 11 g per day, 454 g (1 lb) per 40 days, 4 kg (9 lb) per year and so on.

Similarly it has been suggested that reducing energy intake will reduce body fat by an amount which can be arithmetically calculated. So, a reduction of 1000 kcal per day should lead to a loss of fat at the rate of 111 g (4 oz) per day, nearly 800 g (just under 2 lb) per week, nearly 7 kg (over 1 stone) in two months, 42 kg (6 stone) in a year.

It doesn't work like that in real life. When energy intake goes down, most bodies will ultimately reduce energy output. In the extreme case of starvation, energy is reserved for heart beat, circulation and brain activity, all of which slow down. All other movement is kept to an absolute minimum. When energy intake goes up, some bodies are able to raise their energy output and produce more heat.

Tables of nutrient intakes

In the UK, the Medical Research Council published figures supplied by the British Medical Association in the 1940s. These were *Recommended Allowances of Nutrients*. The United States National Research Council also produced figures at about the same time. The World Health Organisation (WHO) produces guidance figures which are used by people in many countries.

Such tables are useful for the following purposes. National allowances relate to the customary diets of the people in the countries concerned. They are not necessarily applicable to other countries. Together with national food surveys, where these exist, national allowances form a yardstick against which diets of different groups within a community can be measured. Figures given in tables of daily nutrient intakes provide an estimate of both the physiological needs of a community and a basis upon which agricultural and food policies can be formulated.

The UK figures were updated and revised regularly by the Department of Health and Social Security. These tables bore the word *'recommended'* – Recommended Daily Allowances (RDA) or Recommended Daily Intakes (RDI). In 1991, the Committee on the Medical Aspects of Food Policy (COMA) published a completely revised set of figures in its report No. 41 *Dietary Reference Values for Food Energy and Nutrients in the United Kingdom*. The Committee set out to review all the latest literature and research on all of the nutrients known to be required for human health. The COMA Report offers three levels of nutrient requirements but does not use the word 'recommended' because it is not possible to give a recommended intake for all people, even in the same group. The terms 'Recommended Allowance' and 'Recommended Intake' are no longer used.

Dietary reference values

In the 1991 COMA Report, three sets of figures are given within the dietary reference values (DRVs).

*Dietary Reference Values apply to groups of **healthy people**. They are not necessarily appropriate for those with different needs arising from disease, including infections, metabolic upsets, trauma, surgery, long-term drug therapy. The DRVs for any nutrient pre-suppose that requirements for energy and all other nutrients are met.*

These figures:

- represent a range of requirements for each nutrient;
- are 'estimates of reference values and not recommendations for intakes by individuals or groups';
- are to be used as yardsticks, as above, for guidance when planning meals or for food-labelling purposes;
- should be used together with other areas of knowledge within the fields to which they are being applied.

DRVs are based on the judgements of the Committee interpreting the information available to them, some of which is imperfect and uncertain. The three sets of figures are:

- *Estimated Average Requirement [EAR].* Figures represent an average requirement for nutrients in a group of individuals assumed to have fairly standard needs.
- *Reference Nutrient Intake [RNI].* Figures represent a higher than average requirement for nutrients for some individuals within the group.
- *Lower Reference Nutrient Intake [LRNI].* Figures represent a lower than average requirement for nutrients for some individuals within the group.

> *All DRVs should be treated with caution and used as indications of required amounts only.*
>
> *In some instances it is necessary to use figures from more than one set of tables.*
>
> *In some cases there is an assumption that body stores of a nutrient will be available, thus preventing the need to emphasize a dietary intake.*

Table 7.1 *Reference nutrient intakes for healthy people in the United Kingdom, 1991*

Group	Age years	Energy kcals	Protein[1] g	Calcium mg	Iron mg	Vit A µg	Vit B₁[2] mg	Vic C[3] mg	Vit D[4] µg	Fibre[5] g
Boys	< 1	545–920	12.5–14.9	525	1.7–7.8	350	0.2–0.3	25	8.5	
	1–10	1230–1970	14.5–28.3	350–550	6.9–8.7	400–500	0.5–0.7	30	7.0	
	11–14	2220	41.2	1000	11.3	600	0.9	35	*	
	15–18	2755	45.0	1000	11.3	700	1.1	40	*	
Girls	< 1	515–865	12.5–14.9	525	1.7–7.8	350	0.2–0.3	25	8.5	
	1–10	1165–1740	14.9–28.3	350–550	6.9–8.7	400–500	0.5–0.7	30	7.0	
	11–14	1845	41.2	800	14.8	600	0.7	35	*	
	15–18	2110	45.0	800	14.8	600	0.8	40	*	
Men (moderately active)	19–49	2550	55.5	700	8.7	700	1.0			
	50–59	2550	53.3	700	8.7	700	0.9	40	*	12–24
	60–64	2380	53.3	700	8.7	700	0.9	40	*	12–24
	65–74	2380	53.3	700	8.7	700	0.9	40	10	12–24
	75>	2100	53.3	700	8.7	700	0.9	40	10	12–24
Women (most occupations)	19–49	1940	45.0	700	14.8	600	0.8	40	*	12–24
	50–74	1900	46.5	700	8.7	600	0.8	40	10	12–24
	75>	1800	46.5	700	8.7	600	0.8	40	10	12–24
(pregnancy)		2400	51.0	700	see note 7	700	0.9	50	10	12–24
(lactation)		2390–2510[6]	53.0–56.0	1250	"	950	1.0	70[8]	10	12–24

1 The protein figure given is calculated to provide the required percentage of kilocalories for that group. All protein figures assume that the protein will be from foods of animal origin.

2 Vitamin B₁ (thiamin) is usually calculated in relation to the total kilocalorie content of the diet.

3 Vitamin C (ascorbic acid) is calculated to exceed the amount required to prevent scurvy. For older people, vulnerable groups and those recovering from illness, it is advisable to aim for an even higher intake.

4 Vitamin D: For many groups, no figure is given. It is assumed that fair-skinned people will make sufficient Vitamin D during the summer months to lay down a store for the rest of the year.

5 Fibre: A figure is now given. It does not apply to children under 5 years of age. Older children should increase their fibre intake as a percentage of their overall food consumption. It should not prevent them from taking other nutrients at times when nutrient requirement is very high.

6 Protein and energy requirement during lactation: The protein and energy requirement varies according to the duration of breast-feeding and according to whether it is the only source of nutrients for the baby.

7 Iron requirement during pregnancy and lactation: no increase is given as it is assumed that the mother's stores will be adequate.

8 Vitamin C requirements during pregnancy and lactation: an increased amount is recommended in the RNI figures to maintain the mother's stores. Vitamin C is needed during lactation to provide a supply to the baby via the milk.

Based on DRVs for food energy and nutrients for the UK (COMA, No. 41, 1991)

One of the three figures may be appropriate for situations in which the DRVs may be used. These include assessing diets of individuals or groups of people, prescribing therapeutic or other special diets, estimating the provision of food for groups of people, estimating needs for agricultural provision, and for food labelling purposes. The Committee that has produced these guidelines stresses that anyone planning for the feeding of individuals or groups should seek the guidance of a professional qualified in the field of applied nutrition, i.e. a dietitian or clinical nutritionist.

7.2 National Food Surveys

These are produced by MAFF, and are published by HMSO. The annual survey contains many lists and tables relating to food, prices, amount spent on certain items, amount of household income spent on food, contribution of foods to nutrition of households of different composition, averages of intake of foods per head. etc. Tables are compared with other years; regions, income groups and household groups are compared. All the information is based on different methods of collecting data to give as broad a picture as possible. It is, however, primarily statistical.

Each year a different aspect of the food scene is surveyed in more detail. In the 1993 survey, for example, the contribution and prevalence of convenience food was surveyed. The National Food Surveys can be used together with other food tables to assess overall nutritional trends, food policies and agricultural needs. Taken alone they can sometimes seem alarming. Like all sets of figures, they have to be interpreted and used with understanding in the situation to which they are being applied.

ACTIVITY 7.1

1 Visit your local library and ask to see the latest National Food Survey. (It will relate to last year or the year before as the data takes a long time to collate and publish.) Find the information from the Survey that relates to the region in which you work and compare it with the average for other areas. Do the people in your area eat more chocolate for example, or drink more beer than the average?

2 Select a particular client group: children, the elderly, those on a low income for example, and discover as much information about that group from the NFS as possible.

3 Each year a particular aspect of food consumption or policy is surveyed in detail and depth. From the Survey that you are looking at, write brief notes on that year's special topic.

7.3 Food tables

Tabulated figures for the nutrient content of a food are usually derived by chemical analysis. Some nutrients in foods are determined by calculation from analyses carried out elsewhere or from recipes. As with food intakes, it is not possible to give a totally accurate analysis of foods. Analysing a food for all nutrients is time-consuming and costly. It can take up to 10 years to revise a book of tables such as *'The Composition of Foods'*. Analysts work on several samples of the same food stuff to obtain an average figure or range of figures that can be useful. Over time, the conditions in which foods are grown, the processes through which they may go or the manner in which they are stored can undergo considerable change. The food that is being eaten today is not the same food as was originally analysed.

Food tables compiled and used responsibly are indispensable:

- for assessing the nutritional adequacy of diets, meals, menus;
- for compiling therapeutic diets;
- for checking recipes;
- for food labelling;
- for planning food production strategies.

Used in conjunction with figures such as the DRVs and National Food Surveys, where these exist, food tables can provide a snapshot of nutritional status over a broad area.

McCance and Widdowson: *The Composition of Foods*

In Britain, the first coordinated food tables were produced by the government in the mid-1940s: *The Nutritional Value of Wartime Foods*. Two of the co-authors of this work, Dr R.A. McCance and Dr Elsie Widdowson, continued with the work, producing *The Chemical Composition of Foods* in 1946 and *The Composition of Foods* in 1951. The work expanded as more and more foods required to be analysed.

The fifth edition, published in 1991 by The Royal Society of Chemistry and MAFF, includes nearly 1200 food items in its main section. Each item is analysed for 40 nutrients or factors. (These tables are also available as computer software.)

The Composition of Foods is still popularly referred to as 'McCance and Widdowson' by the professionals who use it regularly.

Using food tables

People use tables and programs, such as *The Composition of Foods*, to calculate diets, menus and recipes but as with all figures, food tables must be used with caution for the following reasons:

- the foods being assessed today are not those that were originally analysed;
- the recipes being calculated may not be the same as the ones in the book;
- cooking methods may vary;
- judgement about portion size may be inaccurate;
- figures from one country's tables are not necessarily valid for another country.

Although the 5th edition of *The Composition of Foods* is the most up-to-date, earlier editions, especially the 4th, have facilities which can be helpful in certain circumstances. In the 4th edition the nutrients in the foods are given in two tables: amounts per ounce and amounts per 100 grams. Some people still find it easier to measure and calculate using the imperial system of weights and measures [ounce (oz), pound (lb), stone (st), pint (pt), gallon (gall)] especially where older recipes are being assessed.

The 4th edition also includes a section on the amino acid and fatty acid content of foods. These have been expanded and published as a supplement to the 5th edition. A volume of *Miscellaneous Foods* was published in 1994. This gives information about a very wide range of common and not-so-common foodstuffs. Other supplements to the main volume have been published which include analyses of many specific foods for different groups of users, including a volume of Immigrant Foods published in 1985. Some figures from *The Composition of Foods* are included in the *Manual of Nutrition*. Again, earlier editions of the manual include two tables: nutrients per oz and nutrients per 100 g.

If using tables produced in text-books or reference manuals, it is necessary to check their origin. Some publications have been licensed to use the figures from *The Composition of Foods* and licensing agreements have also been issued to some agencies for the use of the computer software packages. Such permission will be credited in the text. Tables in other books may be based on the UK figures, figures from other countries or sources such as the World Health Organization. These sources will be credited in the text. Where figures are not attributed they should be treated with caution and, where possible, checked against reliable figures.

All the items included in *The Composition of Foods* are explained and users of these tables can usually find an item similar to the one they are assessing. For example:

- No 1053 – Coffee, infusion, 5 minutes. (This is followed by an explanation, i.e. liquid coffee as drunk.)
- No 1054 – Coffee, instant, 10 jars, 2 brands. (This refers to the powder not yet diluted for drinking.)

Where parts of these food tables have been reprinted in other books or articles, these explanations are not always available. Common sense is needed when interpreting them. For example: 'Coffee, instant powder has 100 kcal per 100 g.' It is likely that this is the Calorie value of the whole jar of coffee, not one cupful as drunk.

> *It is unwise to use figures that are not applicable to the country or people being assessed.*

7.4 Portion sizes and handy measures

The UK has accepted the change from imperial measures (pounds, ounces, pints, gallons) to metric measures (grams, kilograms, litres, millilitres, etc.). Carers need to understand how to convert figures fairly quickly. Many people, especially older people, may prefer to record their intake of food in the imperial system. Recipes frequently still use the imperial system, not always with a metric equivalent. Often people will say what they eat in terms of handy measures such as slice, spoonful, cupful. A guide to *Food Portion Sizes* is produced by the Ministry of Agriculture, Fisheries and Food (MAFF).

Table 7.3 on pages 135 and 136 is designed to be a guide only. For checking a person's intake the handy measurement weight will give a rough guide and may be all that is required to satisfy concern about the adequacy of the diet. If there is a need for greater accuracy, food should be *weighed*.

Handy measures

Descriptions used include 'slice', 'portion', 'cupful', 'teaspoon', 'tablespoon', 'each', 'portion', 'serving'. Some of these are very vague terms and the actual quantity will depend on the size of the handy measure in each case. The 'cup' may be a teacup, a coffee cup, a mug, or an American 'cup', for example. The proverbial pinch of salt or handful of rice can be very difficult to convert into a handier measure!

Since the introduction of the metric system into the UK, manufacturers of cutlery have changed some designs. Tablespoons, dessertspoons and teaspoons may now be shallower and smaller than those bought earlier this century when many older people learned to cook using handy measures only.

When monitoring liquid intake for some clients, it is often more convenient to use handy measures and convert the total to pints or litres at the end of the monitoring period. Thus six cups of tea can be recorded as approximately 2 pints or 1150 ml. Table 7.2 gives metric and imperial equivalents for fluids and solids.

Table 7.2 *Metric and imperial measures: approximate conversion factors*

Imperial measure	Metric measure
1 ounce (oz)	28.4 grams (g)
1 pound (lb)	454.0 grams (g)
2.2 pounds (lbs)	1000 g
[16 ozs = 1lb (imperial)]	[1000 g = 1 kilogram (kg)]
1 fluid ounce (fl oz)	28.4 millilitres (ml)
1 pint (imperial)	568.0 ml
1¾ pints, approx.	1 litre (l)
[20 fl oz = 1 pint (imperial)]	[1000ml = 1 litre]

It might be helpful to note also that 1 fluid ounce of water weighs 1 ounce, 1 pint (imperial) of water weighs 1¼ pounds and 1 litre of water weighs 1 kilogram.

Other liquids will weigh heavier than water according to how much solid material is suspended in them. Liquid fats (oils) weigh lighter than water, as they are less dense.

Converting figures

When converting estimates of handy measures and imperial measures into metric figures for calculation, it is important to be consistent.

One ounce is almost equal to 28.4 g but for quick mental arithmetic, many people use the conversion factor of 25 g; and some use a conversion factor of 30 g. People sometimes rely on calculators but it is useful to know how to check that the answer is correct in case the battery is running down. It is important to bear in mind which conversion factor has been used in the mental arithmetic and round up or down accordingly when assessing a person's intake of food or liquid.

The balance of a recipe must remain consistent, too. For example:

Short crust pastry uses a proportion of one part fat to two parts flour (or ½ fat to flour). This can thus be 1 lb flour and ½ lb fat or 500 g flour and 250 g fat.

CAUTION: American measures are different:

When using recipes from America, it should be remembered that the American pint is equal to ⅘ of the imperial pint, i.e. 450 ml or 16 fluid ounces.

The American 'cup' measurement is based on an 8 fluid ounce cup or half an American pint. This is more than the average UK teacup which holds ⅓ of an imperial pint or 6½ fluid ounces.

Sets of American measuring 'cups' are available for use with recipes written in this way.

Table 7.3 *Some examples of handy measures*

Food item	Handy measure	Approx wt in grams	Approx wt in ounces
Breads			
large sliced loaf	1 slice medium[1]	35	1¼
small sliced loaf	1 slice medium[1]	28	1
chapati	average size	58	2
naan bread	plain loaf	160	5½
rolls	burger bun	50	1¾
	bap – 6″ diameter	112	4
Breakfast cereals			
cornflakes type	medium portion	28	1
	1 tablespoon	7	¼
muesli type, (not crunchy)	medium portion	56	2
	1 tablespoon	14	½
porridge, made up	medium portion	112	4
weetabix type	1 biscuit	20	¾
Fats			
butter	per slice of bread[2] (average spread)	7	¼
margarine, soft	per slice of bread[2] (average spread)	5	<¼
	on hot baked potato	20	¾
oil	1 tablespoon	10	⅓
Jams or marmalade	per slice of bread (average spread)	14	½
Sugar	1 rounded teaspoon	7	¼
	1 rounded tablespoon	21	¾
Eggs (hen's)	average	56	2
	(size range 1–4)	70–50	2½–1¾
Cheese			
cheddar type	average piece	56	2
cottage type	1 tablespoon	40	1½
processed	1 slice	20	¾
Yoghurt	pot sizes vary	125–150	4½–5½
	(check labels)	454	16
Cereal grains			
flour	1 rounded tablespoon	28	1
pasta (raw)	1 rounded tablespoon	28	1
(cooked)	medium portion	230	8
spaghetti (boiled)	medium portion	220	7½
rice (raw)	1 rounded tablespoon (1 teacupful provides 3 average portions)	40	1½
(boiled)	medium portion	180	6½
Meat			
bacon, rasher	average, grilled	28	1
beefburger	average, raw	56	2
mince or stew	average portion	100	3½
chicken, roast	average portion	100	3½
lamb chop	average portion (meat only)	57	2
pork, roast	average portion	100	3½
sausages, raw	chipolatas (each) (av. 16 per pound)	28	1
	standard (each) (av. 8 per pound)	57	2
Fish			
white fish fillet	average portion, raw	120	4½
shop fried, in batter	medium portion	180	6½
herring/mackerel type	1 whole, filleted	115	4

Food item	Handy measure	Approx wt in grams	Approx wt in ounces
Potato			
boiled	medium portion	140	5
jacket	average, with skin	180	6½
chips	chip shop, average portion	200	7
crisps	1 packet, sizes vary (check labels)	27–75	1–2½
Green vegetables			
cabbage, sprouts, cauliflower, etc.	average portion	85	3
Root vegetables			
carrots, parsnips, turnips, etc.	average portion	60	2
Peas, green beans	average portion	70	2½
Baked beans	1 large can	420	15
	1 tablespoon	40	1½
Fruit			
apple (raw)	1 medium (average, 4 per pound)	114	4
orange	1 medium, whole	170	6
banana	1 medium, whole[3]	140	5
tomato	1 medium, raw	85	3
Biscuits			
plain (rich tea type)	1 biscuit	7	¼
semi-sweet (digestive)	1 biscuit	13	½
sweet (custard cream)	1 biscuit	13	½
chocolate (bourbon)	1 biscuit	13	½
cream cracker	1 biscuit	7	¼
Cakes			
currant bun	average size (from baker)	60	2
sponge (Swiss roll)	average slice	35	1¼
rich fruit cake	average slice	70	2¼
Puddings			
milk pudding	average portion	200	7
custard	average portion	130	4½
cheesecake	average portion	130	4½
fruit pie	average portion	110	4
sponge pudding	average portion	110	4
Miscellaneous			
peanuts (salted)	1 small packet	28	1
toffees	each	7	¼
chocolate (bar)	medium size	56	2
Mars bar	medium size	65	2¼

Beverages	Handy measure	Approx vol. in millilitres	Approx vol. in fluid ounces
fruit juice (unsweetened)	average glass	155	5½
	1 wineglass	125	4½
squash (concentrated)	average measure	55	2
carbonated drinks (can)	sizes vary	250–500	8½–17
wine	average wineglass	125	4½
sherry	average sherry glass	55	2
spirits	measure in UK	25	<1
beer/lager	half pint or pint	280–560	10–20
tea and coffee	1 teacup[4]	185	6½ (⅓ pint)
milk (not evaporated or condensed)	1 pint	570	20
	average per cup of tea or coffee	28	1

1 Water is lost in toasting which reduces the weight of the slice but does not alter its nutrient content.
2 More will be used on toast if spread while still hot.
3 The skin can be up to half the total weight of the banana.
4 Black tea and coffee are not usually calculated for nutrients but must be included in a fluid balance chart. See earlier for sugar content.

The conversion factors used in Table 7.3 and the guide shown here are approximates. For further information on handy measures and portion sizes for a very wide range of foods refer to MAFF 1993: *Food Portion Sizes*; available through HMSO.

Imperial (oz)	Metric (g)
¼	7
½	14
1	28
2	56
3	85
4	114
5	140
6	170
7	200
8	227
16 (1 lb)	454

7.5 Nutrition labelling on food stuffs

The rules governing nutrition labelling in the UK are the *UK Food Labelling Regulations* (1984) and the *EEC Directive on Nutrition Labelling of Foodstuffs* (1990). Nutrition labelling is not compulsory unless a nutrition claim is being made. Food producers can use the available food tables to calculate the nutrients in their products. Larger companies may analyse their foods in their own laboratories.

The figures given for nutrients on a food label for the percentage contribution to the nutritional requirement use a set of figures agreed across the European Union and are expressed as a percentage of an accepted average for recommended daily intake (RDI) or recommended daily allowance (RDA). The UK's dietary reference values are not used for this purpose. The ingredients given on a food label are listed in descending order of quantity.

E Numbers

Many of the foods we eat have been processed and packaged in some way. Certain substances may be added in varying amounts to improve keeping qualities, to ensure the product is safe from bacteria or other spoilage organisms, to add colour, flavour or nutrients. All such substances have to be approved for use in food and have an 'E' code number. The E coding was introduced in the *Food Labelling Regulations* in 1984. The coding is inten-ded to indicate that an additive has been properly tested and found to be safe.

A few people have found that they react badly to some additives and E numbers in general are regarded as bad by some. This has led to some manufacturers giving the chemical names of additives instead of the E number coding. Others give both.

First find the information?

A clear label

Some of the substances used as additives are, in fact, natural food substances. For example, carotene, the orange pigment found in fruits and vegetables (which the body can make into Vitamin A) is used to give colour in manufactured foods such as margarine.

All substances added to preserve, colour, flavour or enhance a product must be listed on the label. A small packet of Smarties, for instance, will have at least seven E numbers, one for each colour.

Checking labels

It is essential to check the labels of packaged foodstuffs when planning meals for people with special dietary needs. It is also interesting to see what food manufacturers put on their labels and the different ways in which they present the information. It can sometimes be difficult to find the information you need and often even more difficult to read it.

Many foodstuffs carry nutrition information together with the list of ingredients. It is sometimes possible to work out the amount of ingredient in a product using these two pieces of information. Some guesswork is needed as manufacturers do not give the recipe for their product for commercial reasons. This is a useful exercise when comparing the merits of a packet mix with a homemade recipe.

Many packet mixes, when made up, can look just as good as the 'real thing'. Can you tell the difference between the two victoria sponge cakes illustrated overleaf? One is homemade and the other is made from a packet mix. The packet is also illustrated and, using information from the ingredients list, nutritional value and cost of the two cakes can be compared.

> ## ACTIVITY 7.2
>
> Refer to Activity 1.2 when you looked for sources of information about food and nutrition. What information did you collect from the labels on tins, packets and jars?

Two sponge cakes – spot the difference

Recipes	Nutritional value (totals)	Cost
Packet mix (taken from the information on the packet)		
55 g egg	1170 kcal	75 pence
35 g fat	15 g protein	
195 g flour and sugar (ratio unknown)		
(Total weight 280 g plus one egg)		
Home-made		
110 g egg	1800 kcal	50 pence
110 g fat	26 g Protein	
110 g sugar		
110 g flour		
(Total weight 440g)		

VICTORIA
sponge mix

just add one egg and filling

SERVING SUGGESTION

VICTORIA
sponge mix

INGREDIENTS
Flour, Sugar, Oil; Hydrogenated Vegetable and Vegetable with Emulsifier E471; Raising Agents; Sodium Bicarbonate, Sodium Aluminium Phosphate; Acid Sodium Pyrophosphate; Dextrose, Salt, Flavourings, Colour; Beta Carotene.

NUTRITIONAL INFORMATION
Average Nutritional Content of Baked Product

	Per 100g	*Per av. serving
Energy	1538 kJ	615 kJ
	(367 kcal)	(147 kcal)
Protein	6g	2g
Carbohydrate	52g	21g
Fat	15g	6g

*This information is based on product made up according to directions using one Size 3 egg.
*Average serving is calculated as $\frac{1}{8}$ of the cake.

Victoria sponge mix ingredients

The comparison shows that the homemade cake yields 1½ times the nutrients for ⅔ the price. The work and oven heat will be the same in each case so it is clear that the protein and Calories in the homemade cake will cost just *half as much* as that in the packet mix. The homemade cake will contain many other nutrients as well. Remember that domestic flour has added calcium, iron and B vitamins and domestic margarine has added vitamins A and D.

ACTIVITY 7.4

Calculation exercises

The aim of these exercises is to enable you to:

- assess the balance of your own intake;
- become familiar with the 'handy measures' your clients might use;
- calculate some of the main nutrients in food and to understand the ways in which such calculations can give rise to difficulties.

In chapter 6 you wrote down one day's intake of food from your own diet. Hopefully you selected a day when you ate well and with variety and have included beverages such as tea, coffee, alcoholic and soft drinks. Some of the exercises you have already completed about what nutrients you *think* will have been contributed by your diet will be used later for reference.

1 Table 7.4 is an example of how to lay out your day's food intake for calculation purposes. Follow the suggested layout and the tips and guidance given here. You may prefer to calculate the example shown, in preference to your own day's intake. Alternatively you can do both.

Tips and guidance

- Unless the actual amounts are known, use 'handy measures', e.g. slices, cups, tablespoons, etc. and convert them using the amounts given in Table 7.3.
- Separate items where necessary and list separately. For example, toast and marmalade and a cup of tea becomes:
      bread (toasted)
      butter or margarine
      marmalade
      tea
      milk
      sugar (if taken).
- It is usual to add up the milk and sugar (if taken) for the day and assess it as a total. The other items should be written under meal headings. Put in meal times if necessary (for shift workers, for example) in order to assess balance throughout the day.
- Keep descriptions simple, for example Black forest gateau can be described as a cream sponge;
- Some dishes may have to be divided into two or three main ingredients, for example spaghetti bolognaise may be recorded as:
      spaghetti
      beef (minced)
      cheese.
- Try not to analyse a whole recipe.

ACTIVITY 7.3

1 Look at a selection of packets and tins of convenience foods and note the ingredients and nutrition information on the labels. Select one with at least 10 different ingredients including additives (count a list of vegetables in a vegetable soup, say, as one ingredient). Write down each ingredient and alongside say why it is there ('main ingredient', 'flavouring', 'preservative', 'filler', etc.). Tomatoes in a tomato sauce would be a main ingredient, for example. Check on your label to see where the 'main ingredient' comes in the list of ingredients.

2 Try to find out as much as possible about any additives and their function (anti-oxidant, anti-caking, staling-inhibitor, etc.).

ACTIVITY 7.5

1 Use the tables for the composition of foods given in the *Manual of Nutrition* or *The Composition of Foods*, to calculate your own day's meals or the one shown in Table 7.4 (which may be quite typical but is not necessarily recommended).

Assess the food items for:

- energy,
- protein,
- iron,
- calcium,
- vitamin A and
- vitamin C.

2 How accurate were you in your estimates of nutrients provided in the Activities in Chapter 6? What percentage of your protein came from animal sources? What percentage came from vegetable sources?

Table 7.4 *Example menu for calculation*

Food item	Handy measure	Approx Wt g	Energy kcals	Protein g	Iron mg	Calcium mg	Vit. A µg	Vit. C mg
Breakfast								
Orange juice	½ glass							
Cornflakes								
Bread (toasted)	1 slice							
Margarine								
Marmalade								
Tea								
Mid-morning								
Coffee								
Plain biscuit	1							
Midday								
Tomato sandwich								
(bread,	2 slices							
margarine,								
tomato)	1, medium							
Mars bar	1 standard bar							
Mid-afternoon								
Tea								
Banana	1, medium							
Evening meal								
Spaghetti bolognaise								
(spaghetti,								
minced beef								
tomato,								
onion,								
cheese)								
Fruit yoghurt								
Wine	2 glasses							
Coffee								
Bed-time								
½ milk drink								
Biscuit	1, sweet							
Daily								
Semi-skimmed milk								
for drinks and cereals								
Sugar for drinks and cereals								
Totals								

Summary

When planning food for ourselves or others to eat, it may not always be thought necessary to know what is in it. Indeed, many would argue that they would prefer not to know. However, if we are looking after someone else's health, at some point we have to be aware of their nutritional needs, the food's nutritional value, the differences between a homemade or bought product, the function of the additives and the possible harmful effects in certain medical conditions.

Generally, the dietitian will be able to undertake the work of accurate assessment but all carers need to be able to make an initial assessment in order to ask intelligent questions of the dietitian.

References and further reading

Bender and Bender 1991: *Food Labelling, a Companion to Food Tables.* Oxford University Press

COMA 1991: *Dietary Reference Values for Food Energy and Other Nutrients for the UK.* No. 41, HMSO

Hanssen 1987: *The New E for Additives.* Thorsons

MAFF Annually: *National Food Survey.* HMSO (The 1993 survey includes a special report on the contribution of convenience foods.)

MAFF 1993: *Food Portion Sizes.* HMSO

MAFF 1991: *Food Protection.* A Food Sense Booklet

MAFF: *About Food Additives.* A Food Sense Booklet

MAFF: *Understanding Food Labels.* A Food Sense Booklet

RSC and MAFF 1991: *The Composition of Foods.* HMSO
    Suplements: *Cereals and Cereal Products* (1988); *Milk Products and Eggs* (1989); *Vegetables, Herbs and Spices* (1991); *Fish and Fish Products* (1992); *Fruit and Nuts* (1992)

8 Food and kitchen safety

8.1 Whose kitchen?

In an interview, a few years ago, the head of a children's home was asked about the importance of the kitchen in the daily life of young people in care. He was asked how everyday tasks there could act as an important opportunity to do a lot more than just prepare food.

He replied:

'It is very important. Within this establishment, the kitchen is certainly the hub. There is always something going on, there are always meals being prepared, washing up being done ..... We have a large kitchen table – at one end there'll be food preparation and at the other there'll be homework being done, although we do have plenty of rooms where homework could be done other than in the kitchen.

The younger element certainly gravitate to the kitchen – this is where the mother figure – for want of a better term – is always to be found. Problems can be aired. We find that kids will communicate much more readily and easily if they are sharing something, sharing a job, sharing washing up, sharing food preparation.

The essential point is that kids are much more likely to talk about what interests them, what's bugging them maybe, at ordinary times of day, than at a special time and a special place. We must get away – and we've always followed a policy of getting away – from the formal across-a-desk situation, because young people just sit there looking at their hands or their feet and they don't say a word. Whereas, if they're sharing a task with you they will certainly talk a lot more about their problems and their fears (very much so the fears – fears of the unknown, fears of the future, what's going to happen to them, where they're going to go to, where they would like to go to), which is very important.'

Just like being at home, really. Which, of course, is the aim to be achieved in all places where people are cared for.

In any ordinary household: Where will teenage son wash his hands after fixing his motor bike? Where will the cat expect to be fed and where will the vegetables from the garden be dumped?

In the kitchen, probably. In most households, people come and go through the kitchen, often helping themselves to titbits on the way past.

Does it matter? Perhaps not in an ordinary household, but it does matter in any place where food is being prepared for other people to eat.

Current legislation in the shape of the Health and Safety at Work Act and the Food Safety Act, designed to ensure that food and kitchens are safe and do not cause illness or accidents, have left kitchens out of bounds for all but a very few. This makes it very difficult to establish a homely atmosphere for those in residential care who are used to the comfort that a kitchen can provide. Even where clients are able to work in the kitchen under supervision, carers can find themselves restricted by regulations.

You may comment: 'Anyone can go into the kitchen; it's just another room in the Home (nursery, school, office)' 'People have a right to go into the kitchen; they have to do certain jobs there, it's part of their duties'.

Well, maybe, but a kitchen has a dedicated purpose: the provision of food for other people to eat. That purpose, and all the hazards and dangers that go with it, needs to be clearly understood by all who use a kitchen, even if it is only to make a cup of tea or boil a kettle. Many residential establishments find they are unable to fulfill their desire to make their Home a true home-from-home because of regulations. One aim of a Home is to enable clients to feel that they are *at home*. For those who have enjoyed cooking all their lives, to suddenly find they are not even allowed to make tea for their guests can seem a gross infringement of their liberty.

Some residential establishments are able to offer kitchenette facilities to enable residents to make refreshments for themselves and their guests. Such facilities will need to be carefully managed and kept clean to prevent food-stuffs, for example milk, biscuits, etc. being overlooked or clients being upset if their property is discarded or broken.

When carers help clients with their food preparation in their own homes, they too, must attain the same standards of food and personal safety as if they were in a residential home kitchen. Understanding the laws and the reasons for the laws is essential for all health-care professionals.

8.2 Health and safety at work

Every year, over 500 people die at work and several hundred thousand lose time through illness or injury; some of them suffering serious disablement. This alarming statistic has brought health and safety at work to everyone's attention and strengthened the enforcement of the Health and Safety at Work Act, 1974. This Act makes it everyone's responsibility to ensure that the work-place is safe and that it is kept so. It recognises that all places of work are different. It requires people to carry out the general duties under the Act 'so far as is reasonably practicable ...'. The local authority's Environmental Health Officers will willingly advise on this.

There are some things that have to be done at all costs; no allowance is made for the size, nature or profitability of an organisation; the risk must be removed. The most obvious example of this would be the regulations in respect of fire risks and their prevention.

Kitchens are dangerous places

Despite the alarming statistics mentioned above we should remember that most accidents are preventable. Complying with the law is not just a chore or disagreeable nuisance, it is probably the best way to save money, time and an awful lot of pain. In all kitchens, both large and small, we are likely to find:

- boiling oil;
- sharp knives;
- blunt instruments;
- hot metal;
- slippery surfaces;
- electric points and wires;
- poisonous substances.

The larger the kitchen and its equipment, the more hazards it can present. We need to take certain protective measures. Staff need to understand the hazards, be aware of them and prevent accidents from happening by removing the hazard or safeguarding the situation.

Food and kitchen safety can be affected by the size and type of equipment and the size and type of stock (sacks of potatoes or flour, for example). At some point, the way we cook at home stops being convenient for larger numbers, but the way caterers produce food in bulk isn't always convenient for smaller numbers:

- catering for 20 is not the same as catering for 4 multiplied by 5;
- catering for 20 is not the same as catering for 100 divided by 5.

A care situation, be it a residential home, day-care centre, for children or adults, is often somewhere in between. Always aim to get the best of both worlds.

It is easy to be wooed into buying unnecessary equipment or food in bulk. It is necessary to think what is wanted and what is the best way to achieve it in the particular caring situation that is being planned for. It is better not to confine thinking to the ways used either in the domestic situation or the large-scale catering world, but to be willing to explore the

Defences are needed

Table 8.1 Food poisoning: sources and control

Bacteria and preferred conditions for growth	Sources and means of transfer	Symptoms and duration	Onset (hours)	Control, prevention and destruction
Salmonella spp. (many varieties) Produces a toxin in the body; both the organism and its toxin cause illness. Aerobic; likes warm, moist conditions; lies dormant in the cold	The main source is the intestines of animals and birds. Can be transferred to eggs via the bloodstream of infected fowl. Transferred from raw to cooked food and from infected hands	Abdominal pain, diarrhoea, vomiting, fever. Can last 1–7 days. Some people can become carriers	12–36 hours after eating infected food	Follow all measures to prevent harm being caused by bacteria. Refrigerate high-risk foods. Separate raw and cooked foods in the refrigerator. Thaw frozen foods in a refrigerator. Cook meat, etc. thoroughly. Both the bacteria and the toxin can be destroyed by taking the food above 100°C (above 63°C at the centre of the food) for at least 30 minutes
Staphylococcus aureus Produces a toxin in the food. Aerobic; likes warm, moist conditions; can reproduce in very high salt concentrations, e.g. Marmite. Lies dormant in the cold	Most human nasal passages, throats, mouths are infected some of the time. Also found on the skin, hair, in boils, cuts, hangnails, whitlows	Symptoms are like acute sea-sickness. Abdominal pain, vomiting, prostration, low body temperature. Lasts 6–24 hours	1–6 hours after eating infected food	Follow normal measures to prevent harm being caused by bacteria. Keep cuts, sores and whitlows covered with waterproof dressings. Avoid touching skin, nose, mouth, hair. Keep hair well tied back and use very little make-up, if any, and no nail varnish. Exclude food handlers with respiratory infections, boils or deep wounds. Discard old stocks of goods such as Marmite, Bovril or Oxo. Cool high-risk foods quickly, then cover and refrigerate
Clostridium perfringens Produces a toxin in the body. Anaerobic; likes warm, moist conditions; lies dormant in the cold. Produces heat- and cold-resistant spores which germinate when conditions become favourable again	Transferred from the soil via insects, dust, animal (including human) faeces	Abdominal pain and diarrhoea; vomiting is rare. Milder illness than *Salmonella* poisoning. Can last 12–48 hours	Onset 12–18 hours after eating infected food	Boned and rolled meats are especially risky as air is excluded. Thorough cooking to the centre of the joints is essential. Keep large pans of stew, stock or gravy stirred and aerated. Cool rapidly and refrigerate. Keep raw and cooked foods separate
Bacillus cereus Produces a toxin in the body and also in the food. The food toxin is virtually indestructible. Aerobic; likes warm, moist conditions; produces heat- and dry-resistant spores which germinate in more favourable conditions	Cereal grains, especially rice; also found in flour, corn-flour, dried mixes, soups, potatoes, milk powders, etc.	Vomiting, abdominal pains, diarrhoea. Symptoms from the toxin in the food last 12–24 hours, and up to 2 days from the toxin produced in the intestine	1–5 hours after eating infected food; 8–16 hours if the toxin is produced in the intestine	Rotate stocks of dry goods regularly. Thorough cooking and rapid cooling of dishes containing cereals (especially rice) is essential. Store food at correct temperatures. Avoid reheating rice dishes. If in doubt, throw away as the toxin is very heat-resistant. Avoid cross-contamination
Escherichia coli (E.Coli) Causes an abdominal infection and produces a toxin. Aerobic; likes warm, moist conditions	Normal inhabitant of human and animal intestines; only some cause illness. Transferred to food from faeces via unwashed hands	Abdominal pain, fever, diarrhoea, vomiting. Lasts 1–5 days	12–24 hours after eating infected food	The presence of *E. Coli* in food indicates poor standards of personal and kitchen hygiene. Hands must be washed, using a firm nailbrush, after visiting the toilet. Store cooked foods below 4°C
Clostridium botulinum Produces neurotoxins (nerve poisons) in food. Anaerobic; likes warm, moist conditions. Produces very heat-resistant spores in unfavourable conditions	Transferred from the soil via animals, fish and vegetables. Most food-poisoning outbreaks occur due to cross-contamination	Paralysis of nerves leading to difficulties in swallowing, breathing and vision (botulism). Death is common. Recovery for survivors is very slow	Usually 12–36 hours after eating infected food but may be longer. Not always diagnosed at first	The temperatures used for the commercial processing of foods, e.g. canned meats and fish, are determined by the heat resistance of the *C. botulinum* spores. Strict control of food stocks is essential. Discard old stock, especially cans that have 'blown'. Store frozen foods at correct temperatures and rotate stocks regularly
Listeria spp. Causes illness; may be transferred in ways other than by food. Aerobic; likes warm, moist conditions; tolerates salt. Can grow in very cold conditions and can be resistant to heat	Transferred from animal and human carriers and the environment; cross-contamination from infected foods, especially pre-prepared, chilled foods which are not usually re-cooked	Fever, septicaemia, meningitis. Especially dangerous in young babies, the elderly, the ill and during pregnancy when it may induce abortion. Can cause death	A long onset period; listeriosis may not be diagnosed at first	Vulnerable groups, especially pregnant women, should avoid eating soft cheeses, paté and reheated meals. Prevent cross-contamination during storage. Set refrigerators at the correct temperature. The storage temperature for refrigerators has been established by the lowest temperature at which *Listeria* stops growing

possibilities offered by both. Some conventions used by caterers, save time, energy and money in any context. Ways to cope with individual needs learned in the domestic situation can be extremely valuable when caring for individual needs at work.

Choosing suitable equipment

When offering food in any caring situation, apart from a person's own home, there will be times when decisions have to made about the merits of the equipment in use, especially if it needs to be replaced. Residential homes are currently registered with their local authority's social services department and advised by the authority's environmental health officers. Not all officers are trained in the provision of food, nor do they all have access to good catering advice. They may suggest equipment that is inappropriate to the size of home or the numbers catered for. Some smaller establishments may be governed more by the cost of equipment than its suitability to carry out the task effectively.

For some items of equipment there is, at present, only a choice between the domestic size and the large-scale version. It should always be the aim to buy the equipment that is most useful for the job it has to do. Weigh up the pros and cons:

- how many people are being catered for?
- what use will it get?
- will it stand up to heavy use?

Consider the hazards or costs involved, for example:

- in lifting large boxes of canned goods, flour bought in bulk, sacks of potatoes;
- in opening a large can of meat for a small number of people;
- in opening 12 small tins of beans with a manual tin-opener;
- in throwing away herbs and spices because they have lost their flavour.

ACTIVITY 8.1

In your workplace, consider for example:

- the tin-opener;
- the potato peeler;
- the mixing machine;
- the frying pan;
- the oven space.

Is the domestic size right or wrong?

Is the catering size right or wrong?

Give reasons for your answers.

ACTIVITY 8.2

1 Consider the kitchen in your own household and also the one you are most closely associated with at work (this might be in a care home, hospital, day centre, school or community meals distribution centre).

2 Compare the sizes of the equipment as well as the other differences: fuel used, size of food packages, numbers of people working there.

- What differences do you find in the way hazardous items are handled?
- How do you prevent accidents in both situations?

8.3 Food safety and hygiene

Since food is an essential part of caring and most care workers will have to prepare, cook or serve food at some time, it is essential that all those who work with clients understand the basic principles of safe food handling. For basic food hygiene and safety it is as important to know the *reasons* as it is to know the *rules*.

Safe food handling is designed to prevent or reduce the growth of harmful (pathogenic) bacteria in food. The main purpose of the Food Safety law and the Food Hygiene Regulations is to prevent food poisoning.

Food poisoning

In the UK, food poisoning is a notifiable disease; the environmental health officers (EHOs) of the local authority must be notified of any occurrence.

This is the name commonly given to a group of diseases caused by certain bacteria which have been allowed to grow in food before it is eaten. Some food poisoning may be caused by other substances: viruses, some metals, chemicals, for example. Food poisoning can cause death, especially in people who are frail or sick. Symptoms nearly always include diarrhoea and sometimes vomiting. Death is caused by dehydration (loss of water and essential minerals from the body) as well as stress and exhaustion.

About bacteria

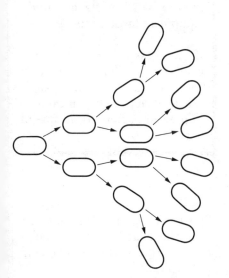

Bacteria dividing

Bacteria are an essential part of life so it is not a good idea to destroy them altogether. Only a small number of the hundreds of bacteria that exist cause food poisoning. A bacterium is a single living cell which, in the right conditions, multiplies by simple division, one divides into two which each divide into two and so on. The aim is to prevent the harmful bacteria from multiplying in the food by handling food safely. Given the right conditions, one bacterium becomes 7 000 000 000 (7 billion) after 12 hours. In addition, we don't start with only one bacterium in the food. It is possible for there to be 10 000 on the sharp end of a pin. As they multiply, bacteria produce waste products that are poisonous to humans. In some cases it is the poisons (toxins) that cause the disease and in others it is the bacteria themselves.

Many species of bacteria exist, most of which are useful to us. Only a few species are harmful and of these, only about seven cause food poisoning.

ACTIVITY 8.3

Instead of counting sheep one night, imagine a clock face. Starting at 12 o'clock with 1, double the number every quarter of an hour: 1 – 2 – 4 – 8 – 16 – 32 – 64 – 128 and so on.

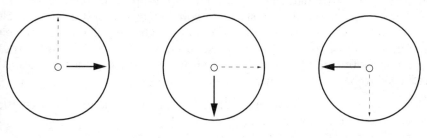

You could fall asleep quite quickly but you will still have counted up to several thousand in a very short space of time.

The right conditions

Bacteria like to have those things around them that make people feel comfortable too – warmth, food, moisture, air to breathe (some can live without air) and plenty of time to enjoy themselves:

- *Food* is the food that is being prepared or served, especially protein foods.
- *Warmth* – bacteria prefer a temperature of around blood heat.
- *Moisture* – bacteria don't grow well in very dry foods.
- *Air* – most bacteria grow better in air; these are the aerobic bacteria. Some, the anaerobic bacteria, prefer not to have air around.
- *Time* – you have already worked out what happens if you give bacteria time to grow.

Given the 'right conditions', the bacteria which cause food poisoning multiply very rapidly and produce large amounts of toxic waste products.

Sources of harmful bacteria

Bacteria are all around: in the air, in the soil, on the skin, on clothes, in animal and human faeces (some bacteria thrive in the intestines of humans and animals so they are passed out in the faeces). Some are transferred from place to place by insects and vermin.

The main food-poisoning bacteria are *Salmonella* spp., *Staphylococcus aureus*, *Clostridium perfringens*, *Listeria* spp., *Clostridium botulinum*, *Bacillus cereus* and *Escherichia coli*. The last three bacteria all form heat-resistant spores in unfavourable conditions, i.e. hot, cold or dry states in which they cannot grow. As a more favourable state returns, the spores germinate and the bacteria reproduce more quickly than normal to make up for lost time. As these spores are heat-resistant, the temperature required to destroy them is much higher than is required to kill the bacterial cells. Table 8.1 gives further information on food-poisoning bacteria.

Food safety

The UK Food Safety laws are designed to prevent food poisoning and contamination at all points in the food production and service chain. The Food Safety Act 1990 relates to all parts of the food chain from growing to serving. It enables ministers to make regulations, as appropriate, for the individual parts of the industry. The main aim of the Act is to ensure that food does not cause harm to the people who eat it. It is mainly based on *common sense*. It is an offence to cause illness by *preventable contamination* of food. It is a criminal offence if the contamination occurs deliberately or knowingly. Penalties include closure of premises, large fines and/or imprisonment. The Act strengthens the local authorities' powers of enforcement.

Food safety is one of the tasks laid upon managers and staff at all levels. The main aim at the service end of the food production chain is to prevent contamination of food by harmful bacteria, and this will include cross-contamination from products already infected, as well as other sources. All staff need to be aware and understand:

- how food can be contaminated and cross-contaminated and how risks can be eliminated or reduced;
- the nature of the risks involved in food handling;
- the reasons for good practice in safe food handling;
- the need to ensure that proper facilities are available for safe food handling;

KEY CONCEPT
Pathogenic: an organism or substance which causes disease.

Aerobic bacteria need air as part of the 'right conditions' for living and multiplying.
Anaerobic bacteria thrive better in the absence of air.

ACTIVITY 8.4

1 Think of the kitchen at home or at your workplace. List the places where bacteria could hide, for example cracks in tiles, joins in the work-surfaces, under equipment, around the drains.

2 Suggest other areas where bacteria might lurk if you are not very careful. Make a list of all the practical steps that you can take to prevent bacteria from spreading.

Spp. means species. This indicates that there are several species or varieties within one group of bacteria.

- the need to ensure that everyone understands the reasons for their actions in relation to food handling and that they willingly use these good practices.

All staff must be committed to the prevention of food-borne illness and cooperate in a commitment to achieve this end. It is necessary for people involved in food handling to be able to adapt their understanding of the issues to the situation in which they work. It is not sensible to make hard and fast rules and expect them to apply to all situations.

Staff need to understand the reasons for safe food handling so they can explain to others why they should adopt certain practices in a way that makes them willing partners. It is not enough to blindly follow the guidelines and rules made by others. Some of the people who make up the guidelines know very little about food or the variety of situations to which these guidelines are intended to apply.

High risk foods

Some foods are much more likely to allow the growth of harmful bacteria than others. Bacteria need protein for growth (as do all living cells) so foods which have a high concentration of protein allow bacteria to multiply if kept in the right conditions (see page 148). Good sources of food protein include meat, fish, cheese, eggs, milk, yoghurt, pulses, nuts and some cereal grains. (Gelatine also provides a good growing medium for bacteria.) Moist protein-rich foods which have been cooked or processed and are not to be reheated or recooked are particularly high risk. These include:

- soft cheeses, patés, cooked meat and poultry;
- cooked dishes containing meat, fish, eggs, cheese, cereals, pulses or vegetables;
- cooked pies, pasties, sausage rolls, gravy, stock and soup;
- mayonnaise and made-up salads in dressing;
- cream and artificial cream, cream cakes, custards, dairy desserts;
- shellfish and molluscs, smoked or cured fish;
- cut or sliced smoked or cured meats;
- sandwiches or filled rolls containing meat, fish, egg, soft cheese, etc.

In addition, cooked rice should not be stored unless it has been cooled very quickly. Storage of all these foods must be *at or below 5°C*. However, bacteria do not thrive where there is little moisture or an acid environment. Some foods which are good sources of protein will not allow bacteria to grow during storage, for example, hard cheeses, dried pulses, nuts and cereals.

Medium risk foods

Raw protein-rich foods, e.g. meat, poultry and fish may harbour bacteria. Until these foods are cooked they should be stored *at or below 5°C*. To prevent cross-contamination, raw meat and fish should be kept away from the high-risk foods listed above. If in the same refrigerator, keep all foods well covered and keep raw foods on the lower shelves.

Low risk foods

Dry foods, for example bread, biscuits, cereals, powdered foods, flour, etc. do not provide a good growing medium for food-poisoning bacteria. If they are not stored well, however, they can deteriorate for other reasons and will have to be thrown away. The spores of *B.cereus* can survive in dried goods such as cereal grains, especially rice, dried milk and soup powders. Dried foods must be stored in a cool, dry place and good stock rotation and control is essential to prevent possible contamination.

Canned foods do not carry a risk of food poisoning or cross-contamination. They should be stored in a dry, cool larder to prevent damage to the tin. Cans can become 'blown' by the production of gases if they have not been processed or sealed properly. The rings at the top of the tin expand and the tin develops a domed shape. If the tin is opened there will be a hiss of escaping gas. *The food from 'blown' tins must not be eaten.* It is useful to make a note of the brand, the batch number and the date the blown tin was purchased and to notify the environmental health officer and, if possible, the supplier and the manufacturer. Canned goods should not go beyond their 'use-by' date. Once opened, treat the contents of a can as if it were fresh and follow the advice given for the equivalent fresh product.

Vegetables and fruits are low risk as they are usually acidic. However, root vegetables are likely to carry bacteria from the soil. Cross-contamination with high risk foods must be prevented. Fruit and vegetables should be stored away from other foods.

Jams, syrup, honey and other preserves are low risk due to the high sugar content.

Destruction and control of food-poisoning bacteria

Time and *temperature* are the two main tools for control.

Time: Fresh foods must not be left for long periods of time as this will enable bacteria to grow. If they are to be stored, the temperature and environment of the storage must be such that bacterial growth is prevented. Cooked foods should be eaten straight away, maintained at or above 63°C if being served from a hot counter, or cooled rapidly and refrigerated.

Temperature: Bacteria prefer warmth; they grow most rapidly at blood heat. Strict regulations are in force which determine correct refrigerator, freezer, cooking and hot trolley temperatures as well as those required for some food processes. These temperatures have been set according to the conditions which certain bacteria can tolerate.

Temperature regulations

Regulations with regard to temperatures for the storage of foods are set out in the Food Safety Regulations 1990.

During cooking: Most bacteria will be destroyed if temperatures are held *above 100°C* for at least 30 minutes. Temperatures *above 63°C* have to be reached in the centre of bulky food, for example a large joint of meat or a big pan of stew. The toxins that bacteria produce will be destroyed by the same heat process, except for the toxin of *B. cereus.* If serving hot food from a counter or trolley over a period of time, it must be kept at a minimum temperature of 63°C during service.

Cooling: Bacterial growth is slowed and may cease altogether at low temperatures. Current regulations on refrigerator temperatures for food storage are based on the fact that *Listeria* ceases to grow at 5°C or below. This temperature has to be achieved at the centre of bulk food so it is recommended that refrigerators are kept *at or below 4°C.* Cooling should be as rapid as possible. However, be aware that if hot food is put into a refrigerator, it will warm up the surrounding air and allow bacteria to grow in other foods. Commercial blast chillers reduce food to these temperatures very rapidly.

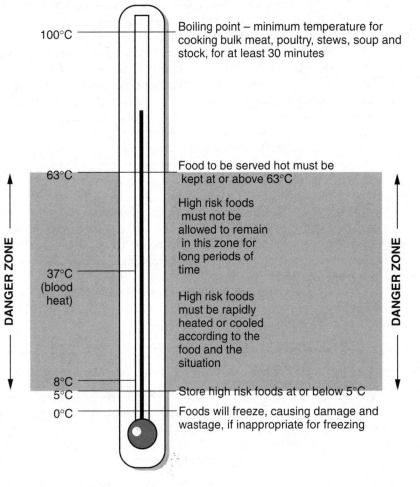

100°C — Boiling point – minimum temperature for cooking bulk meat, poultry, stews, soup and stock, for at least 30 minutes

63°C — Food to be served hot must be kept at or above 63°C

High risk foods must not be allowed to remain in this zone for long periods of time

37°C (blood heat) —

High risk foods must be rapidly heated or cooled according to the food and the situation

8°C —
5°C — Store high risk foods at or below 5°C

0°C — Foods will freeze, causing damage and wastage, if inappropriate for freezing

DANGER ZONE

Temperature controls

Other methods of controlling the growth of bacteria

Air supply: Aerobic bacteria grow better in airy conditions. Keep foods covered; if possible, create a vacuum in a pan by covering with a tight-fitting lid whilst the food is still at boiling point and the pan is full of steam. Anaerobic bacteria can grow at the bottom of large pans of gravy, stew and custard unless they are aerated. Stews and stockpots should be stirred regularly. Dishes such as trifles should just be eaten as soon as possible.

Dehydration: Removing water effectively stops bacteria from reproducing. However some spores, especially those of *B.cereus*, can survive in dried goods and will regain their activity when liquid is added. Other microorganisms can grow in badly stored dry goods, causing food to deteriorate. This is wasteful even if it does not cause food poisoning.

Preservation in sugar or salt: Strong solutions of sugar or salt dehydrate most bacteria (by osmosis) and thus stop them reproducing. *Staphylococcus aureus*, however, can survive and grow in very strong salt conditions, e.g. Marmite.

Preservation in acid: Most bacteria will not grow in very acid conditions. Altering the acidity of their surroundings, by pickling in vinegar for example, prevents them from multiplying.

> *The constant opening of refrigerator and freezer doors will cause the temperature inside to rise. Such doors should not be left open at any time.*

Freezing: All bacterial growth ceases when food is frozen and some bacteria may be destroyed by lack of available water. However, during thawing, bacteria may pass through their optimum growth temperature when they will reproduce even more rapidly than normal to compensate for being dormant. To prevent this, food should be thawed in the refrigerator at or below 5°C. Freezers must be kept at a maximum of –18°C.

The prevention of food-borne disease

> As a general rule the main risks of food poisoning are poor hygiene, cross-contamination and storage at warm temperatures. Control must include the education of all staff, high standards of personal hygiene and good practices, especially temperature control.
>
> R.A. Sprenger 1991: *Hygiene for Managers*. Highfield Publications

> *It is vital that foods are taken rapidly through the critical temperature for maximum growth and foods which could cause food poisoning are heated or cooled quickly.*

A combination of sensible and manageable measures can be taken to prevent bacteria causing harm to people. Measures taken by staff should cover the buying, storage, cooking, service and disposal of food. They should include standard practices in relation to cleaning, maintenance, repair and replacement of equipment, both large and small.

Personal hygiene is part of a care worker's normal practice and all care workers who handle food must be aware of the possibility of cross-contamination. Monitoring all aspects of the provision of food is now included in food safety laws and aims to ensure that good practices are maintained at all levels. Monitoring includes the upkeep of records for inspection by the environmental health officers of the local authority. All measures are based on *common sense* and an understanding of bacteria (and other organisms) together with a knowledge of the optimum conditions for their growth.

Guidelines for good practice

Good practice and ideals are sometimes written down as rules. Some of these rules are more practical in large-scale kitchens whilst others favour smaller kitchens. Rules need to be made to suit the particular kitchen and circumstances of the care situation. They must ensure food safety and the safety of everyone who works in the preparation and service of food.

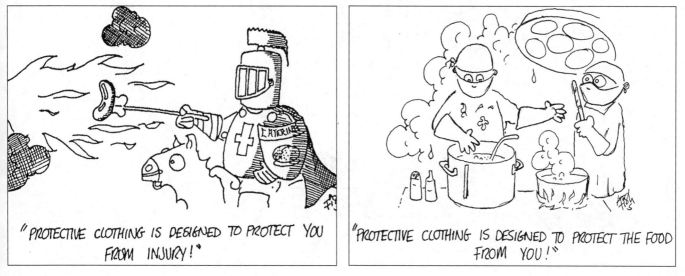

Protective clothing

Good practice for the kitchen:

- all cooked food should be kept covered;
- all cooked and raw foods should be kept separate, even in the refrigerator;
- all food must be kept separate from non-food items, e.g. drugs;
- all surfaces should be non-stick, easy to clean and be cleaned thoroughly, at least once daily;
- large equipment should be mobile, flush to the walls or able to be cleaned round;
- small equipment such as tin-openers, slicing machines, food processors, should be cleaned and sterilised regularly;
- ideally, kitchens should be designed to allow a work flow-through which prevents cross-contamination. For example, raw vegetables should not be in the path of cooked meats;
- cupboards and storerooms need to be cleaned on a regular rota basis;
- fridges and freezers must be kept at the required temperatures (see pages 151 and 153) and be defrosted and cleaned regularly;
- all cloths, tea towels, oven gloves, etc. should be washable (preferably able to be boiled) and must be laundered frequently. Paper towels can be used for wiping plates before service;
- disposable towels are recommended for hand drying and mopping up spills;
- floor mops need to be kept clean and in good condition (inspect and replace regularly). They must be stored away from food-handling areas.
- rubbish bins and swill bins must be kept well away from food preparation, preferably outside the cooking area. All bins should be cleaned and disinfected regularly.

Kitchen staff must be aware of the way in which bacteria can be transferred from one place to another and from one food to another.

ACTIVITY 8.5

1   Using the lists of ideals for good practice, compile a set of rules to ensure food safety that you think would be practical in your workplace.

2   Test some of them by asking others at work to comply with them, and seeing if this is possible.

Mohair cookery

8.4 Hazard analysis – prevention is better than cure

The development of a HACCP-type technique will only be successful where the principles of good hygienic practice are already in place and understood. It is necessary to understand what constitutes a hazard and what preventive measures are appropriate in that situation.

Food hygiene regulations cover the preparation and service of food in hospitals, nursing and residential homes, day-care centres and schools. It also includes the provision of community meals and food in restaurants, hotels, cafeterias, canteens, etc. All are regarded as 'food premises' within this law. In addition to the regulations that have been in force since 1970, the Food Safety (General Food Hygiene) Regulations 1995, require the owners of any food premises to introduce a system of prevention to ensure that clients do not come to harm through the food eaten on those premises.

Any system for analysing and preventing hazards should be designed to prevent problems arising and should include identification of the dangers or hazards and the areas where those dangers are likely to occur, the taking of measures to prevent them and the establishment of a system to check that those measures are being carried out. One system has been called the *Hazard Analysis Critical Control Point* (HACCP). This technique has been developed to enable all those involved in food handling to assess the risks of food poisoning and so take steps to prevent it. The main feature of the technique is for staff to decide what are the main stages in *their* food-related activities which must be controlled to ensure the safety of the final product.

- A hazard is anything which can harm the client.
- Control of points at which the hazard is likely to occur involves taking preventive action in advance so that the hazard does not occur. (Remove the spider's web before the fly drops into the soup!)
- Monitoring the control system regularly ensures that standards do not slip.

Monitoring the system involves managers and supervisers setting up systems for checking that controls are in place at the critical points in the food production and service process and that they are effective. Local authorities may want to see the evidence of control in writing so some documentation has to be maintained, for example cleaning schedules, maintenance contracts, stock control records, temperature logs for refrigerators and freezers. The environmental health officer may ask for samples of meals to be kept in the refrigerator for a period of time in order that occasional laboratory checks can be carried out.

A HACCP-type system enables staff to:

- identify the potential hazards that may be involved with food preparation and service; note the critical points at which the hazards are most likely to occur;
- assess the likelihood of occurrence of those hazards;
- decide what preventive measures may be necessary for their control;
- decide what can be controlled to minimise risks.

Where's the problem?
Situation 1

A care worker in a childrens' home is making a lunchtime barbecue meal for 12 teenagers who are on an environmental project during the school holiday. The meal will consist of homemade beefburgers (mince and chopped onion), sausages, bread buns, tomato sauce, fruit cake and fresh apples. In the morning, the care worker buys 3 kilos (6½ lbs) of fresh raw mince, 1½ kilos

(3lbs) of thick pork sausages and prepares 1 kilo (2 lbs) of chopped raw onion. He takes these ingredients, together with the other items for the menu and the barbecue equipment, to the site in his car. He intends to make the burgers immediately before cooking them.

What are the dangers (hazards)?

- Food-poisoning bacteria will exist in the mince.
- The sausages, however, will contain preservative to slow down bacterial growth.
- Bacteria can be transferred from the onions and possibly from the apples.
- The other items are low risk.
- There may be no adequate washing facilities to wash hands after setting up the barbecue.

Controlling, preventing and monitoring

Control points	Prevention of hazard
Buying the meats	Check that they are freshly made and have not been stored in an unrefrigerated window or display cabinet
Transporting the food	Keep the mince and sausages wrapped, apart from the other items and preferably in an ice box
Preparing the burgers	Make the mixture as near to cooking time as possible
Cooking	Burgers and sausages need to be cooked through. Keep turning. If part of the grill is too hot, move items to an area where they will continue to cook without burning on the outside.
Clearing away	Keep some left-over cooked burger in a clean food bag to take back to the home for analysis if required later. Dispose of the remaining cooked items in a plastic rubbish bag. Remaining sausages and raw mince and onion can be taken back to the home in the ice box, cooked thoroughly, cooled and refrigerated

Monitoring

As this is not a routine type of meal for this residential home, the usual monitoring system might not apply. Reference to the day's events and the procedures for the meal could appear in the careworker's daily log and some record will be kept of the whereabouts of the samples kept for analysis.

Situation 2

The menu includes homemade apple pie served with ice cream.

What are the dangers (hazards)?

- Food-poisoning bacteria will probably exist in the ice cream. Ice cream will certainly allow them to grow as it thaws.
- Apples are too acid to allow bacterial growth.
- The pastry will not usually be contaminated, nor will it allow bacteria to grow.
- The heat of the oven should destroy bacteria, spores and toxins.

Controlling, preventing and monitoring

Serve the ice cream as cold as possible. If a complete container is not going to be used at one meal, take out only the amount required for that meal and quickly replace the remainder. (It is sometimes less wasteful, although initially more expensive, to buy two smaller containers rather than one larger one.) Once the ice cream has begun to thaw it should not be refrozen. Once-thawed, refrozen ice cream can easily be detected as its texture is different. Stock control of ice cream must be rigid.)

ACTIVITY 8.6

Consider the situation in your workplace. What high risk foods do you handle or advise on?
Draw up a schedule, similar to that illustrated here, to help you assess, control and monitor possible hazards.

Stage	What problems?	How to control	How to check
Buying the food			
Storage Larder Refrigerator Freezer Other			
Thawing routine			
Preparation			
Cooking			
Serving			
Cooling			
Reheating procedures			
Waste disposal			

ACTIVITY 8.7

1 Following the steps outlined on pages 155 and 156, identify the potential problems in the following situations.

- A day-centre lunch menu includes curried chicken, boiled rice and coleslaw in mayonnaise.
- The lunch box to take to school is to contain cheese sandwich with tomato; fresh fruit and shortbread biscuit.
- Monday's lunch menu of fried fish and chips will use frozen cod fillets and fresh potato chips.
- Trifles for service on an evening buffet bar (open for a 2 hour period) will be made from sponge cake, tinned fruit, jelly, custard and cream.

2 Decide the points at which control can take place, what measures should be taken to prevent food becoming a hazard at those points and suggest ways of monitoring the system to see that the measures are carried out.

3 List your suggestions under the headings: 'What problems?', 'How to control', 'How to prevent hazard', 'How to monitor and check'.

8.5 The law, regulations and guidelines

The law

The Food Safety Act 1990 covers all aspects of food safety in the UK. It is applicable to all premises that take part in the production and preparation of food for sale for human consumption. 'Sale' in this context includes food offered on premises for which the provision of food is part of their normal activities and will include all settings where carers provide food for clients or patients. The main provision of the Law in relation to the food itself makes it an offence:

- to treat food so as to render it injurious to health with the intent that the food will be sold in that state. Regard shall be had to the cumulative effect of foods consumed over a long period;
- to sell, offer for sale or have in possession for sale food intended for human consumption which fails to comply with the food safety requirements, i.e. food which has been rendered injurious to health, is unfit for human consumption or is so contaminated that it would not be reasonable to expect it to be used for human consumption in that state.

The Law is an Act of Parliament. The Food Safety Act is an 'enabling' law, i.e. it enables ministers to issue regulations which are legally binding. Regulations are easier to update than laws enacted by Parliament. In this case the regulations that are issued for securing food safety throughout the UK are able to be very specific to the relevant parts of the food chain.

Regulations

The Food Hygiene (general) Regulations 1970 are the most important with regard to the hygienic operations of the majority of food premises, including restaurants, canteens, shops and food factories. They also cover the preparation and service of food in hospitals, nursing homes and residential homes, hostels, day-care centres, schools and the provision of community meals. Their main objective is to prevent food poisoning; to achieve this objective the regulations stress that food must not be exposed to the risk of contamination. Regulations are enforced through the local authority, called the 'Enforcing Body'. The local authority's environmental health officers monitor all food premises, including all places where food is prepared for other people to eat. They are always willing to advise.

The Food Hygiene (amendment) Regulations 1990 add to the above regulations by issuing regulations about effective temperature controls to prevent the multiplication of food-poisoning bacteria, especially in high risk foods. (Refer to page 150 and the diagram on page 152.)

The Food Safety (general Food Hygiene) Regulations 1995 add to and enforce previous regulations. Included in these regulations is the requirement for the proprietors of food premises to establish a system to control and monitor potential hazards and take steps to eliminate them.

Staff involved in food handling are required to receive appropriate training unless working under instruction and supervision of a fully trained operative. There are also specific requirements for the materials, etc. used for walls, ceilings, floors, doors and windows of rooms designed for food preparation purposes.

Guidelines

Local authorities issue guidelines, regulations and bye-laws according to the requirements of their area and the advice of the local environmental health officers.

Defence of due diligence

There are tough penalties for allowing an outbreak of food poisoning or for failing to prevent accidents. They include heavy fines, imprisonment and the closure of the premises. The 1990 Food Safety Act, however, includes a clause to allow for the owners of the premises to plead *'due diligence'*. This means that if it can be shown that everyone in the establishment did everything possible to prevent the problem and that the problem occurred through circumstances beyond reasonable control, they can be found not guilty. The owners of the premises *have to prove* that they have exercised due diligence.

Colour-coding

Some local authorities have issued guidelines through their environmental health officers on colour-coding of some equipment. Coloured plastic boards and spoons have replaced wooden boards and spoons in the belief that they are more hygienic. Knife handles too, have adopted the same colour-coding. The intention is that only one colour will be used for one type of commodity to prevent cross-contamination. However, all food handlers need to know why this is necessary.

Boards, spoons and knives can become infected if not washed and sterilised after use, whether wooden or plastic. Many people have gone back to using wooden boards and spoons as they are no more harmful than plastic, especially once the plastic has become scored and chipped.

References and further reading

DOH 1995: *Assured Safe Catering – a Management System for Hazard Analysis*
DOH 1995: Food Safety – *Food Hazards and Your Business*
DOH 1995: Food Safety – *Guide to the Temperature Control Regulations*
DOH 1995: Food Safety – *Guide to the Food Hygiene Regulations (1995)*
MAFF 1990: *The Food Safety Act and You*. A Food Sense Booklet
MAFF 1991: *Food Safety*. A Food Sense Booklet
Sprenger 1991: *Hygiene for Managers*. Highfield Publications

9 Planning meals and menus

Providing meals for others usually involves us in deciding what food to give, how to prepare it and how, when and where to serve it. Informally, as part of our social lives, you may be asked to plan a party for a special occasion: a wedding, a birthday, Christmas or other religious festival for example, or you may decide to take a group of friends for a picnic. You may become involved with a children's group that is going for a camping holiday for a week. Whatever the circumstances, there are a large number of factors to consider.

ACTIVITY 9.1

Plan a menu for a young relative's wedding party.
List the factors you would consider in deciding what food to offer.

9.1 Menus

In many care situations it is necessary to draw up menus in a more formal way. A menu is defined as a *'bill of fare'*. It is essentially a list of foods which are being served at that time. A menu can be for a meal, a day, a week, a month or a specified period such as Christmas or other religious festival, holiday time, special occasions.

Menu planning is not easy. In the end, what is written is the result of an understanding of all the many factors which influence what to buy, make and serve. The task of the menu planner is to be aware of all these factors (see page 161). Even where a qualified or trained cook or caterer is employed in a caring situation, the menu planning is often undertaken by the care staff, for traditional reasons. It has become part of the carer's role in caring.

The basis of a normal menu

What is normal? In terms of the menu it will depend mainly on regional custom and practice. In the UK, when planning menus formally, it is still convenient to think of the day as being divided roughly into three:

- Breakfast and mid-morning drink/snack;
- Midday meal and mid-afternoon drink/snack;
- Evening meal and bedtime drink/snack.

Many people, of course, omit some of these meals or snacks, but it is a convenient framework which ensures that the day's intake of food is fairly evenly spread.

ACTIVITY 9.2

In Activity 1.5 you decided with your group what you thought was 'normal'. You also discussed with people of other cultural backgrounds, what differences there were in 'normality'.

- Refer to your responses as a basis for considering where to start with your menu planning.
- Refer back to them to see what you thought was 'normal'.

ACTIVITY 9.3

Write down the meal titles that are normally used in menus in your area and alongside them write the titles used in this book.

Naming meals

The names of meals vary from place to place and this can sometimes cause embarrassing situations. For example, it is possible to arrive for 'dinner' at midday instead of being there in the evening or be given a full, three-course meal for 'tea' when only expecting a cup of tea and a biscuit. Dinner may be called supper or tea. Lunch may be called dinner or elevenses. Elevenses sometimes come at 9.30–10.00am and may also be called breakfast. Midday meals do not always appear at noon and bedtime drinks/snacks often appear quite a while before a client goes to bed.

When planning menus, name the meals in a way that clients and staff are used to and happiest with. Throughout this book the names that are used are breakfast, mid-morning, midday, mid-afternoon, evening meal and bedtime. They may be dull but they avoid some of the confusion.

Factors to consider when writing a menu

Many factors influence your decision about what to give people to eat. You may not be consciously aware of them. Factors listed below relate to a residential situation. They can be adapted for community meals, day-centres, schools or the client's own home.

Factors relating to the care situation

- Where is it? (town, village, remote country area)
- How easy is it to travel to and bring supplies to?
- How easy is it to get to the shops?
- What type of house is it? (custom built, adapted, number of floor levels)
- How much money is allowed for food?

Factors relating to the clients (refer to the diagram on page 27)

- How many are there?
- How mobile are they?
- What age group are they, in the main?
- Do they have specific disabilities: visual, speech, hearing impairment, learning or memory difficulties, physical problems, a mixture of disabilities?
- Do any clients follow a religious or cultural regime?
- Are there just one or two clients only who follow such a regime?
- Do a lot of clients have special needs?

Factors relating to the kitchen

- Is it custom built or has it been adapted?
- Does it present problems: size, layout, convenience, nearness to food service area?
- Does the equipment prevent certain dishes being included on the menu?
- What type of cooking fuel is used? Does it affect what can be cooked?
- How is the food served to clients: plated meals, self-service, family service, tray service, trolley service or a mixture of several?

Factors relating to the staff

- How many staff are involved in food preparation and service?
- Are they full-time or part-time?

- Do they have special skills in making some dishes and not others?
- Are there regular meetings with all staff and clients to discuss menus?
- Do all members of the care staff help in cooking and serving the meals?

Does it matter?

Some of these questions might be puzzling, but the answers show how they affect what is put on a menu. For example:

- if there is only one omelette pan, it will not be convenient to serve omelettes to everyone in a large residential home or centre;
- some solid fuel ovens are hard to regulate; making meringues or even sponges can be a bit risky;
- some people are poor pastry cooks so it is best not to put pies on the menu when they are on duty;
- food delivered in a hot trolley can either overcook or go cold.

Writing a menu for a residential or day centre

Writing a menu is like doing a jigsaw puzzle. You have to take into account all the factors which are noted above. A few ideas and tips for beginning the jigsaw are:

- aim to plan a rotating menu, i.e. one that comes round (with variations) over a period of weeks. Four or six week periods are the most common. Remember always that Week 1 follows on again after Week 4 (or 6);
- use a pencil and keep a rubber handy!

Step one

Set out the main-course ingredient at midday and evening meals for the whole week, e.g. beef, fish, egg, lamb, liver, vegetable-base, etc. If offering a cooked breakfast, put these main ingredients in, too. This helps to avoid the same or similar items appearing in nearby meals or on consecutive days. This is the start of the jigsaw.

	Monday	Tuesday	Wednesday	Thursday	Friday	Saturday	Sunday
Breakfast							
Midday	Mince	Liver	Lamb	Pork	Fish	Sausage	Beef
Evening meal	Egg	Chicken	Tinned fish	Vegetable-based dish	Ham	Cheese	Salmon/tuna

ACTIVITY 9.4

1 Using these lists, consider your own care situation. Answer all the questions in relation to your own experience.

2 Begin to compile a list of those factors which you think influence, either consciously or unconsciously, what foods appear on your menu.

3 Look back at your plan for the wedding party menu which you made in Activity 9.1. Do some of these considerations influence what you decided to give to the guests in that example?

ACTIVITY 9.5

1 Write out one day's meals from your current menu (include the between-meal snacks and drinks). Alongside each item comment on why you think it is there. For example:

- the clients like it;
- they always have that on Fridays;
- it's a cheap day, on Monday;
- it covers the vitamin D for the week;
- it's the cook's day off.

2 Think seriously about each item and don't be afraid to say 'I don't know'. It is very easy to get into a rut when planning meals.

ACTIVITY 9.6

Draw up a menu like the one illustrated here but add starters, sweets, breakfasts and in-between meal snacks also (mid-morning, mid-afternoon and bedtime). Compare your choice with the menu on page 165 which has been designed for a residential home with the main meal at midday and a high tea in the evening.

When it is clear that the main items don't clash, balanced meals can be built around each item. For a day-care situation, including a school, the menu can be planned for Mid-morning, Midday and Mid-afternoon.

Menu balance depends on a number of factors (see also Chapter 2). It can be achieved for:

- *colour* – picture the meal on the plate. There shouldn't be a preponderance of one colour. Use garnishes if necessary. Try to imagine it all together on a tray, too;
- *texture* – include foods which need to be chewed (unless chewing is not desirable for that client). Give something crunchy with something soft;
- *nutrients* (see Chapter 6) – some nutrients are needed for absorbtion or use of others;
- *flavour* – one highly spiced item in a meal is enough for most people, so avoid following a curry with a ginger pudding, for example;
- *cost* – it is sometimes possible to average the price of a meal by using a cheaper sweet with an expensive main course or vice versa.

Balance meals out through the week, too, including less popular dishes with the more popular ones to make sure that all tastes are catered for. Use of the oven and cooking space will depend on the numbers being catered for. Some dishes can be cooked in advance. If there is room in the oven, a batch of scones, cakes or biscuits can be baked for a later meal. Baked potatoes and rice puddings, for example, can make of use of the oven heat and space as it heats up or cools down. In large establishments, all the ovens and cooking space may need to be used. When cooking for smaller numbers it may be cheaper to plan to cook either everything on the hob or everything in the oven.

Step two

Fill in the dish that you are thinking of for the main ingredient.

	Monday	Tuesday	Wednesday	Thursday	Friday	Saturday	Sunday
Breakfast							
Midday	Cottage pie	Liver and bacon with onions	Lamb hot pot	Pork chop with apple sauce	Grilled fish and lemon	Bacon, egg and sausage	Roast beef and Yorkshire pudding
Evening meal	Savoury flan	Chicken salad	Sardines on toast	Vegetable and bean soup	Baked potato with minced ham	Cheese on toast	Salmon and tuna sandwiches

ACTIVITY 9.7

1 Using the diagram on page 16 and your answers to Activity 2.7 on page 18, list the nutrients that require other nutrients for their absorbtion or use.

2 Suggest four items of food which would give balance under the headings of:

- colour;
- texture;
- taste.

Step three

Fill in the staple and the vegetables for colour and texture, etc.

	Monday	Tuesday	Wednesday	Thursday	Friday	Saturday	Sunday
Breakfast							
Midday	Cottage pie	Liver and bacon with onions	Lamb hot pot	Pork chop with apple sauce	Grilled fish and lemon	Bacon, egg and sausage	Roast beef and Yorkshire pudding
	mashed potato cauliflower peas and carrots	parsley potato spring greens celery	boulangere potatoes broccoli tomato	sauté potato green beans leeks in sauce	chips peas mushrooms	mashed potato baked beans	roast potato parsnip cabbage
Evening meal	Savoury flan	Chicken salad	Sardines on toast	Vegetable and bean soup	Baked potato with minced ham	Cheese on toast	Salmon and tuna sandwiches
	sliced tomato	potato crisps	lemon and cress	cheese bread	coleslaw	grilled tomato	cucumber relish

Step four

Balance the whole menu across the week by filling in the starter and sweet where appropriate. Use the sweet and starter dishes, as well as the vegetables, to ensure that the meal is nutritionally balanced. Using the same basic main meals, it is possible to plan balanced meals for different cultural groups.

Menus that offer a choice

Giving people a choice at meal times is an ideal that many strive for. It can be a mixed blessing, however.

Often the notion of choice is just that – a notion. It is unrealistic to offer complete freedom of choice in many care situations. The choices built in to the menu are often those which the carer or caterer think should be there and they may well be determined by such factors as cost, ideals of healthy eating, convenience or time.

It is good advice to start with a well-balanced, varied menu and build in choices only if and when necessary. Even one properly balanced menu is not easy to plan. Trying to balance a menu with three or more different choices for each course, which takes in all the factors for the particular situation, is very time-consuming. It can be done, of course, but it takes a great deal of experience, patience and a lot of professional know-how in addition to the time.

Choices are necessary when people of many cultures or persuasions eat together. Where possible, it is best if the main course choices are of equal nutritional value. This makes it a lot easier for the catering as the starters and sweets can often remain the same. There are many pros and cons for a choice menu and all are valid. Each care situation must decide what suits staff and clients best. In some circumstances, offering a choice may be seen as a lack of real caring.

When Mr B feels depressed and alone, he doesn't want to be bothered about food. When the care assistant brings in the menu and asks him what he wants for lunch: chicken casserole, poached cod or ham salad, he agrees to anything and is served the fish because 'he likes fish'.

On another day another care assistant, faced with the same situation, sits down with him. She says: 'I know you like fish and we have some nice fresh fillets. Would you like me to cook you some?' Effectively, she is saying: 'I know you are feeling down and I care.' It is the caring that will cheer him up. The meal remains the same.

Table 9.1 *Some pros and cons of a choice menu*

For	Against
All people like to be independent	It's hard to assess how much of each item to buy
Not everyone likes the same food	It makes for difficulties when writing a balanced menu
It enables the use of leftovers	No matter how much choice you give them there will
Giving a choice can cut down wastage	always be someone who wants something different
It makes catering for special needs easier	It creates more work for the cook
	It increases dependence on convenience foods

The menu as a basis for control

Once you have a menu with which you are fairly happy (you will, of course, always want to improve on it), you can use it as a basis for a great deal of organisation and planning. You can, for example:

- build up the recipes to go with it (try to adapt standard basic recipes and proportions) and have a collection of pictures to enable some clients to choose what they want (see Activity 5.4);
- share the cooking where appropriate. Everyone can use the menu and the recipes;
- display the menu. That way no one should raid the larder and use up a specially ordered item.

An organised menu has other advantages, for example:

- ordering and negotiating special deals helps with the budgeting;
- staff rostering becomes more manageable;
- menus can be adapted quickly for emergencies, holidays, sickness, etc;
- cleaning, servicing and maintenance of all equipment and premises can be arranged on a regular basis to ensure food safety and prevent accidents.

The menu can be very flexible. Dishes/recipes can be varied each time they come round. For example, mince and mash can become cottage pie, burgers and chips, mince hot pot, or meat loaf and roast potatoes. In this way, menus can accommodate holidays, sick leave, sudden absences, etc. without altering the overall balance of cost, popularity and workload. For example, in Christmas week meals can be exchanged between days: Friday's fish and chips can become Tuesday's fish pie and Tuesday's chicken casserole can be exchanged for Friday's (Christmas Day's) roast turkey. It is easier to adapt a well planned menu than to keep starting from scratch. Menu planning mainly requires imagination, intuition, ingenuity and instinct (the four 'I's). Table 9.2 illustrates a sample menu for a residential home with the main meal being at midday and the evening meal, high tea.

Table 9.2 *Example menu*

	Monday	Tuesday	Wednesday	Thursday	Friday	Saturday	Sunday
Breakfast	choice of breakfast cereals, porridge, muesli, etc. milk or yoghurt choice of fruit – fresh or dried – or fruit juice bread, rolls, crispbread or toast – brown or white butter or margarine or spread; marmalade, honey, jam, marmite, etc. tea or coffee; milk, lemon or cream (sugar)						
Mid-morning	tea, coffee, milk drink or fruit drink				biscuit or piece of fresh fruit		
Midday	cottage pie	liver and bacon with onion gravy	lamb hot pot	pork chop with apple sauce	grilled fish and lemon	bacon, egg and sausage	roast beef and Yorkshire pudding
	mashed potato cauliflower sauce peas and carrots	parsley potato spring greens tinned celery	boulangere potato broccoli tinned tomato	sauté potato green beans leeks in sauce	chips peas mushrooms	mashed potato baked beans	roast potato roast parsnip cabbage
	fruit crumble and evaporated milk	rice pudding and jam	apple pie custard	fruit sponge flan	bread and butter pudding	fruit salad and ice cream	jelly whip
Mid-afternoon	tea or coffee or fruit drink				biscuit or cake or piece of fresh fruit		
Evening meal	fruit juice	soup	soup	fruit juice	grapefruit and orange cocktail	soup	fruit juice
	savoury flan	chicken salad	sardines on toast	'main course' soup	baked potato with minced ham	cheese on toast	salmon and tuna sandwiches
	sliced tomato	potato crisps	lemon and cress	cheese bread	cole slaw	grilled tomato	cucumber garnish
	ice cream sweet	shortbreads	pear condé	blackcurrant tarts	butterfly cakes	Dundee cake	sherry trifle
		bread and butter and jam served each evening					
		tea or coffee					
Bedtime	milk drink or tea or coffee or fruit drink			flapjack, digestive biscuit or fruit scone or piece of fresh fruit			

ACTIVITY 9.8

Using the following meal menu, adapt the items in it to produce *two* different meal menus:

chicken in white wine sauce
rice
stir-fry vegetables
fruit flan and cream

For example, grilled fish and parsley sauce, creamed potato, mushrooms, peas, followed by apple fritters with lemon can become:

fish pie with potato topping
mushroom sauce
peas
apple pancakes
or
fried fish with lemon
sauté potato
mushrooms
peas
apple snow
or
poached fish and lemon sauce
mashed potato
mushroom fritters
peas
baked apple and custard

Speciality menus

One person's favourite food will not necessarily be liked by everyone else. However, clients could feel very deprived if they had to go without something they had eaten all their lives. Examples might include jellied eels, tripe and onions, haggis, kippered herrings. A way around this for older clients in care may be to have a speciality menu when they can choose their particular favourite.

Allow clients to help with the planning of the menu if they are able to, especially in a residential establishment where people live permanently. It is their home and the women, especially, could have been planning meals for most of their lives. In day centres, too, the older clients will know a thing or two about planning meals and menus. They are likely to be especially good at cost control.

Those clients with physical, visual or other impairments will be able to offer tips and ideas. Many people, both young and older, enjoy talking about food and a thoroughly enjoyable and satisfying time can be had by all. Make sure that ideas and suggestions are not ignored or overlooked. Some may be impractical or too expensive but this can be talked through rather than discarded.

9.2 Food service

Food service is the 'sharp end' of all our endeavours to care for people through the provision of food. The main aim is to get the right food to the right person at the right time and to see that person eat it and enjoy it. It is at the point of food service that the main aim either succeeds or fails.

However lovingly and carefully the food has been prepared and cooked, whatever choices are offered, however much the client is looking forward to the meal, it is at the point of service that the whole thing can go disastrously wrong and all efforts can be wasted. The way food is to be served is included in the thinking that goes into the menu planning. Some meal items are not suitable for some types of service. Some items need to be served in certain ways. It is a waste of time, money and effort and can give rise to enormous disappointment if food is spoiled or altered beyond recognition by the manner of its service. For example, cooked eggs will harden in a hot trolley and be unappetising when they are served; ice cream will melt if it has to travel over a long distance without an insulated container; sandwiches can dry and curl up and salads can wilt if left on a buffet table for a long period.

The aim, at all times, is that:

- hot food should be served hot, without being spoiled;
- cold food should be served cold, but not limp;
- all food should be as fresh as possible.

There may be difficulties in achieving this aim every time but given thought, ingenuity and imagination, meals can be planned to allow the service to be acceptable to all.

Types of meal service

There are several different types of meal service. They all have their advantages and disadvantages which vary according to the various care situations where food is served to clients. Always aim to select the type or types of meal service that will give you all the advantages and none of the disadvantages. The most common types are:

- hot trolley service
- plated meal service;
- tray service;
- family service;
- buffet service;
- cafeteria self-service;
- restaurant 'silver' service.

Less familiar, but one which is growing in popularity, is the cook–freeze, airline style, plated meal service. Always remember the basic rules of safe food handling in all types of food service. For temperature controls on hot and frozen foods, see pages 151–153.

Hot trolley service

The heated trolley is a very familiar part of food service in many hospitals in the UK. Trolleys are electrically heated, thermostatically controlled and

> ## ACTIVITY 9.9
>
> **1** Using the information on food safety in Chapter 8, make a list of the danger points for each of the seven types of food service given in this section.
>
> **2** Try to assess the hazards associated with each one and suggest ways of ensuring that the food remains safe. You could lay out your hazard analysis as a chart using the same headings that you used for your schedule in Activity 8.6 on page 157.

insulated. There is usually a cold compartment as well. The trolley is pre-heated in the kitchen area and used to carry quantities of food to the point of service. In the case of some hospitals, this may be to wards and departments a considerable distance away. On reaching their destination, the meals may need to be brought back up to temperature if they have had to travel outside in the cold.

In small residential homes and centres, a domestic-style hostess trolley may be used for this method of service. Food is served from the trolley using one or more of the other forms of service: plated meals, tray or family service, buffet or cafeteria service.

Advantages

- Hot food can be prepared centrally and carried for some distance. Food can be presented in different styles for different parts of the same establishment. Clients or patients do not have to travel or be transported to one central dining area.

Disadvantages

- There is a danger of cross-contamination of food during carriage.
- Food deteriorates when kept hot for long periods and when storage temperatures fluctuate.
- Cold food may not always remain cold if the insulation is weak.
- Some foods do not travel well.
- Where there is a wide choice or many special diets, there may not be enough room to preserve everything in an attractive way or at the correct temperatures.

Plated meal service

Food is served directly onto the plate and delivered to an individual client at table, in bed or by the fire. This type of service may be combined with other types, for example hot trolley service or buffet service. Food may be served directly from the kitchen by the care staff in a residential home or centre. Alternatively, it may be delivered in bulk to a service point using a heated trolley.

Advantages

- Carers can serve the food attractively.
- It is possible to assess the colour balance on the plate and use suitable garnishes if necessary.
- Food can be in accordance with the clients needs.
- There is little waste if the exact quantities are known before the meal is cooked.
- There is less risk of cross-contamination as hot food is not being transported or kept hot (unless combined with hot trolley service).

Disadvantages

- This type of service can be very slow.
- Clients have to be near the point of service.
- Hot food can become cold unless plates are hot.
- Clients may not always have the choice of what is put on their plate.
- Clients may like to have a second helping.

Food service: a) Family, b) Plated, c) Cafeteria, d) Tray and buffet

Tray service

All parts of the meal are served onto a tray for delivery to the client or patient. This may be in the form of a full plated meal or food served in individual dishes together with a plate for the clients to serve themselves. This type of service will be used in residential places when clients are ill or want to be alone or where there is a tradition of room service. In many residential homes it is used for serving breakfasts to enable clients to get up and dress at leisure.

Where meals are pre-plated, the total colour combination can be assessed and adjusted if necessary. For example, imagine beef casserole, roast potato and carrots together with orange jelly and shortbread on a brown tray. Colour balance can always be adjusted by the use of a tray cloth, a serviette, a flower or a garnish. In fact, a good menu planner would have imagined this colour combination at the outset and perhaps included a green vegetable in the menu. This second vegetable may only have been omitted at the client's choice so the food server needs to consider the total colour balance also. It would be nice to think that the proverbial white fish, white potato, white sauce and white cauliflower on a white plate on a white cloth, were a thing of the past, but it still happens. Use coloured plates, tray cloths, serviettes and garnishes where possible.

Advantages

- It can free the dining room area and allow staff to carry out other tasks.
- It allows clients to choose the amount of food they want on their plate.

Disadvantages

- It involves a number of extra dishes, unless the meal is pre-plated.
- It can be wasteful.
- Although it may be convenient for staff and more acceptable for other clients, it may be very depressing for the indivdual who has to eat alone.
- Clients may not be able to help themselves if the dishes are small.
- Hot food can become cold during delivery.
- Trays need a special delivery trolley.
- There is a danger of cross-contamination during transport.

Some systems use a plate over a pre-heated pellet or hot water in an insulated base. Plated meals can then be carried over a distance without the need for a heated trolley. This removes some disadvantages of the heated trolley system but limits the distance over which the food will remain hot. The preheated pellet or base may be a hazard in some circumstances.

Family service

Meals are served to a small number of people at a table which may be set in the traditional way with tablecloth, mats, cruet, place settings of the correct cutlery, side plates, glasses and serviettes. Clients may have their own serviette ring. Meals are served in dishes appropriate to the number of people at the table. Food may be cooked in the serving dish or served in attractive china or stainless steel dishes. Clients either help themselves or are served by a carer. Young children may be served by adults or older children joining them at mealtimes.

Advantages

- Older clients feel at home with familiar traditions.
- Clients can choose the size of portion.
- Young children learn to share and discover social behaviour.
- Very young children can learn new tastes with foods eaten together with adults.

- Tables can be made to look very attractive and welcoming.
- Family service frees some staff from food service (some may have to help and supervise in some circumstances).

Disadvantages

- It can be wasteful if appetites are poor.
- Hot food may become cold.
- Some clients may have difficulty with the dishes.
- It increases the number of dishes needed.
- If it is always very formal, some clients may feel uncomfortable and not see it as homely.

Buffet service

Food is served onto a side table or sideboard and clients help themselves to their choice of meal. Cutlery, serviettes and cruets may be included on the buffet table or may be laid onto separate dining tables. Hot food may be kept hot on electrically heated stands, so it is possible to serve a hot or cold buffet. This type of service is often used for the service of breakfasts in residential establishments.

Advantages

- Clients can help themselves to their own choice and size of portion.
- The table usually looks very attractive, colourful and inviting.
- Clients can eat at leisure as there is no need to clear one course before serving the next.

Disadvantages

- Clients may not be able to carry plates themselves; carers need to be on hand to assist.
- Some clients will feel very confused by such an array of food spread before them and will need help to choose.
- There is a possibility of wastage.
- It may not be possible to keep hot food at the right temperature to prevent food-poisoning bacteria from multiplying.

Cafeteria self-service

This type of service is probably the most familiar to most people. It is used in most cafés, high-street stores, schools, factories and works' canteens and restaurants. Clients help themselves or are served with the food of their choice from a hot-plate and/or a cold counter. There are many variations in layout of equipment for this type of service and some have been adapted for vending machines. Clients take their tray of food to the table of their choice.

Advantages

- For most able-bodied, mobile people it is the cheapest and quickest way to provide meals for large numbers in a short space of time.
- It enables clients to see what they are choosing and often to say what size of portion they would like.
- Staff time is efficiently used; in many cases clients clear away their own trays.

The batch system

For large concerns operating a cafeteria-style service, smaller quantities of food may be cooked in batches. This ensures that a steady flow of freshly cooked dishes, especially vegetables, is brought to the service point at regular intervals. Where the number of diners fluctuates, this can present some problems but where large numbers of people require meals over a long time period, the advantages can be considerable.

Food service is often a mixture of some of the types outlined in this section. Carers should think about the needs of the clients, the situation, the staff, equipment, transport and all the many factors involved in safe food handling. Always aim to get the best of all possible worlds. Try not to compromise.

Catering to a standard of 'it will do', won't.

Disadvantages

- Clients need to be mobile and able to carry trays.
- Food can become overcooked unless a batch system of food preparation and service operates.
- Clients eating at the end of the meal break are often left without a choice and sometimes with very unappetising food.
- It is not always possible to serve food onto the plates attractively; foods may be piled on top of one another in a very unappetising way.
- Some clients can be very confused and unable to choose.

Restaurant 'silver' service

Restaurant service is most frequently found in the commercial sector where customers are willing to pay for their meals to be brought to table by a waiter/waitress. Menus may offer a very wide choice and food may be served over a long period. In such cases there is a great reliance on convenience (especially frozen) foods which can be reheated quickly using microwave ovens. This type of service is not very suitable in most care situations although it may be used on special occasions, for example at Christmas when staff wait upon residents, teachers wait upon children in school or the managers wait upon the workforce.

Advantages

- It gives clients a sense of 'occasion'.
- It can offer a very wide choice of foods.
- It enables the right food to be served to the right client.

Disadvantages

- It is an expensive service.
- It can be very wasteful of food unless there is adequate modern technology to support it.
- It is time-consuming for staff.

Barbecues and picnics

Many groups organise occasional parties involving the use of an outdoor method of food service. Arranging food to be served in these ways enables clients to experience a different situation. However, great care is needed in planning these occasions and carers must be aware of the difficulties that some clients will have in handling food served away from their usual routine. Such occasions are a good idea but can cause distress to some if not carefully managed.

Cook–chill

This is a commercial process by which food is thoroughly cooked and then chilled rapidly in a blast chiller to a temperature of 3°C or below within 1½ hours. The food is stored between 0°C and 3°C until required, when it is regenerated (reheated) at the point of service.

Advantages

- The cost-effectiveness of being able safely to prepare large amounts of foods at one time.
- Food of consistent good quality is readily available.
- Efficient use is made of centralised equipment.
- Food may be stored in specialised containers for up to 5 days.
- Food does not need heated trolleys for transport to the point of regeneration.

Disadvantages

- It requires a large capital outlay.
- Specialised, often large, equipment is needed for all parts of the process, including special transport to the point of regeneration.
- Portion sizes do not allow for flexibility.
- Consistency can become boring.

Cook–freeze

This is a process of commercially producing food which is similar to the Cook–Chill system. Food is reduced to a temperature of $-20°C$ in a blast freezer and may be stored at that temperature for up to 12 months. Some catering systems use a combination of the two systems: Cook–freeze food is bought in bulk, regenerated to cook–chill, transported to the service site and regenerated again.

A number of commercial companies are establishing a system for providing plated meals, special and cultural diets and other services for various care situations. These meals use the cook–freeze system. The company may also hire out and service the necessary freezer for individual clients at home (see Chapter 3).

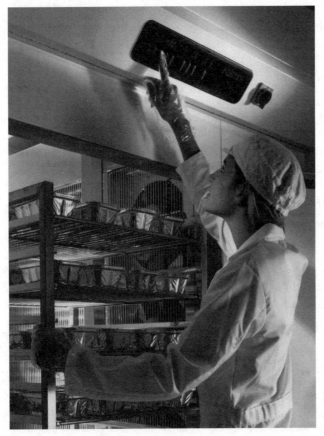

Cook–freeze

Conclusion

'In the end, what we decide to include in our menu is determined by our understanding of the many issues relating to food.' (page 160).

Your menu is now written. You have included in it the choice of food that suits all the circumstances of your situation and all the information gathered throughout this book. Hopefully, it will be acceptable to staff and clients alike. The information you have used has related to clients, their diet, the foods available, nutrition, special circumstances and safety.

However, this is not the end of the story. There is much to be explored, expanded and discovered. Some of our current thinking will be replaced, some of our former thinking will be revived. Foods, attitudes, lives, situations, policies, finances, will all change over time. In this book it has not been possible to go into all the aspects of food in depth nor to explore some of the exciting topics that contribute to our understanding of the whole subject.

Food, diet and nutrition issues can seem like a merry-go-round. It is often necessary to go back to the beginning and start again, but there is really no beginning and no end. With a basic understanding of the food issues in relation to our care for ourselves and each other, adapting to changes can be entered into in the spirit of adventure. More and more people are finding it a fascinating and exciting scene to explore, laying the foundations, as it does, for the future health, happiness and possible evolution of the human race.

Useful contacts

Local help will be available from:

- Local Authority departments: Social Services, Environmental Health and Education departments;
- Health Education department;
- Health authorities;
- Council for Voluntary Services;
- Her Majesty's Stationery Office (HMSO) accredited agents.

Addresses for these will be in the local telephone directory.

Advisory Body for Social Services Catering (ABSSC) 104 Briarwood Drive, Bradford, Yorks BD6 1SE.

Age Concern England (ACE) Astral House, 1268 London Road, London SW16 4ER. Tel: 0181 679 8000.

apetito (UK) Ltd Arctic House, Dunton Green, Sevenoaks, Kent TN14 5HB. Tel: 01732 741816.

Boots the Chemists Health and Food Business Centre, Citygate House, Toll House Hill, Nottingham NG2 3AA.

British Broadcasting Corporation BBC Radio, Broadcasting House, London W1A 1AA. For programmes 'In Touch', 'Does He Take Sugar?', 'The Food Programme'.

British Diabetic Association 10 Queen Anne Street, London W1M 0BD. Tel: 0171 323 1531.

British Dietetic Association Elizabeth House, 22 Suffolk Street, Queensway, Birmingham, B1 1LS. Tel: 0121 643 3483.

Caroline Walker Trust 6 Aldridge Road Villas, London W11 1BP.

Centre for Accessible Environments 35 Great Smith Street, London SW1P 3BJ. Tel: 0171 222 7980.

Clintec Nutrition Ltd. Shaftesbury Court, 8 Chalvey Park, Slough, Berks SL1 2HT. Tel: 01753 550 800.

Coeliac Society P.O. Box 220, High Wycombe, Bucks. HP11 2HY.

Department of Health Skipton House, 80 London Road, London SE1 6LW. Tel: 0171 972 2000.

Disabled Living Centres Council 286 Camden Road, London N7 0BJ. Tel: 0171 700 1707.

Disabled Living Foundation 380–384 Harrow Road, London W9 2HU. Tel: 0171 289 6111.

Gateshead Shopping Service Civic Centre, Regent Street, Gateshead, Tyne & Wear NE8 1HH.

Gluten Free Foods Ltd PO Box 178, Stanmore, Middx HA7 4XN. Tel: 0181 954 7348.

Hearing Concern (Royal National Institute for the Deaf) 7–11 Armstrong Road, Acton, London W3 7JL. Tel: 0181 740 4447/0181 743 1110.

Local Authority Caterers Association (LACA) c/o Bourne House, Horsell Park, Woking GU21 4YY.

Royal National College for the Blind College Road, Hereford HR1 1EB. Tel: 01432 265725.

Royal National Institute for the Blind (RNIB) PO Box 173, Peterborough PE2 6WS. Tel: 01345 023153.

NCH Action for Children 85 Highbury Park, London NA5 1UD. Tel: 0171 226 2033.

Nutricia Dietary Products, Ltd Newmarket Avenue, Whitehouse Business Park, Trowbridge, Wiltshire BA14 OXQ.

Schools Nutrition Action Group [SNAG] Martineau Education Centre, 74 Balden Road, Birmingham B32 2EH. Tel: 0121 428 2262.

SHAP c/o The National Society's Religious Education Centre, 36 Causton Street, London SW1P 4AU. Tel: 0171 932 1194.

Teleshop Services Ltd 15 Berkeley Court, Manor Park, Runcorn, Cheshire WA7 1TQ. Tel: 01928 579 755.

Trufree Foods Larkhall Natural Health, 225 Putney Bridge Road, London SW15 2PY.

Women's Royal Voluntary Service (WRVS) 234–244 Stockwell Road, London SW9 9SP. Tel: 0171 416 0146.

Bibliography

ABSSC 1990: *A Recommended Standard for Community Meals*. ABSSC *Advanced GVNQ Health and Social Care*. Hodder and Stoughton
Allison, S.P. 1995: *Cost-effectiveness of Nutritional Support in the Elderly.* The Proceedings of the Nutrition Society, Vol. 54 No. 3, Cambridge University Press.

BBC 1994 and annually: *In Touch – a Guide to Services for People With a Visual Handicap*
BDA 1987: *Child's Diets and change*. British Dietetic Association
BDA 1990: *Countdown*. British Diabetic Association
Bender and Bender 1991: *Food Labelling – a Companion to Food Tables.* Oxford University Press

Coeliac Society: *Coeliac Handbook*. The Coeliac Society
Committee on the Medical Aspects of Food Policy (COMA) Reports: HMSO
  1991: No. 41 *Dietary Reference Values for Food Energy and Other Nutrients for the United Kingdom*
  1992: No. 43 *Nutrition and the Elderly*
  1994: No. 45 *Weaning and the Weaning Diet*
  1994: No. 46 *Nutritional Aspects of Cardiovascular Disease*
Coultate and Davies 1994: *Food – the Definitive Guide*. Royal Society of Chemistry
CPA 1990: *Community Life – a Code of Practice for Community Care*. The Centre for Policy on Aging
Crawford, Michael and Marsh, David 1989: *The Driving Force*. Heinemann Ltd

Dant and Gully 1994: *Coordinating Care at Home*. Collins Educational
DOH 1991: *While you are Pregnant – Safe Eating*. Department of Health
DOH 1994: *Nutrition and Health – a Management Handbook for the NHS.* Department of Health
DOH 1995: *Assured Safe Catering*. Department of Health
DOH 1995: *Food Safety – A Guide to Food Hazards and Your Business*
DOH 1995: *Food Safety – A Guide to the Food Hygiene Regulations 1995*
DOH 1995: *Food Safety – A Guide to the Temperature Control Regulations*
Drummond and Wilbraham 1991: *The Englishman's Food – a History of Five Centuries of the English Diet*. Pimlico.

Edwards and Bazalgette: *BBC Food Check – a Practical Guide to Safe Food.* BBC Books

Eversole and Hess 1981: *Towards Healthy Aging – Human Needs and Nursing Response*. CV Mosby Co.

Francis 1986: *Nutrition for Children*. Blackwell Scientific Press

Garrow and James 1993: *Human Nutrition and Dietetics*. Churchill Livingstone

Hall 1984: *Feeding Your Children*. Judy Piatkus Ltd
Hanssen, Maurice 1987: *The New E for Additives*. Thorsons
Haslam 1985: *Eat It Up! – a Parent's Guide to Eating Problems*. Macdonald & Co.
HEA 1993: *Enjoy Healthy Eating*. The Health Education Authority
HEA 1993: *The Health Guide*. The Health Education Authority
Henley 1983: *Caring for Hindus and Their Families*. National Extension College
Henley 1983: *Caring for Muslims and Their Families*. National Extension College
Henley 1983: *Caring for Sikhs and Their Families*. National Extension College
HMSO 1991: *Dietary Reference Values – a Guide to Report No. 41*. HMSO

Influences on Health and Well-being. Longman

Karmel 1991: *The Complete Baby and Toddler Menu Planner*. Ebury Press

Lewis 1993: *Eating Well on a Budget*. Age Concern England
Lindon 1993: *Caring for the Under 8s*. Macmillan
Lindon 1994: *Caring for Young Children*. Macmillan

MAFF 1990: *The Food Safety Act and You*. A Food Sense Booklet
MAFF 1991: *Food Protection*. A Food Sense Booklet
MAFF 1993: *Food Portion Sizes*. HMSO
MAFF 1995: *The Manual of Nutrition*, 10th Edn. HMSO
MAFF annually: *National Food Survey*
MAFF: *About Food Additives*. A Food Sense Booklet
MAFF: *Healthy Eating for Older People*. A Food Sense Booklet
MAFF: *Understanding Food Labels*. A Food Sense Booklet
McCance and Widdowson 1992: *The Composition of Foods*. Royal Society of Chemistry (RSC) and Ministry of Agriculture, Fisheries and Foods (MAFF), HMSO
Supplements: 1988: *Cereals and Cereal Products*; 1989: *Milk Products and Eggs*; 1991: *Vegetables, Herbs and Spices*; 1992: *Fish and Fish Products*; 1992: *Fruit and Nuts*
Minett 1985: *Childcare and Development*. John Murray
Moonie, Neil: *Intermediate GNVQ Health and Social Care*. Heinemann Educational

NACNE 1983: *Proposals for Nutritional Guidelines for Health Education in Britain*. Health Education Council
NAGE 1992: *Food and Health Policies for Elderly People*. British Dietetic Association
NAGE 1992: *Nutritional Assessment and Checklist – a Screening Tool*. NAGE
NAGE 1993: *Eating Through the 90s*. British Dietetic Association
NAGE 1993: *In the Minority Through the 90s*. British Dietetic Association
NCC 1995: *Budgeting for food on benefits*. National Consumer Council
NCH 1992: *Poverty and Nutrition Survey*. NCH Action for Children

NCH 1994: *A Lost Generation.* NCH Action for Children
Nilson, B 1981: *Cooking for Special Diets.* Penguin

Orton and West 1991: *Working with Older People – a Guide to Services.* Open University
OU 1985: *Open University Guide to Healthy Eating.* The Open University
OU 1991: *Working With Children and Young People.* The Open University
OU: *The 1989 Children's Act* – a Resource Booklet. The Open University

Pay 1986: *Cooking for Kids the Healthy Way.* Macdonald Optima

Rawcliffe and Rolph 1985: *The Gluten-free Diet Book.* Martin Dunitz

SHAP: *Shap Calendar of Religious Festivals.* SHAP Working Party on World Religions in Education
Smyth, Terry 1992: *Caring for Older People.* Macmillan
Sprenger 1991: *Hygiene for Managers.* Highfield Publications

Tan, Wenlock and Buss 1985: *Immigrant Foods – a Supplement to The Composition of Foods.* HMSO
The Care Sector Consortium's Care Standards and Qualifications 1992: *National Occupational Standards for Working with Young Children and their Families*
The National Diet and Nutrition Surveys (Children aged 1 to 4 years)
    Vol. 1 *Report on the Diet and Nutrition Survey*
    Vol. 2 *Report on the Dental Survey*
Thomas 1994: *The Manual of Dietetic Practice.* Blackwell Science
Turner, Michael (ed.) 1983: *Food and People.* John Libby and Co. Ltd

1985: *The Oxford Illustrated Book of Food Plants.* Oxford University Press
1992: *Nutritional Guidelines for School Meals.* Caroline Walker Trust
1995: *Eating Well for Older People.* Caroline Walker Trust

Index

Many foodstuffs are mentioned throughout the book in different contexts, and are not listed individually in the Index. Information can be found under entries such as budgeting, cooking and processing, food (groups, intake, portion sizes, safety/hygiene), healthy eating, meals, menus, nutrients.

Bold numbers indicate the main entry.